D0870508

WHY AM I
SO *Angry?*

DEBI PRYDE

Iron Sharpeneth Iron Publications
Newberry Springs, California

THE IRONWOOD TOOLBOOK SERIES

The Ironwood Toolbook Series is designed to address specific facets of ministry and to provide practical instruction in areas such as leadership, management, counseling, team building, youth work, music, and service ministries. The tried and tested contents of this series, an integral part of Ironwood, are now available to assist individuals and ministries. To God alone be the glory for the countless hours of service that have made this series possible.

Copyright 2006 by Debi Pryde

ISBN 978-1-931787-20-8

LOC 2006932186

Unless otherwise noted, Scripture quotations are from the Authorized King James Version.

For information concerning the Ironwood Toolbook Series or any other resources listed in this book, contact us at www.ironwood.org.

Managing Editor, Ron Perry
Cover Design, Susanna I. Capetz
Content Layout, Allison Pust

Iron Sharpeneth Iron Publications
Newberry Springs, California

TABLE OF CONTENTS

WHY AM I
SO
Angry?

PART ONE 1

WHICH WAY *Out?*

CHAPTER ONE

Have you ever helplessly watched as a sparrow tried to find his way out of a large building in which he accidentally became entrapped? Typically, the bird will fly frantically in every direction looking for a way to escape. When no opening is found, the bird gives up and perches as high as he possibly can, trembling in total exhaustion. Our compassions go out to the little creature, and we find ourselves wishing we could explain how easily he could escape if he would only let us show him the open window located much lower than he is flying. This, however, would require the bird to fly down when his survival instinct is telling him to fly up. Furthermore, the sparrow would have to leave the safety of his perch high in the rafters just to see the way out. It is not unusual for birds to die rather than venture lower or follow a human that freely leaves the building and returns at will. The way of escape is available, but how to find the opening eludes the unsuspecting little bird.

A Christian who resigns himself to living in bondage to habitual anger, believing it is impossible to be free from it, is like that bird.

According to the Bible, habitual anger entraps *every* human being and makes *every* human being subject to a cruel taskmaster whose goal is to torment and destroy. In *Ephesians 2:1–3*, Paul reminds us that we who are believers *were*, by nature, the children of wrath, even as others who do not know Christ. However, because we have been given new life in Christ and have become energized by the indwelling Holy Spirit, we have a new direction, new motivations, and new attitudes that thoroughly transform our character and behavior as we learn to practice God's Word. We are told in Romans 6:14 that sin cannot have dominion over a believer because the believer is freed from the enslaving power of sin the moment he comes to Christ in repentance and faith. Whereas once we were hopelessly entrapped by the power of sin, now the prison door has been opened; and we have the means to walk out in freedom.

When we recognize we are enslaved by sin as a way of life and come to the cross of Christ and trust Him alone for salvation and forgiveness, the windows of heaven are opened for us. We can remain entrapped in sin, or we can find the open window and escape; but we are no longer trapped without hope. Yes, being free from bondage does require us to fly down when our instinct tells us to fly up; and freedom does require us to leave the familiar safety of our perch. But the way out is available for *every* believer, and freedom is possible just as soon as we discover how to get there. Freedom from the controlling chains of anger is not only possible for a believer, it should be expected. We who are the Lord's children do not need to resort to worldly methods in order to *manage* anger. We are given the means to *conquer* anger and become increasingly more like Christ in the way we respond to life's difficulties and disappointments. We have hope because our Father in heaven delights in our growth and promises to transform our character as we learn how to think and respond biblically (*Romans 12:1–2*).

Human instinct will tell us the way out is up, but we cannot be fooled by this philosophy. The way out is always down. When we humble ourselves in the sight of the Lord, the Scriptures promise

He will lift us up (*James 4:10*). The ability to conquer anger begins with honest self-evaluation, as opposed to our more natural tendency to engage in subtle self-deception. An honest evaluation of our angry expressions and emotions requires an enormous amount of courage, humility, and God-given grace. Honest self-evaluation is not for the fainthearted or shortsighted! Self-evaluation requires, above all else, humility and a willingness to reject our own reasoning and submit ourselves to God's standards instead. According to *James 4:6*, we will discover God's enabling grace and mercy to conquer sinful anger *only* when we humble ourselves and submit our will to God. Insisting on our own way and stubbornly clinging to our prideful excuses and self-sufficiency render us incapable of obtaining God's overcoming power. Because God resists [is opposed to] the proud (*James 4:6*), no amount of pleading or remorse elicits God's help until our heart is humbled and dependent on Christ alone. So then, the journey begins here, with a humble willingness to listen to what God, not man, has to say about the matter.

Where, then, does God say animosity and fighting among people originate? And what triggers that split-second outburst of angry thoughts or words that can immediately fill a believer with remorse? James answers these questions for us in the Bible (*James 4*). His answer is swift and simple but not exactly what we like to hear. The problem lies within us, not in the circumstances around us. God clearly informs us that anger originates in our corrupted human nature and is the outward manifestation of inward self-motivated desires. "But," we often object, "what about righteous anger? And isn't anger just an emotion? Surely being angry can't be wrong or selfish when someone has just wronged me or treated me with cruelty! Wouldn't expressions of anger be justified in such cases?"

Anger can be described as both an emotion and an expression of displeasure. Yes, there is such a thing as righteous anger; and yes, anger can be an appropriate emotion. We will tackle those issues later; but for now, let me address anger as it appears in the vast majority of cases. Most expressed anger is incited by real or imagined personal injury that is accompanied by split-second hatred or a desire for vengeance and retaliation, which is clearly sinful. Because expressions of anger come so naturally to us, we do not readily like to admit that we could actually be reacting in a sinful manner. In fact, even mature Christians may be unwilling to evaluate their angry reactions in light of God's Word or to use biblical criteria to determine whether they are expressing righteous or unrighteous (sinful) anger.

My Way or God's Way?

Anyone who has ever supervised grade-school children at play has witnessed the unfolding drama of our sinful human nature. Johnny hits Tommy because he cut in line and then justifies his action because Tommy is so selfish. Mary calls Susie a hurtful name and, when confronted, explains that she was just kidding. Steven cheats in a game of basketball and loudly protests that he only made a mistake. When we watch what triggers tempers and observe how the children explain away their sinful actions (and reactions), we begin to see how the human heart naturally gravitates toward wanting to excuse, justify, or re-define what God calls sinful. If our reprehensible behavior is provoked by the unjust behavior of another, we are quick to conclude that our response is reasonable and justified. How easily we excuse our own angry reaction by explaining that someone or something has *made* us mad; and how quickly we exonerate ourselves, while at the same time condemning the very same actions in others. We easily become irritated by the sins and failures of those with whom we interact, even while we are incredibly tolerant of our own sins and failures.

We quickly recognize the sinfulness of anger when it is directed toward us, but we have difficulty seeing the sinfulness of anger when we must evaluate our own angry emotions and actions. To better understand how we see another's sin more easily than our own, we need to remember that God has declared every human heart to be "deceitful above all things, and desperately wicked," with no exceptions (*Jeremiah* 17:9). This verse means that every one of us is quite capable *and even prone* to deceiving our own selves, and all of us naturally behave in ways that cater to our selfish and prideful nature. Rather than face anger as a sin and conquer it by God's power and grace, we would much rather ignore its significance and dismiss it as an excusable reaction. Rather than conform our way of thinking and reacting to God's standards, we are much more comfortable making God's Word conform to our own human standards and code of conduct. We often have no real desire to eliminate anger itself but are content instead to merely learn how to keep anger under control enough to keep us out of trouble and disgrace. Our self-deception and ability to paint sin in virtuous colors keep us from recognizing the perils of our anger and prevent us from experiencing freedom from the sin. For this reason, understanding the role pride and humility play in anger is crucial to understanding and conquering anger.

People become angry for a vast variety of reasons; yet in every angry contention, the Bible tells us that the starting point of the contention is the sin of pride. We read in *Proverbs 13:10* that "*only* by pride cometh contention: but with the well advised is wisdom." Pride is the one common denominator in all sinful anger, no matter what other factors enter into the problem. The pride the Bible speaks of in this passage is a presumptuous arrogance, or an unreasonably confident presumption that one's own view is correct. To be thus proud is to confidently rely on one's own reasoning, to act in such a self-sufficient way that one does not see the importance of censoring one's own thoughts and attitudes to reflect God's point of view. We are told that God resists, or is opposed to, the one who is proud or self-sufficient. In contrast, God is gracious toward those who rely on Him and exchange their thoughts and ways for His thoughts and ways. Giving up our own way, however, does not come naturally to us. It requires faith and a deliberate act of our will to die to, or deny, ourselves daily as our Lord described in *Luke 9:23*, in order to follow Him.

The Way Up Is Down

The whole essence of the victorious Christian life is summed up in the words of Christ when He said, "If any man will come after me, let him deny himself, and take up his cross, and follow me. For whosoever will save his life shall lose it: and whosoever will lose his life for my sake shall find it" (*Matthew 16:24–25*). The believer loses victories in this life that could be his, as well as eternal rewards that are promised to all who truly follow Christ. In order to follow Christ and be truly free from sin's enslavement, one must be willing to deny (die to) one's own self-will and ways, one's own plans and personal ambitions. To deny one's self is to remove self from the heart's throne of governing power and yield instead to the loving lordship of Christ. Who and what governs our life at any particular moment will always determine its course and actions. Though believers do not bear the curse of the cross, for Christ bore it for us, they are to be willing to suffer for the cause of Christ and take a stand against sinful human reasoning. Self-will dies when it is replaced with a will to trust and follow Christ. Every act of obedience to the Word of God strikes a blow to our human self-sufficiency and pride. Notice the contrast between God's way and man's way in the following passages of Scripture:

- We naturally want to be exalted, and we earnestly desire the respect and consideration of others; yet we are taught by our Lord that before honor is humility, and before being exalted, one must be abased (*Matthew 23:12*).

- We naturally want to receive God's blessings, yet Christ teaches us we receive by giving (*Luke 6:38*).

- We like to lead, but the way to become a good leader is to become a good follower (*1 Corinthians 11:1*).

- We naturally want to fight back, but Christ tells us the way He wants us to fight is to love our enemies (*Matthew 5:44*).

- We want to be honored, but Christ tells us the way to be honored is to serve others, not our own aspirations (*Matthew 20:27*).

- We want to conquer the devil, but Christ tells us the way we conquer the devil is to submit to God (*James 4:7*).

- We like being strong; but Christ tells us when we are weak, we are strong (*2 Corinthians 12:10*).

- We want to be praised openly; but Christ teaches us to pray secretly, and he will praise us openly (*Matthew 6:6*).

- We like to be first, but Christ teaches us to be last (*Mark 10:31*).

As we study God's Word carefully, we begin to recognize that God's ways are designed to produce humility and an appropriate reliance on Christ rather than on self. Truly, nothing less than a supernatural work of God has the power to transform our human nature or to cause us to delight in governing our lives by principles such as these. We grow in wisdom and spiritual understanding only as we live in obedience to His Word and are dependent upon the transforming work of the Holy Spirit within us. Apart from spiritual growth and a work of God's grace in our hearts, we bristle at words such as *abase, follow, lose, serve, submit, weak, poor*, or *last*. Yet how many squabbles and outbursts of anger would be immediately silenced if these were the rules that governed our reactions, and those on the playground! If we are to experience freedom from the sorrows and destructions of anger, we must be willing to live by the laws of a gracious and wise God rather than the laws of our sinful human nature.

My Wisdom or God's Wisdom?

Wisdom is the ability to apply truth in everyday living. It gives us spiritual perception that enables us to understand the ways of God and the dangerous subtleties of human nature. By wisdom we see the delights of God's truth and experience the joys of incorporating it into our lives. Wisdom prevents us from being deceived and destroyed by Satan's traps. The Bible teaches us that it preserves and keeps us from evil and delivers us from deceptions of every kind. "The law of the wise is a fountain of life, to depart from the snares of death. Good understanding giveth favor: but the way of transgressors is hard" (*Proverbs 13:14–15*). "When wisdom entereth into thine heart, and knowledge is pleasant unto thy soul; Discretion shall preserve thee, understanding shall keep thee: To deliver thee from the way of the evil man, from the man that speaketh froward things" (*Proverbs 2:10–12*).

In contrast with God's wisdom, the wisdom of this world exalts self-reliance and self-will. It generates a false sense of confidence and determination to live life in pursuit of what one believes will make him happy, rather than what God tells us will bring true joy and peace. When we set our hearts on obtaining things we believe we must have in order to be happy and are then denied that which we passionately desire, we will naturally express our displeasure and react in anger. Wanting what God does not give is to reject God's wisdom and to choose instead our own understanding. In this frame of mind, what we want at the moment is of far greater importance to us than what God wants to accomplish in our lives. Though we are warned that only a fool puts unquestioned trust in his own human heart (or human reasoning), we tend to ignore the warning or believe it does not apply when we are angry over some perceived wrong or when we have our hearts set on pursuing our own direction.

The wise, in contrast to the foolish, starts with the premise that one is not wise in and of himself and should not rely on his own understanding apart from God in any matter. Such a person is able to respond to disappointment and mistreatment with Christlike graciousness rather than anger because he understands such things in the context of God's bigger picture, rather than seeing the provocation as an isolated incident. If our only concern when we are faced with irritation is our own comfort and aspirations, we will naturally be shortsighted and react in sinful ways. If, however, our greater concern is submission to a wise and intimately involved heavenly Father whom we believe oversees every detail of our lives , we are not so quick to see the offense apart from God's greater work on our behalf and the good of others as well.

God describes those who are slow to wrath as those who have *great* understanding, according to *Proverbs 14:29*. The Bible says, "The fear of the Lord is the beginning of wisdom: and the knowledge of the holy is understanding" (*Proverbs 9:10*). As we hear God's Word with the ear of faith, we learn to fear, or respect, God. When we believe and respect God, we develop wisdom that enables us to understand and apply God's principles to our lives. This ultimately produces spiritual perception that governs our lives like a compass in order to navigate us around life's pitfalls so that we will ultimately enjoy the rewards of faith. The Bible repeatedly associates anger with foolishness, pride, and self-will; whereas it associates the ability to patiently control the way one responds to irritation with wisdom, humility, and the fear of the Lord.

Our typical response when our desires are thwarted is to bristle in anger, believing any frustration of our will is an unjust interference with our quest for happiness. Only eyes of faith and understanding see a loving, faithful Creator working behind mundane irritations and provocations that often seem so senseless. Suffering that results because we are imperfect people living in an imperfect world along with other imperfect people is part of our human experience that God both allows and uses. The Scriptures offer an eternal perspective to such suffering and exhort us, "Wherefore let them that suffer according to the will of God commit the keeping of their souls to him in well doing, as unto a faithful Creator" (*1 Peter 4:19*).

My Will or God's Will?

Though God does not cause offenses and irritations, He does use them and make them work together for our good and His own glory. Our choice to cooperate with or to fight against God's methods reveals either our pride or humility. When faced with irritations, misunderstandings, disappointments, setbacks, or personal failures, either we will fight and war to have our own way; or we will submit and yield our lives to the wise management of our heavenly Father. Sometimes we forget that these kinds of disruptions in our lives are included in the "all" of "all things work together for good to them that love God, to them who are the called according to his purpose" (*Romans 8:28*).

Humility always leads to obedience and submission to God's divine will and always elicits God's gracious mercy and favor. As we are weaned from dependence on our own understanding and grow in our dependence on Christ, we begin to produce the fruit of His Spirit as a result. Listed among the characteristics of Christ's divine nature is the character quality of temperance, or self-control. Rather than being something we are commanded to develop by our own power or strength, temperance is something that develops by God's power and strength as we simply humble ourselves to submit, believe, and obey His Word. Genuine happiness and peace are things the world longs to experience but finds elusive. How precious that God freely gives both of these to those who humbly put their trust in Him on a daily basis! *Proverbs 22:4* assures us that "by humility and the fear of the Lord are riches, and honor, and life."

Jesus provided the perfect example of humility and submission to the Father that we are to follow. Though perfect in every way, our Lord and Savior lived in dependence on God and declared, "I can of mine own self do nothing… I seek not mine own will, but the will of the Father which hath sent me" (*John 5:30*). Paul understood that apart from Christ he could do nothing and humbly confessed, "I know that in me (that is, in my flesh,) dwelleth no good thing" (*Romans 7:18*). David understood the futility and sorrow of following the desires of the flesh as well as the joys of living in submission to God. He too spoke with humility and confessed, "I am poor and needy" (*Psalm 86:1*). Like Jacob, we receive God's enabling power to conquer anger when we can say as he, "I am not worthy of the least of all the mercies, and of all the truth, which thou hast showed unto thy servant" (*Genesis 32:10*).

Many Christians wonder why they cannot live the Christian life they desire, why they cannot seem to conquer their anger, why their prayers seem unanswered, or why they are so unhappy. The answer can often be found in their attitude of pride (self-sufficiency) and lack of humility (submission to Christ). Blaming people, circumstances, or anything at all for our anger or unhappiness reveals a lack of understanding and an immature refusal to acknowledge the fact that God Himself uses people and circumstances to accomplish His will and purpose in each of our lives. The instruction then is to submit wholeheartedly to the work of God through any means He chooses and to think differently about all those unwanted difficulties and frustrations that come our way. Consider the words of Peter: "Likewise, ye younger, submit yourselves unto the elder. Yea, all of you be subject one to another, and be clothed with humility: for God resisteth the proud, and giveth grace to the humble. Humble yourselves therefore under the mighty hand of God, that he may exalt you in due time" (*1 Peter 5:5–6*).

The Bible tells us that angry people become increasingly more unreasonable, less approachable, and less willing to humble themselves or admit wrong. Those who stubbornly refuse to evaluate their own sin or see any fault except the faults of others are blinded with pride and in danger of its terrible consequences. Anger entraps every willing participant; and in the end, anger leaves nothing but misery in its wake. No one conquers the world, the flesh, and the devil by fighting in worldly ways or exerting his own will and determination. The only means of escaping the wiles of the devil or conquering the sinful nature of man is to submit wholly to Christ alone. To submit to God's will is to resist the devil. Humility and submission to God's will opens wide the window of freedom in anger's prison.

My Strength or God's Strength?

Some Christians are at a place in their lives where they recognize their frailty and feel helpless to change. They might be inwardly lamenting as Paul was and saying as he, "O wretched man that I am! who shall deliver me from the body of this death?" (*Romans 7:24*). The answer given is one of great hope, for not one believer is left out of God's promises; and not one who trusts in Christ, being willing to confess his sin, is a "hopeless" case without sufficient resources for change. God's help is withheld from those who live in self-righteous pride, not those who are weak and prone to fail. Those who humbly recognize their weakness and need for God's grace and mercy find He lavishly pours out upon them His help and comfort. Paul asks *who*, not *what* will deliver him, and then happily replies, "I thank God through Jesus Christ our Lord" (*Romans 7:25*).

Have you come to a place where you are willing to admit, "I am an angry person"? If you can, you have already taken the most important first step toward freedom. It requires a tremendous amount of courage and humility to truthfully admit a problem. In fact, for every person who will plainly identify and admit sin, there are a great many who will not. Nevertheless, as important as this step is, simply admitting the problem does not get you where you want to go. You will need to prepare yourself for a spiritual journey that may take you many places before you reach your desired destination, keeping in mind that the journey is much shorter if you continue walking in the right direction.

Consider the spiritual path that brought the following men to a place where they began to seek answers from God in order to find freedom from a troubled conscience and strength that is more powerful than any sinful habit.

A Self-made Man

There once lived a fabulously wealthy young man who had spent his life working hard to be both honorable and successful. His zeal and character earned him a prestigious title and an abundance of luxuries. Yet for all his accomplishments at such a young age, he remained troubled about spiritual matters concerning his own soul. The respect of his colleagues and adoration of his community did not satisfy his gnawing uneasiness or give him the assurance that God was pleased with him. Peace eluded him; though he sought it carefully by studying the law of Moses and striving to do all the right things contained therein. He had sought the advice of religious leaders who held him in high esteem but found no comfort in their instructions or praise. He gladly would have traveled to the ends of the world if he thought there was someone there who could help him.

You can imagine this man's excitement when he began to hear about a religious teacher who not only performed incredible miracles but also taught with astounding wisdom capable of challenging even the most astute Bible scholars and intellectuals in his circles. The things he heard filled him with excitement and renewed hope; for perhaps, thought he, this was someone who could tell him what he most wanted to know—that he had indeed earned eternal life, or that he would, provided he did some good thing. He wasted no time setting aside all his important meetings and activities so he could personally travel to meet this man in the city where He was teaching.

By the time the young man's entourage neared the place where people were gathered to hear, he was filled with excitement and anticipation. Rather than stand back and wait, he saw an opportunity to get close and ran to meet Jesus, kneeling in His presence to show his respect and eagerness to listen. "Good master," he said, "What good thing shall I do, that I may have eternal life?" The young man waited for a reply, fully expecting to hear something that would immediately resolve his dilemma and give him peace of mind. Imagine his utter surprise when Jesus asked a question that seemed unrelated to his problem: "Why callest thou me good?"

Jesus understood exactly what troubled the young man and began immediately to draw his attention to the crucial things he must believe before he would have what he most desired. The rich man's salutation was one used to address a respected teacher, not someone he believed to be the promised Messiah, the Son of God. And so Jesus, desiring him to understand Who He was, replied that "there is none good but one, that is, God." In other words, Jesus could only be truly good if He were sinless, if He *were* God. Then the Lord addressed the man's efforts to earn God's favor and told him what others had, "If thou wilt enter into life, keep the commandments."

At that, the young man asked which commandments, believing he might have left one out. When Jesus reviewed the commandments listed in the law of Moses having to do with one's neighbor, the young man became excited, believing he had kept them all. "All these things have I kept from my youth up," he anxiously replied. "What lack I yet?" At this, Jesus proposed a challenge in order to show the young man that he could not keep the commandments of God perfectly as he supposed. He said, "If thou wilt be perfect, go and sell that thou hast, and give to the poor, and thou shalt have treasure in heaven; and come and follow me." Upon hearing this, the young man became very sad, because he had much wealth and possessions—so he quietly turned away.

His choice to walk away from Christ revealed what Jesus already knew—that he was covetous and did not truly love the Lord with all his heart, as the commandments require. His money was the idol of his heart and of greater importance than his love for God; yet he walked away rather than admitting his sinful condition or asking, "What must I do to be forgiven or saved?" The young man went away lost, not because he was selfish or covetous, but because he did not believe he was a sinner in need of God's mercy and did not believe Jesus was the promised Savior Who alone could grant him forgiveness and assurance of salvation. (You can read this story in *Matthew 19:16–26; Mark 10:17–30;* and *Luke 18:18–30.*)

Notice how our Lord turned the rich young man's attention to the law, not to show the man his righteousness, but to show him his sin and his need. This is exactly what the law was intended to do, as Paul stated in *Romans 3:20*: "Therefore by the deeds of the law there shall no flesh be justified in his sight: for by the law is the knowledge of sin." Just as a mirror reflects dirt on our faces, so the law reflects the dirty condition of our heart. The purpose of the mirror is not to wash the face but to reveal what needs to be washed. One who never sinned would not need a Savior or a substitute lamb to atone for sin. Therefore, God shows us what sin is in order to bring us to a place of understanding and repentance. It is only then that we are able to recognize the futility of our own efforts and are willing to admit our inability to live a sinless life making us dependent upon God's mercy for salvation.

A Successful Failure

The rich young ruler was much like the Pharisee who rejected the idea that he was unworthy of salvation but relied instead upon his own good works to commend himself to God. As he stood in the temple praying, he said, "I thank thee, that I am not as other men are, extortioners, unjust, adulterers, or even as this publican. I fast twice in the week, I give tithes of all that I possess." God was so unimpressed with this man's dialogue that He refused to acknowledge the Pharisee's speech as a prayer to Him at all, but tells us he prayed with himself.

On the other hand, the Lord tells us the prayer of the publican, with whom the Pharisee compared himself, was heard and answered. This man recognized his sin and his need of a Savior and came to God in repentance and humility, beating on his chest and crying, "God be merciful to me a sinner." This man, Jesus told us, went home justified, or forgiven. (You can read this story in *Luke 18:9–14*.)

The human heart naturally wants to be saved by good works and likes to believe one is made holy by human efforts and discipline. Man's way of salvation by works rather than by God's grace honors man instead of God and exalts man's pride. God's way is that we believe and rely upon the work of the Lord Jesus Christ and is the only acceptable way to find God's mercy and forgiveness. No human being is able to earn salvation, for no human being is sinless. "For by grace are ye saved through faith; and that not of yourselves: it is the gift of God: not of works, lest any man should boast" (*Ephesians 2:8–9*). Salvation is granted to those who receive it as a gift that cost God His Son's life but costs us nothing. It is wholly given on the basis of what God has done, not upon what we do.

Many come to Christ, believing He is Who He said He was—God in human form—and willingly rely upon Him alone for salvation. Yet rather than acknowledge the fact that they also need to rely upon the power of God to change their character, they often proceed to live as though they are saved by faith but made holy by their own efforts apart from Christ. Paul addressed this error when he wrote to the believers living in Galatia. His explanation began, "O foolish Galatians…" Paul wanted them to know how utterly silly and futile it was for them to think they could change their own heart by sheer determination alone. He asked the rhetorical question, "Received ye the Spirit by the works of the law, or by the hearing of faith? Are ye so foolish? having begun in the Spirit, are ye now made perfect [mature] by the flesh [human efforts]?" (*Galatians 3:1–3*). Paul wanted the believers to recognize that it was God's power that saved them when they relied upon Him in faith, and it was God's power that would change them as they obeyed His Word and relied upon Him to transform their hearts.

Sooner or later in our journey of faith, we come to understand that apart from Christ, we can do absolutely nothing at all and are powerless to change our own hearts. Sometimes it takes failing repeatedly to be what we know God wants us to be in order to bring us to the end of ourselves and to the feet of our Lord and Savior. Some give up altogether and turn away in frustration while others live in pride and self-deception, believing God is pleased with their outward behavior and human accomplishments apart from an inward change of heart that is wrought by God. Yet there are others who come to Christ as the publican did, confessing their helpless condition and begging the Lord for His mercy. It is these who find the supernatural grace of God to become like Christ and these who give honor to God for His mercy and love.

A Man of Strength

We can see in the life of David the effects of both self-reliance and reliance upon God. David was never stronger than when he saw himself as nothing and God as everything. And David was never weaker than when he was trusting in his own strength and reasoning and ignoring God's strength. Throughout his songs of praise, we read about his agony when he was defeated by sin and his overwhelming joy when by faith, he put his trust in the mercy of God. David's journey led him through valleys dark with sin and upon mountaintops bright with victory; but in the end, David always came to realize his strength was in the love and mercy of his Lord, not in his human efforts or achievements. It is what led him to sing so often of God's faithfulness and love and what gave him qualities that caused God to tell us he was a man after His own heart. David's worship was not empty or mechanical; it sprang from his experiences of spiritual defeat as well as spiritual victory. Knowing the reality of God's promises and God's Word caused his heart to overflow with joy and gratitude.

Words like these, found in *Psalm 138*, express David's deepest emotions and love for God. He tells the Lord, "I will worship toward thy holy temple, and praise thy name for thy lovingkindness and for thy truth: for thou hast magnified thy word above all thy name. In the day when I cried thou answeredst me, and strengthenedst me with strength in my soul…Though the LORD be high, yet hath he respect unto the lowly: but the proud he knoweth afar off… The LORD will perfect that which concerneth me: thy mercy, O LORD, endureth forever; forsake not the works of thine own hands" (*Psalm 138:2–3, 6, 8*).

So you see, if you have exhausted your own efforts to conquer sinful anger and are ready now to confess that you cannot change apart from God's work in your life, you are among the few who are ready to discover that He delights to show Himself strong on behalf of those who rely upon Him rather than upon their own strength. All who come to Him in humility and repentance find He is ever gracious and merciful. It is not the proud and self-sufficient that enjoy the peace and happiness found in Christ, no matter how polished and successful they may appear on the outside. Rather, it is those who quickly admit their own weakness and depend on Him for every victory that experience the joy of the Lord.

The Truth That Sets You Free

"Then said Jesus to those Jews which believed on him [Jesus is speaking to believers, not unbelievers], If [provided that] ye continue in my word [obey the Word of God], then are ye my disciples [followers] indeed; and ye shall know the truth [God's truth], and the truth shall make you free [free from any sin that would enslave you or steal your joy]...Whosoever committeth sin is the servant [slave] of sin...If the Son therefore shall make you free, ye shall be free indeed" (*John 8:31–32, 34, 36*).

If we will be free indeed from the power of sinful anger, we must make a deliberate choice to continue learning and obeying God's Word; for it contains God's truth, which is our road map that leads to freedom from enslaving sin. Apart from the Word of God, we cannot and we will not grow or survive spiritually. Virtually every success in the Christian life can be traced back to knowing the Word of God; for it is the foundation on which every doctrine, every blessing, and every Christian discipline is established.

It is the Word of God with the Spirit of God (*Philippians 2:13*) that has the power to change our hearts and produce in our lives the liberating and delicious fruit of God's Spirit. Paul wrote, "For this cause also thank we God without ceasing, because, when ye received the word of God which ye heard of us, ye received it not as the word of men, but as it is in truth, the word of God, which effectually worketh also in you that believe" (*1 Thessalonians 2:13*).

God's Word miraculously works in us who believe, changing us in ways that nothing else can! No wonder the Scripture tells us we do not live by bread alone, but by every word that proceeds from the mouth of God. The Bible not only sustains and strengthens us, it illuminates our way and leads us out of darkness. When Israel found themselves in trouble and cried to the Lord, he delivered them from their distress and destructions and healed them by sending them His Word. (See *Psalm 107:19; Proverbs 2:1–6; Psalm 31:19.*)

We are so much like that little bird whose instinct tells him to fly up, while wisdom tells him to fly down. As we sit exhausted on the highest beam, we must make a choice either to follow God's Word or to follow our own impulses. If we follow the path of wisdom, we will be led to safety and freedom; but if we follow our own reasoning, we will live our lives in captivity, a prisoner of our own foolishness. The door is open, dear believer; *fly down!*

THE MANY FACES OF anger

CHAPTER TWO

W hen we think of an angry person, we tend to picture someone whose face is tightened into an angry scowl, loudly expressing his outrage or venting threats as to what he is going to do about whatever has thwarted his will. We can imagine him slamming doors, hurling insults, or even lunging toward an offender with clenched fists. What we do not usually imagine is an angry person who is always smiling, quiet in nature, easy to get along with, or easily brought to tears. The face of anger may not look anything at all like the stereotype we think of. Soft-spoken, funny, sociable, or quiet people can be just as angry as those who are more serious or expressive. In fact, sometimes the most soft-spoken among us are inwardly the angriest!

Expressions of hostility and anger are normally easy to recognize, but not always. While many people react by speaking hatefully, yelling, hitting, or slapping; others use subtle sarcasm, excessive teasing, or biting humor to vent their buried hostility. Crying, clamming up, refusing to cooperate with others, exposing or portraying others in an unfavorable light, or quietly sulking is used just as easily and often. Those who are inwardly seething with quiet anger may not even perceive it in themselves, because they assume anger is always expressed in its more easily distinguishable forms. Such people typically learn to use words that can be masked expressions of anger. These include "I'm annoyed," "I'm irritated," "I'm fed up," "I'm hurt," "I'm aggravated," or "I'm frustrated." In all honesty, words such as these might more accurately be replaced with, "I'm angry."

Anger Concealed

Hidden anger is far more deadly than blatant forms of anger. It can deceive the heart of one who is angry, making it easy for him to excuse anger or believe it does not exist. Yet most often it is an intentional ruse designed to mislead the one who is the target of hidden anger or those who are observing and might discover it. The Bible compares such a person to a mad man who hurls deadly flaming arrows at another and then says, "Hey, I was just kidding!" The Bible says, "As a mad man who casteth firebrands, arrows, and death, so is the man that deceiveth his neighbor, and saith, Am not I in sport?" (*Proverbs 26:18–19*) Further on, the Bible compares the lips that speak burning words and the heart from which they originate to a clay pot that is dipped in silver (*Proverbs 26:23*). It may look like a fine silver vase on the outside, but in reality it is a cheap imitation that deceives the eyes of the beholder.

Some people are able to intentionally keep their anger so well hidden that others never suspect they have a problem with it. The human mind begins honing the skill of covering up, excusing, justifying, and hiding sin almost as soon as it begins to reason and exert a will of its own. Listen to the way little children artfully defend themselves when confronted, and note how they retell a contentious quarrel in such a way that they appear faultless in the ordeal. They are so clever at making themselves look good that even the most discerning parent is sometimes fooled. Give them several years of practice, and they may soon become adults who are able to defy discovery unless they encounter someone with unusual perception and understanding of sin's power to corrupt the human heart. And if they are discovered and confronted by someone close enough or wise enough to see through the deception, they will often react with surprising contempt and malice.

Anger Exposed

A wise prophet by the name of Hanani lived during the reign of Asa, king of Israel. He had enough courage and love for Asa that he came to visit him shortly after Asa had enlisted the help of Syria to defeat a common enemy. The battle had been won, Asa's objectives were met, and the spoils of victory were appropriately divided. The fact that Asa had rejected God's provision and instructions and relied instead on a godless nation for the victory did not seem at all unreasonable or sinful to Asa. The battle plan he had devised was a complete success as far as he was concerned. So when Hanani said, "Because thou hast relied on the king of Syria, and not relied on the Lord thy God, therefore is the host of the king of Syria escaped out of thine hand" (*2 Chronicles 16:7*), Asa became furious. Hanani went on to tell Asa that he had acted foolishly and, as a result, would have wars with Syria. The Bible tells us that Asa was so angry that Hanani had exposed and confronted his self-willed reliance on the king of Syria that he had the prophet thrown into prison.

Such ruthless retaliation was a common reaction toward God's spokesman then, and it continues still today. Jesus warned that we, like Him, would sometimes be hated and rejected for speaking the truth, even when it was done out of love and concern for the welfare of others. Very few are humble enough to immediately recognize their own sin and error when confronted. Rather than responding with contrite repentance as David did when Nathan pointed out his sin, people typically do as Asa did and use whatever means they can to defame, demoralize, and torment those who recognize and confront anger and sin. This is often why the first words out of the mouths of those confronted are hurtful remarks hurled at someone else and have nothing to do with the problem being raised. Vengeance such as this betrays a heart that has been deceived by its own hidden anger and pride and that is desperately trying to maintain its facade of respectable innocence. Quiet words or a calm countenance may hide our angry thoughts, but our actions reveal them.

Another common way people disguise anger is by quietly withdrawing from others to be alone. This reaction seems reasonable and innocent enough because it is often an honorable thing to withdraw in silence and spend time alone in quiet contemplation before responding to something troubling. In many cases, however, the meditation is not at all constructive or honorable. Rather than seeking God and re-orienting one's thoughts and meditations to reflect a Christlike, biblical point of view, people more typically withdraw in order to mentally rehearse over and over the many reasons why they *should* feel hurt and angry about something. The more one persists in such thinking, or more accurately, sulking, the more one is able to deceive himself into believing he has a right to feel sad, angry, or vengeful. Before long, such pouting and self-pity will become full-blown bitterness or depression. Very often, the sulking continues and the hidden anger builds until it explodes with astonishing fury at the slightest provocation. It might surprise everyone who witnesses it, but it never surprises God.

Consider the story of Ahab who withdrew in silence when Naboth refused to sell him his vineyard. When he did not get what he wanted, the Bible tells us that he refused to eat and instead lay down on his bed and turned his face to the wall. When his wicked wife Jezebel found him she asked, "Why is thy spirit so sad, that thou eatest no bread?" (*1 Kings 21:5*). Ahab then rehearsed for Jezebel the conversation he had with Naboth, making certain he sounded perfectly reasonable and Naboth perfectly *unreasonable*. He was all too happy to let Jezebel devise the means of Naboth's murder so he could then take possession of the forbidden vineyard upon which he had set his heart. Jezebel openly expressed her outrage and used force to get what she wanted, but Ahab's style was to hide his anger alone in his room, choosing instead to manipulate and plot in silence. When he finally got what he wanted, the sulking ended and his appetite "miraculously" returned.

We are horrified to think Ahab and Jezebel would go so far as to murder in order to remove what they saw as an impediment to Ahab's happiness. Yet we often respond just like self-absorbed Ahab, attempting to soothe our hurt feelings by withdrawing in self-pity and focusing on our own disappointment or bitterness. Like Ahab, the sulking often abates only when we have successfully won the sympathy of others, devised a plan to get what we want, or gotten revenge on those who seem to stand in our way. When our focus is riveted on what we want rather than submitting to what God may want, we are able to quickly forget He is a sovereign King who sees all, weighs all, and has the power to withhold or give anything He chooses. Like Ahab and Jezebel, we reap the appropriate consequences of our anger and soon find that getting what we want does not bring the happiness we thought it would. Unless God Himself grants our requests and God Himself grants subsequent happiness, all self-pity, pouting, sulking, whining, complaining, or any other means of expressing anger and displeasure will not bring satisfaction to our sinful human hearts.

Anger Disguised

Those who know Christ know that it is sinful to express anger the way unbelievers commonly do. This truth presents an enormous conflict for those who secretly want to maintain angry habits yet at the same time want to be respected as godly Christians. The more Christians want to maintain the appearance of godliness and the admiration of others, the more they will be motivated to expend considerable effort to hide or disguise any sinful expression of anger. These Christians learn to act patient, loving, and forgiving without being patient, loving, or forgiving. Instead of facing sinful attitudes hidden in their hearts and repenting, they often learn to conceal their hostility by disguising it as something virtuous.

There are numerous methods one might use to mask anger. One very common means of disguising displeasure or contempt is to clothe it in a cutting form of humor or teasing that provides fun for some at the expense of others. As long as people laugh, people who use humor as a weapon think nothing of the wounds their words and actions inflict. They ignore objections voiced by those brave enough to call cruelty by its rightful name and convince themselves they are "just having fun." They further evade personal responsibility for their cruelty by putting blame on their victim, telling him he's a poor sport or overly sensitive if he objects to teasing. Anger-induced teasing might take the form of tickling someone until he cries, playing roughly until one gets hurt, taking a normally acceptable practical joke to the extreme, or initiating conversation that humiliates or embarrasses another person. Angry people often take pleasure in seeing those they secretly resent wounded or trapped in helpless embarrassment, particularly if they believe retribution for offenses is deserved. They will often laugh the loudest when someone they secretly disdain or consider worthy of rebuke becomes the object of someone else's cruel humor.

Anger That Appears "Respectable"

Others disguise hostile attitudes by hurting those who displease them with silence of various kinds. Because they know yelling and venting is wicked, they resort to ignoring people with icy silence instead, presuming it is a righteous, innocent, or even disciplined way to respond. Silence can certainly *look* godly and can provide a veneer of respectability because it effectively conceals the malice of the heart. In reality, it is often a subtle attempt to disguise bitterness, inflict despair, evade responsibility, or control the emotions of others.

Silence can be justified by twisting the meaning of passages that tell us those who hold their peace and control their words are wise. Self-control that is wise (the fruit of God's Spirit) can be distinguished from self-control that is sinful by examining the motives of the heart. One has only to determine whether or not the silence is kind and loving to determine whether or not it is a sinful weapon of defense, a bludgeon to intentionally cause pain, a means intended to elicit sympathy, or a means of responding with the character and love of Christ. Silence that is being used as a weapon or an expression of anger or disdain is hurtful and self-focused. In sharp contrast, godly silence is *always* loving and concerned for the welfare of others. It is self-sacrificial, as opposed to self-protective, and is never used as a way to inflict sorrow, gain sympathy, win an argument by default, manipulate others, or provoke another to anger.

People devise many other ways of spiritualizing anger so that it looks justified or righteous. Moral people commonly change swear words just enough to make them sound honorable. *Darn, dang, shoot, gosh, freakin, geez, son of a gun*, and others are words designed primarily to express contempt or anger without the stigma of using vulgar or blasphemous words. The words themselves are not what make saying them a problem. Saying, "Oh peanuts!" is not particularly offensive; rather, the underlying expression of displeasure that can be rooted in anger is the problem. Most of us are unaware of the significance of many words we pick up simply by hearing them spoken by others. It is natural for us to search for words that will satisfactorily express strong emotions, and we seldom pause long enough to think about what it is we are really saying. Although not all exclamatory words are motivated by anger, we would do well to examine our responses to determine if they are, in fact, substitute words that cloak sinful anger in respectability.

One of the most common ways Christians camouflage sinful anger with explanations that seem innocent and spiritually justified is to espouse a cause that is righteous and then campaign for it with angry passion. Righteous causes provide an outlet for anger and self-righteous attitudes when people use them as an excuse to express outrage toward those who do not agree with them. These suppose they are expressing "righteous indignation" toward sin that is intolerable, when in truth they are exalting themselves in pride by condemning others and violating God's warning to forsake wrath because the wrath of man does not accomplish the righteousness of God (*James 1:20*). Anger vented in response to the sins of others is a common expression of resentment, unforgiveness, and bitterness. It is the practice of unmerciful people whom the Bible describes as "foolish." In the end, sinful anger evokes resentment and rebellion rather than humility and true repentance. Few Bible conversations illustrate this human tendency more clearly than one recorded in the New Testament between a father and son. In it, we can see anger that is motivated by something many would call a seemingly righteous hatred of selfishness and sin. Upon closer scrutiny, however, we will find it is nothing more than contention rooted in pride and self-centeredness.

Righteous, But Angry

The story Jesus tells in *Luke 15* centers on a young man who decided he wanted to leave the family farming business and make a living in the city where he could live life by his own rules. He asked his father for his inheritance and then packed everything he owned and took off for what he thought would be a fun and adventurous life. Instead of using his money to establish himself in a business of his own, he squandered all his money in immoral living and partying. When finally his money was gone, he became a destitute, homeless young man, scrounging for food in a pigpen, forsaken by all his worldly friends. In this low and desperate condition, he came to his senses and acknowledged his sin against God and his father. He decided to humble himself and go back home in order to make things right with his father and beg for mercy and a job. The loving father saw him coming and in great excitement ran to meet him and embraced him with love. The son immediately told his father all he had rehearsed. "Father," he said, "I have sinned against heaven, and in thy sight, and am no more worthy to be called thy son." But the father, instead of scolding and rejecting him, rejoiced to hear his son's repentant words and ordered his servants to prepare a feast so all could celebrate and rejoice with him.

The older son, meanwhile, was off working in the fields and was not aware that his brother had come back home. At the end of the day, he headed for home and upon nearing the house, heard the laughing and singing of people enjoying a feast over some happy event. He immediately asked a servant what was going on and was told of his brother's return and his father's joyful invitation for all to rejoice with him in celebration. The Bible then tells us, "And he was angry, and would not go in: therefore came his father out, and intreated him. And he answering said to his father, Lo these many years do I serve thee, neither transgressed I at any time thy commandment; and yet thou never gavest me a kid, that I might make merry with my friends; But as soon as this thy son was come, which hath devoured thy living with harlots, thou hast killed for him the fatted calf."

Notice the words and actions of this older brother who portrayed himself as righteous, deserving the father's mercy, and his brother unrighteous and deserving no mercy. He did not base his righteousness on God's imputed righteousness that is given by faith to those who recognize and repent of their failure to keep God's perfect commandments. Rather, he based his righteousness on a comparison with his brother whom he judged as vile and disobedient. This allowed him to see himself on a human level as perfectly obedient and godly and therefore deserving of the honor his brother was wrongfully receiving, while at the same time seeing his brother as someone who deserved the misery of his sinful past, as well as the disdain and rejection of those he had wronged. This older brother had a grossly inflated view of his own worthiness and a pathetically inaccurate view of God's love and grace.

Observe the way the older brother reacted when he heard the news of his brother's homecoming for the first time. He did not express any joy or sigh of relief for his brother's safe return. He could not even bring himself to express joy for his father who had been living in grief, hoping one day his wayward son would repent and come home. Instead this son became jealous and angry and sulked alone, refusing to greet his brother or join the celebration. His thoughts were centered exclusively on himself as he mentally rehearsed his brother's sins in comparison to his perceived goodness. Upon hearing of his older son's refusal to join the feast, the kind father left the party and urged his older son to come in. At this, the bitter words began pouring out of the older son's mouth, betraying his self-righteous attitude and unwillingness to forgive or extend mercy. Yet notice the particular way he justified his anger in his own mind. He pointed immediately to the basis on which he rested his opinion— "I have never sinned against you or rebelled as my brother has."

As many angry people do, the son wrapped his defense in an accusation with the intention of placing the blame for his unhappiness on someone other than himself. In this case, the son accused the father of failing to recognize and honor his righteous obedience, implying that he, not his brother, was the one deserving a happy celebration. Before we quickly condemn the obvious immaturity and selfishness of his reactions, we might want to remember that we too have been guilty of self-righteous, rather than righteous, indignation when someone we viewed as undeserving was honored or treated with kindness. We are prone, just as he, to point out the sins of others and contrast them with our own perceived righteousness in an effort to soothe the bitterness of jealous feelings or perceived injustice. We too say in so many words, "*I* would never stoop so low as to do such a thing!" and then proceed to justify our contempt and disgust. In doing so, we reveal an attitude of pride and spiritual blindness just as this young man did in his conversation with his father.

Finally, may I call to your attention the cold and subtle way the angry son referred to his brother. He did not call him "my brother." Rather, he chose to distance himself and refer to him as "your son," further demonstrating contempt for his brother and disgust for the way his father had chosen to respond to him. He reminded the father of his brother's irresponsible and wicked use of his hard-earned money and then implied that the father was rewarding evil with good. In a truly amazing and godly response to the self-centered and angry words of this son, the father responded with characteristic compassion and patient longsuffering. "And he said unto him, Son, thou art ever with me, and all that I have is thine. It was meet [suitable] that we should make merry, and be glad; for this thy brother was dead, and is alive again; and was lost, and is found."

Self-righteous anger focuses on what one wants, what one believes others should or should not do, and what one *demands* others agree or comply with. It seeks to force and intimidate others into obedience, rather than entreat and respond in the loving way the father did in this story to those who sinned. Both young men were given the freedom to make choices, even when they were sinful choices. Both were treated patiently, and both were loved and spoken to with kindness even when they were being unreasonable and rebellious. The father was quick to forgive wrongs done to him and put aside his own discomfort and sorrow. He showed wisdom in reminding his pouting son that everything he owned was his as a result of his faithfulness, while his brother had forfeited everything he inherited by squandering it in sinful choices. Unlike the angry son, the father did not have any desire to punish his son further in an attempt to satisfy his anger. As a type of God the Father, he exemplified the characteristics that Paul refers to in *Romans 2:4* when he says, "Or despisest thou the riches of his goodness and forbearance and longsuffering; not knowing that the goodness of God leadeth thee to repentance?"

Self-righteous anger is concerned about the letter of the law, not the intent, and values outward behavior rather than an inward change of heart. Like the Pharisees, many today hide anger and contempt with pious-sounding words and actions. They speak as the Pharisee whom God said prayed to himself, saying, "God, I thank thee, that I am not as other men are, extortioners, unjust, adulterers, or even as this publican. I fast twice in the week, I give tithes of all that I possess." How surprised that Pharisee would have been to hear that

God had no regard for his prayer, his lavish gifts of money, or his righteous deeds, but heard instead the prayer of the repentant and humble man that he viewed with disgust. Jesus remarked that "this man went down to his house justified rather than the other; for every one that exalteth himself shall be abased; and he that humbleth himself shall be exalted" (*Luke 18:11–12, 14*).

The most fatal error the older son made is the same fatal error that condemned the unbelieving Pharisees and others like them who still want to angrily rant and rave about those who violate God's law and believe their harsh treatment of them is justified, as well as their lack of compassion and mercy. They are quick to pick up stones and hurl them at a woman caught in adultery but slow to remember that God is watching and will show the same mercy to them that they show to others. The self-righteous see people in two categories: the guilty and the righteous. Jesus, on the other hand, sees only one category: the guilty. "*All* have sinned," the Bible tells us. *All* have "come short of the glory of God" (*Romans 3:23*). *All* are guilty.

God Gives Grace to the Humble

Paul reminds us in *Romans 3:19*, "Now we know that what things soever the law saith, it saith to them who are under the law: that every mouth may be stopped, and all the world may become guilty before God." Guilt is removed only when one humbles himself and admits his need of God's grace and unworthiness to be God's son. Yet God seeks to arouse guilt in those who feel none even while supposing they merit God's favor. He is opposed to those who attempt to commend themselves by comparing their righteousness with the sinfulness of others but warmly welcomes home those who come to Him in true humility, pointing fingers at none but themselves. When we see ourselves as undeserving recipients of God's mercy and grace and really understand that our *own* hearts are deceitful above all things, and desperately wicked—not just the hearts of murderers, adulterers or thieves—we are not so quick to compare our supposed righteous behavior with that of others. Somehow our ability to jump ten feet further than someone else does not matter a bit when we must jump a chasm hundreds of miles wide to get to the other side. We are just as helpless and inadequate to jump across as one having no legs at all.

Those who stand outside the prison and cheer when a murderer is executed sin according to *Proverbs 24:17*. It is right, according to God, for appointed authority to execute a murderer. But it is not right to be happy about the death of any human being for any reason. It is a fearful thing for a murderer to enter eternity with the blood of his victims on his hands. It is not something appropriate to rejoice over. Those who flash signs that say "Repent or else!" at football games bring shame upon the cause of Christ and misrepresent His character and heart. It is right, according to God, to warn the lost and urge all men everywhere to repent of their sins and put their faith in Christ Who, in love for their souls, bore the punishment for their sins. It is not right to imply that God or any mature believer takes pleasure of any kind in the death of the wicked who die in their sins, and it is not right to warn people to turn from sin without also telling them to turn to Christ for mercy and forgiveness. Those who angrily hurl insults and Bible verses at people who enter abortion clinics do not represent Christ or believers who follow His example of humility and self-control when persecuted for righteousness' sake. It is right to speak out on behalf of innocent babies who are being destroyed by their own mothers, but it is not right to use anger and hate as weapons against those who do not recognize abortion is murder or understand the significance of what they are doing.

May we realize that we have been called to follow Christ's example and suffer for the sake of others as He has suffered for us. Peter tells us there was no guile found in His mouth when others mistreated Him. He did not retaliate against those who hurt Him and did not threaten those who caused His pain and sorrow. May we put aside all anger and malice and instead pray like Christ, "Father, forgive them; for they know not what they do" (*Luke 23:34*) and be as our Lord Who is truly good and always ready to forgive and exercise mercy to all who call upon Him. When Christians are incited by their passions to spew hateful threats at the lost or shake their fists in the face of those who hate the Word of God, they are being motivated by passion for self-exaltation and vengeance, not passion for righteousness and truth.

Authority Misapplied

The mis-application of God-given authority is yet another way in which anger is often disguised and hidden. Those in positions of authority sometimes insist they have a right to be angry simply because they are to be honored and obeyed. Mothers might excuse anger directed toward their children by calling it "discipline," husbands might excuse anger directed toward a wife, pastors might excuse anger directed toward church members, police officers might excuse anger toward those they apprehend, or teachers might excuse anger toward students under their supervision—simply because they have a God-given responsibility to command and govern those under their care or because what they are saying to others is righteous. There is no question that God created an authority structure for the local church, the home, and government to insure harmony and leadership. However, all delegated authority is accountable to God Himself and is commanded to operate within the limitations set by God, and in a manner that glorifies God as the head of every human authority.

The Scriptures are very clear—the wrath of man does not glorify God, is not blessed of God, and does not produce the righteousness of God in others (*James 1:20*). Yes, it may stop wrong behavior; and yes, it may successfully command the attention of others or make them conform to one's will; but it does not transform their hearts nor produce the kind of change that is accomplished by the power of the Holy Spirit. Sooner or later, the consequences of such misapplied authority will surface. Most who are subjected to angry authority grow to resent and turn against those who govern in anger. Some may learn the art of angry manipulation themselves, mistreating others under them as they have been mistreated. Still others develop problems with depression, anxiety, self-destruction, or fear, while others simply become unhappy, angry people. The fruit of anger is anything but sweet.

Those to whom God has delegated authority do not receive authority to treat others with cruelty, anger, or harsh demands. The New Testament emphasizes the responsibility of leaders in authority to be humble, to entreat with patience and kindness, to exercise restraint, and to lead by example in the attitude of a servant. Leaders are warned not to treat others with heavy-handed dominance nor to exercise authority by demanding compliance in a harsh manner. Fathers are warned not to provoke children to wrath in the way they handle a child. Pastors are warned not to assert themselves or their will in an attitude of entitlement. Husbands are warned not to act in bitterness toward their wives. Employers are warned not to oppress and demean employees. The power granted by God to those in authority is granted for the purpose of leading, guiding, protecting, and teaching others for *their* benefit—not for the benefit of the leader.

God Grants Limited Authority

All authority is subject to God's Word. Never does God give any human authority the authority to demand loyalty towards himself above loyalty to the Word of God or Christ Himself. Blind trust in *any* human authority is never called for in Scripture, for every person's loyalty must first and foremost be to the Word of God and Christ. No church constitution, pastor, husband, school, parent, or government official has greater authority than the Word of God. A pastor does not have authority from God to ridicule and treat those who sin with contempt. He does not have authority to command church members to cater to his whims and desires any more than he has authority to command church members to drink Kool-aid laced with cyanide. A father does not have authority to command his children to engage in sexual favors for his perverted pleasure, nor does he have authority to use his power to vent his outrage or beat his children. A husband has no authority to command his wife to rob a bank or to submit to his abuse. Never does God give husbands the authority to force a wife to submit to him. A police officer does not have authority to enter a home without a search warrant nor to harass or abuse one in custody. In other words, all human authority is subject to the law of God, is limited by God, and accountable to God. Jesus alone can say, "All power is given unto me in heaven and in earth" (*Matthew 28:18*).

It is a fearful thing for one in authority to misuse the power granted to him or her by God. Those in authority are held to a higher standard of conduct, not a lesser standard than those they lead. Leaders are clearly warned that God Himself sees the manner in which they handle His sheep and He will deal with offenses committed against those under their authority. The apostle Paul solemnly warns every believer who would oppress another believer in any matter that, "The Lord is the avenger of all such, as we also have forewarned you and testified" (*1 Thessalonians 4:6*). Anger and harshness are not excused in the least, under any circumstance, simply because one is in a position of authority. The law of love is to prevail in any authoritative action for "love worketh no ill to his neighbor" (*Romans 13:10*).

Anger Expressed by Rebellion

Just as those who are in positions of authority often express their anger by abusing and over-controlling others, so do those *under* authority often express their anger by rebelling and defying those who govern. Anger may be expressed toward any kind of authority with quiet noncompliance or subtle resistance just as easily as it might be expressed with raised voices and outbursts of open rage. It is not unusual for angry people to express their disappointment, grief, and anger in ways that defy the boundaries they have been taught to respect or know to be right. In doing so, they tend to gravitate toward other angry and disgruntled people or anyone who sympathizes and reinforces any justification for their discontent. They may tend to find satisfaction in music that is defiant in nature or in activities that involve risk. One thing is certain—the inner tension and turmoil of unresolved anger will always look for an outlet to express itself, whether that outlet is directed inwardly or outwardly.

When angry people believe they are helpless to resolve their problems, they sometimes derive a sense of power over their despair by deliberately behaving in ways that are unacceptable or shocking to others. The more they win the disapproval or disgusted reactions of others, the more they experience the temporary satisfaction of a rather twisted type of revenge. Indulging in activities that satisfy the flesh and require angry people to abandon self-restraint tends to relieve the inner tension of anger, even while it produces a new tension of guilt and confusion and in the end, more anger. Again, it is a distorted means of defying whatever is troubling them or whatever has hurt them and is a means of assuaging the ravages of their anger. For a brief time, such rebellion may seem satisfying and empowering; but sadly, it only enslaves and destroys the one who attempts to express and manage anger in such ways. God's way is to go right to the heart of the matter, dealing first with whatever problem is fueling the anger rather than the way anger is being expressed.

Bitterness Disguised as Zeal

It was a great day when Simon the town sorcerer, whom many people feared, became a believer in the Lord Jesus Christ. As Philip began baptizing the many people in Samaria who believed, Simon also submitted himself for baptism. Then he followed close to Philip and listened as he taught and used miracles in order to point others to Christ. Shortly thereafter, Peter and John arrived and met with the new believers who had come to Christ. As Simon watched Peter and John pray for the young converts and lay their hands upon them, asking God to fill them with the power of the Holy Spirit, he envied their ministry and power. Simon wanted that power in order to be exalted among others, and so he offered the apostles money to obtain it. Immediately Peter discerned Simon's true motives and called upon him to repent of his sin because his heart was not right in the sight of God. Then Peter went straight to the hidden source of Simon's behavior and told him, "For I perceive that thou art in the gall [poison] of bitterness, and in the bond of iniquity [enslaved by sin]" (*Acts 8:23*).

Who would have guessed that Simon's real problem was anger and bitterness! He appeared to be an enthusiastic young convert, anxious to learn all he could and eager to please those who taught him. Yet below the surface lay a hidden reason for his desire to obtain the power of God. He wanted the preeminence over others, for he had a desire to assuage his own bitterness and anger by lording it over others in the same way he had done before he became a believer. Power is a dangerous thing in the hands of one who is poisoned by his bitterness, no matter what that power is—whether it be power to inflict suffering, power to do what one wants, power to manipulate others, or power to defy the wishes of others in authority.

Anger as an Emotion

Emotions are a wonderful God-given part of our nature and serve very useful and important functions. All emotions have their proper time and place—even sad ones—and are not in themselves sinful *when they are experienced or expressed properly.* All emotions have the potential of being misused and corrupted by our sinful nature. Human emotions become evil or good depending on what motivates them. When they are motivated by thoughts and desires that are pure and godly, they are an expression of the image of God that is stamped on our hearts. But when they are motivated by sinful perceptions, evaluations, assumptions, and beliefs, emotions become a sinful expression of our corrupt human nature.

For instance, we do not often think of joy as a sinful emotion; yet upon more careful scrutiny, it is easy to identify it as sinful if we know that it is motivated by something such as delight in seeing an enemy suffer in some way. The emotion of joy is not wrong—it is the *reason* behind the emotion that God condemns in *Proverbs 24:17* when He says, "Rejoice not when thine enemy falleth, and let not thine heart be glad when he stumbleth." Criminals experience joy committing crimes, and sin itself can provide temporary joy. We read in *Ecclesiastes 7:4* that the heart of foolish people is in the house of laughter. Finding joy and laughing inappropriately over the wrong things can be sinful; but again, what makes it wicked is what motivates it, not the emotion itself. This same principle applies to the emotion of fear.

Reasonable fear that aids in a quick and accurate response for the purpose of survival and safety is much different than fear that develops as a result of doubting God's faithfulness. Helpful fear can be quickly transformed into needless and sinful worry or paralyzing anxiety if our view of God's faithfulness and character is in any way immature or faulty. In a similar way, sorrow and grief are emotions that Jesus Himself experienced and did not condemn in others. Yet sorrow that is not accompanied with hope in God's promises, or sorrow that is provoked by sinful disappointment is not righteous in the least and leads to despair and spiritual defeat. In *Ecclesiastes 7:2–6*, God tells us that sorrow over the right kind of things actually makes the heart better, not worse. In *James 4:9–10*, we are taught to "let [our] laughter be turned to mourning and [our] joy to heaviness" when we must deal with our sin and confess it humbly before God. In this sense, sorrow is not sinful at all, but rather a mark of spiritual maturity and wisdom.

Anger is an emotion that is also a part of our human make-up and can be both sinful and righteous. It is not necessarily sinful to experience anger as an emotion in reaction to another person's sinful behavior in the way God experiences anger for the same reason. Paul instructs us to "be ye angry, and sin not: let not the sun go down upon your wrath: neither give place to the devil" (*Ephesians 4:26–27*). In other words, Paul is acknowledging the emotion of anger as a part of our human experience. Even so, he admonishes us not to express the emotion of anger in sinful ways (no matter how terribly we have been wronged) and not to leave anger unresolved; for to do so gives the devil an opportunity to use it destructively.

Righteous and Unrighteous Anger

How do we know our anger is sinful and not righteous? The same way we know other emotions are an expression of sin—when they arise out of sinful, selfish motives and are expressed in sinful ways.

Notice how Paul followed his instruction with guidelines for our attitudes. "Let no corrupt communication proceed out of your mouth, but that which is good to the use of edifying, that it may minister grace unto the hearers...Let all bitterness, and wrath, and anger, and clamor, and evil speaking, be put away from you, with all malice: and be ye kind one to another, tenderhearted, forgiving one another, even as God for Christ's sake hath forgiven you" (*Ephesians 4:29, 31–32*).

The Bible clarifies the difference between righteous and sinful anger by distinguishing righteous anger as anger that imitates God's and is exercised in submission to God's authority. God *does* express anger, and God *does* exercise vengeance, yet He is able to do so without any sinful motive, injustice, or lack of control whatsoever. Because God limits the authority given to any human being, He puts limits on how we are permitted to deal with the emotion of anger and requires our response to pass the test of love and obedience to Him.

Vengeance, for example, is expressly forbidden. The Bible says, "Dearly beloved, avenge not yourselves, but rather give place unto wrath: for it is written, Vengeance is mine; I will repay, saith the Lord" (*Romans 12:19*). Only God has the ability to carry out wrath and vengeance in perfect justice, for He alone knows and understands each human heart. We are to follow instead the pattern Jesus set for us by committing Himself to Him that judges righteously rather than retaliating and doing to others as they have done to us (*1 Peter 2:23; Proverbs 20:22*). Jesus prayed as David did in *Psalm 94:1* when he acknowledged God's right alone to exercise vengeance and simply asked the Lord to defend and intervene on his behalf. In cases where a crime has been committed against us, we are instructed to commit our case to governing authorities to whom God has delegated the responsibility to defend and protect the innocent (governing officials, police officers, military leaders according to *Romans 13:1–8*). We are to submit ourselves to God, trusting Him for the outcome, regardless whether or not our situation warrants using God's provision of governing authorities (*Proverb 28:25*).

Next, it is important to understand that God's anger is always on behalf of others and is always controlled and with purpose. It is expressed without sin of any kind and is perfectly just and reasonable. Righteous anger is not accompanied by hatred, malice, or resentment; it is not selfish, but rather, it expresses appropriate hatred of sin and injustice or stems out of genuine care and concern. The purpose of righteous anger is to correct or curtail destructive behavior, never to break relationships. God's anger is directed at injustice or willful disobedience. Likewise, righteous anger is always expressed on behalf of another who is oppressed, abused, or betrayed. It is not anger that is incited by wrongs done to one's own self.

Man's anger, in contrast, is usually uncontrolled and without patience; it is characterized by an unforgiving spirit, hatred, malice, resentment, and selfishness. Sometimes man's anger is used as an expression of one's indignation. This sinful anger destroys individuals, is often an expression of revenge or resentment, and is intended to hurt others or elicit sympathy for one's pain or mistreatment. It is an expression directed toward those who hurt or violate us, and is always a reaction to offenses against ourselves. Throughout the centuries, man's sinful anger has left a trail of destruction more devastating than drugs or any natural disaster. Nothing has destroyed more relationships and families, caused more children to rebel, or discouraged more Christians than anger. Nothing has destroyed churches, governments, nations, organizations, or partnerships quite like anger. Anger is deadly. Jesus connected anger with hatred and murder; and, indeed, anger does kill and destroy.

Righteous anger is directed toward the same things, in the same way, and for the same motives as God's anger. Yet even when anger is a righteous response, it is to be controlled and kept in its proper place, lest it destroy others and us by turning into bitterness and resentment. We are specifically warned not to use a righteous cause as a guise for getting our own way or taking vengeance on others, but are exhorted instead to love and serve one another in a Christlike attitude of humility, forbearance, and patience. Paul warns, "But if ye bite and devour one another, take heed that ye be not consumed one of another" (*Galatians 5:15*). We are never allowed freedom to retaliate against anyone out of righteous anger but are to trust God to be God and to execute proper vengeance in His time. We are permitted to use the righteous and just means God has provided for us to use in dealing with offenders and offenses, but not our own human methods. These God-given means may include the use of law enforcement, the court system, church discipline, and godly confrontation and appeal. Apart from these, we are commanded to entrust our case to Him Who has both the power and right to execute justice.

Righteous anger is extremely rare in human beings. The Bible cites many instances of expressed anger and provides enough information for us to know that it is almost always motivated by fear, jealousy, selfish demands and desires, prideful demands for respect and honor, unforgiveness, guilt, self-exaltation, vengeance, humiliation, misunderstood truth, or human frailties of many kinds. In very few cases does anger pass the test of righteous motives and methods of expression. One example might be Jonathan's anger expressed on behalf of David who was being unjustly persecuted by his father Saul (*1 Samuel 20:34*). Another might be Moses' anger toward Pharaoh recorded in *Exodus 11:8*. But we do not see many more examples than these where man's anger could be called "righteous." God's anger and wrath, on the other hand, is mentioned in the Bible hundreds of times and is always just.

The many faces of anger are diverse and sometimes incredibly well hidden behind a vast variety of behaviors. Those that have been discussed in this chapter are simply some of the more common ways anger might be covertly expressed. By learning to recognize the symptoms of anger, we can more accurately identify the destructive desires and beliefs that fuel it; for there is a much larger problem that lies hidden beneath the surface of what is seen.

THE HEART
OF THE
matter

CHAPTER THREE

P erhaps no other circumstance triggers anger more easily than a busy metropolitan freeway loaded with rush hour traffic and a sea of tired drivers all anxious to get somewhere. It is quite possibly the easiest place in the world for the true character of people to be revealed! Imagine you are driving alone on your way to the airport during one of the busiest times of the day. There is barely enough time to get to the airport, park, and catch your flight. As you are driving along, you realize you need to get over to the left in order to exit onto the interchange and another freeway. But as soon as you signal that you want to move into the left lane, the driver next to you slows down, making it impossible for you to move into the lane. When you speed up to get in front of him, he speeds up too. Because there are now other cars blocking access to the left lane and the exit is just yards away, you miss the exit. Immediately you experience a strong sense of anger (the emotion) and bang the steering wheel with your hand (an angry expression), then frown disapprovingly (another angry expression) at the young teenage driver who would not let you over. As he passes, you make sure he sees your obvious displeasure (another angry expression); and he, in return, smiles (an expression communicating his defiance) and makes an obscene gesture (an expression of contempt), and then races off. You angrily get off at the next exit, frowning and mumbling about the trouble you now have to go through in order to get back on the right road. All the way to the airport, you ruminate about the incident, thinking about the selfishness of the teenage driver whose license should be taken away and hoping the teenager's foolishness one day lands him in an accident that will teach him a lesson.

Now suppose that instead of being alone, you are driving someone else to the airport. Riding next to you is someone you do not know very well but highly respect—perhaps your pastor or his wife. The same thing happens again, and again, you sense the emotion of anger as soon as you are cut off from the exit. This time, however, you control your response without any problem at all and make a light-hearted comment about the teenager's maneuver. Instead of yelling something nasty, you smile, and then say, "Oh dear, I waited too long to get over to the left. Let's just hope we still make it to the airport in time!" At that, you continue in conversation, laughing and enjoying the company of your pastor as you drive to the airport, never thinking again about the selfish teenage driver—until you are on your way back home after dropping off your passenger. Once alone in the car, you begin thinking about the incident and are still irritated about it when you arrive back home and begin angrily telling the first person you see what happened.

Let's alter the story a little differently this time and see if this scenario better fits your typical response. You are alone, driving to the airport, when a teenager rudely cuts you off, causing you to miss your exit. In a split second, you sense the strong emotion of anger. This time, you immediately make a conscious decision to pray for the teen, instead of cursing him in some way, as you feel like doing. You ask God to protect him from harm and give him a heart to receive the gospel if he is not a believer, and then you ask for God's grace to fill your heart with a spirit of love and forgiveness, rather than hatred and revenge. You ask, too, that the Lord help you get to the airport on time if it be His will for you to make your flight, and then conclude by asking for grace and faith to trust the Lord's wisdom if you should miss the flight. As soon as you are done praying, you put on a favorite gospel CD and sing along the rest of the way to the airport, deliberately choosing to commit this incident to the Lord and focus your mind on pleasant things. You never think about the incident again as it seems insignificant in light of the things you have chosen to center your life on.

So…are you laughing just picturing yourself praying and behaving in this rather uncommon manner? This response is not a typical response at all, and in fact, might not even seem human. Perhaps you are thinking that there must be a happy medium somewhere or that in this situation, you would have every right to be upset. But let's look at these hypothetical reactions a little closer and see if, in fact, the driver did have a right to be angry, as we might suppose.

All of us like to imagine we are fairly righteous and good—that only certain conditions provoke us to be unnaturally sinful. The truth is that adverse circumstances reveal what we really are inside—they do not cause us to behave the way we do. Our circumstances do not determine the way we behave; but rather, our character determines the way we behave in any given circumstance. For example, in the first freeway scenario, the driver behaved in a very different way than in the second scenario. When no one else was present in the car, he expressed himself freely. From the example given, we have many clues as to what he was thinking and what was motivating his behavior.

First, we notice that he had a specific focus and goal—to get to the airport on time. When someone thwarted his progress toward his goal, he immediately became indignant. Perhaps he was thinking something like, "I can't believe that driver would do something so selfish!" Needless to say, he became upset and felt compelled to express his displeasure in such a way that the teen would *know* he was disgusted. When the teen responded with obvious disregard and contempt, and the exit was missed, he became even angrier. He did not pull out a gun—after all, he is a Christian—and he did not swear, return the obscene gesture, or call the highway patrol. He was certainly exercising a measure of control, which was good, but his focus was very much on himself and the trouble this teen had caused him. The fact that this teen is likely an unbeliever who is headed toward misery and an eternity without Christ did not even cross his mind. Thoughts of love, forgiveness, mercy, or trust in God were the furthest things from his thinking. Instead, he found a measure of relief mulling over the incident and hoping the teen, at the very least, would be pulled over by a policeman and cited for reckless driving. Those rather vengeful thoughts, together with his anxiety over being late and possibly missing his plane, were what wholly occupied his mind.

In the next scenario, the fact that someone else was in the car with the driver definitely changed things. The provocation was exactly the same, but the different circumstances made a difference in how he openly reacted. Not wanting to offend his passenger or appear ungodly, he was motivated to control his speech and respond in a lighthearted manner. He even accepted a measure of responsibility by noting that he waited too long to change lanes, and he acted as if missing the plane would be no big deal. (Of course, it was not his plane that would be missed but his passenger's!) All and all, it would appear that he handled things in a rather mature and godly way— until that is, he dropped off his passenger and began driving home.

What took place once the inhibiting factor was removed revealed more accurately his motives and his true beliefs. Soon his thoughts gravitated toward the selfish teenage driver and the trouble he caused—and could have caused. The smoldering continued as he fed the fire more wood and ruminated all the way home. By the time he walked in the door, the fire had turned into flames and he wasted no time finding someone who would share his outrage and appease his anger. His initial outward behavior was not a true reflection of his heart: it was merely a show designed to make him appear that he was acting in a genuinely godly manner. The moment the audience he wanted to convince was gone, he relaxed and expressed his true character, thoughts, and beliefs. Like in the first scenario, his major focus was on himself, his presumed right to be treated with respect, and on the inconvenience he had experienced.

In the third scenario, the driver's response was much different. His reaction was not designed to impress anyone, for no one saw him nor heard his prayer. As in the first two situations, he was definitely angry when he was cut off; but he refused to sin as he recognized the tension and emotion of anger rising within himself. He did not pretend that the teen was a sweet and innocent youngster, but rather, acknowledged the teen's selfishness. Doing so led him to make a deliberate choice to think about the spiritual welfare of the reckless teen and to pray for him. Rather than to curse the teen or wish God would avenge his wrong, he prayed for God's blessing and mercy on the rude driver. He also did not pretend he was not prone to dwell on the wrong done and the irritation he was experiencing as a result of missing the exit. This prompted him to pray for himself as well as the teen, asking God to give him supernatural love and grace, together with enough trust to accept the outcome as God's will if he should miss the plane. His prayer completed, he did not immediately launch into a pity party or indulge in congratulating himself for his righteous outlook. He deliberately chose what he would focus his mind on and engaged himself in singing and thinking about the work he was doing.

What he did in response to the provocation was to apply to his own life Christ's command to "love your enemies, bless [speak well of] them that curse [speak evil of] you, do good to them that hate you and pray for them which despitefully use you and persecute you" (*Matthew 5:44*). Passages such as *Philippians 4:8* were more to him than a memory verse or a nice text for a sermon. Paul's admonition to think about things that are true, honest, just, pure, lovely, of good report, virtuous, and worthy of praise was a genuine spiritual truth meant to be put into practice.

In all three scenarios, the driver had a predominant goal in mind when he encountered the irritating teen. In scenario number one, his focus was on getting to the airport in time. In scenario number two, his focus was on preserving his testimony and reputation. In scenario number three, his focus was on cooperating with whatever purpose God had in allowing him to experience the irritation. In all but the third instance, he held to the belief that he and his desires were of the utmost importance. Only in the third instance did he think of pleasing God over pleasing himself. What made the difference in each situation? The beliefs and desires in his life at the time of each situation. Each time, he made choices about the way he wanted to live his life and respond to its irritations and problems. His choices were a reflection of his core beliefs about himself and others, his purpose for living, and his relationship with God.

An orange tree produces oranges because it is an orange tree. If we control the environment of the orange tree by depriving it of light or nutrients, it may not produce oranges—but it is still an orange tree. All we have to do to prove the tree's identity is expose the tree to normal conditions favorable to orange trees so that it will once again produce oranges. People may not produce sin when there is no provocation; however, if we introduce to their lives normal conditions of life such as financial pressure, a disagreeable neighbor, a lack of sleep, or unjust treatment, such as came from the rude teenage driver, there may be an instant change in their behavior. That which is deep inside the heart rises to the surface in a split-second reaction and immediately identifies the condition of the heart. Words and actions are like fruit on a tree—they identify what kind of fruit tree it is. Jesus reminds us that "every good tree bringeth forth good fruit; but a corrupt tree bringeth forth evil fruit" (*Matthew 7:17*). "A good man out of the good treasure of the heart bringeth forth good things; and an evil man out of the evil treasure bringeth forth evil things" (*Matthew 12:35*). Our character reveals itself best in adverse conditions, not when things are going exactly as we would like.

We can sum it up as Christ did when he said, "But those things which proceed out of the mouth come forth from the heart; and they defile the man. For out of the heart proceed evil thoughts, murders, adulteries, fornications, thefts, false witness, blasphemies" (*Matthew 15:18–19*). When the Bible speaks of the heart, it refers to our inner beliefs and the place of our affections and desires. Our heart is who we really are inside, where no one else can see but ourselves and God. The heart is where all behavior, right or wrong, originates. It is the center of our being, where faith and love for God reside, as well as doubt and fear and selfish ambition.

But I Want…

Sometimes we react in anger so quickly that we are not aware that we actually thought and evaluated the provocation in our hearts before we responded to it. In fact, reactions happen so fast that we tend to conclude that something or someone *made* us mad, and our response could *not* be controlled! While it is true that we can be provoked to anger, it is not true that our reactions to the anger cannot be controlled. We might truly believe someone or some thing is the direct cause of our anger and say, "Now look what you made me do!" But the fact is, *no one*—not even the devil—*makes* us sin! "But every man is tempted, when he is drawn away of his own lust and enticed" (*James 1:14*). Although we like to say, "Such and such or so and so MADE me angry," as if someone or something held a gun to our heads and forced us to react in anger, it is not our circumstances, but the desires (or lusts, as the Bible describes it) in our own hearts that cause us to react the way we do. While adverse circumstances may indeed provoke strong emotion in us, it is our individual interpretation of circumstances and our own desires and choices that ultimately incite our anger.

James tells us that our anger originates from within us, "even of your lusts [selfish desires] that war in your members" (*James 4:1*). When our hearts are filled with "I want," "I need," and "I deserve," sinful anger is lurking at the door just waiting for us to let it in. When our desires become something we believe we are entitled to and are in some way being wrongly withheld from us, we react in anger. The desire itself may not necessarily be wrong; our desires may actually be quite noble and good. The problem is the place of importance that we give to our desire and whether we are willing to sin in order to get it or sin if we do not. For instance, it would not be sinful in the least for a single young woman to desire a husband. If, however, she desires a husband to such an extent that she impatiently seeks the companionship of an unbeliever and marries him, she has allowed a good desire to become a sinful desire. In her self-willed determination to obtain that which she desired apart from God, she forsook the God she professed to love and trust and was willing to sin to satisfy herself.

A desire that has become a requirement for our happiness or a demand of any kind completely leaves God out of the equation, whether it is the desire of a mother that her children sit quietly or the desire of a husband that his wife balance the checkbook properly. The place of importance we give to our desires must never supersede the importance of learning to rely on God and love both Him and others. Anger is essentially an expression of our heart that says, "I don't like what has just happened, and I am extremely unhappy about it." Our feelings and wants become the prime issue at the moment we express this kind of anger. We are far from being focused on God's work in the matter, what He wants to accomplish, or how He wants us to respond to disappointment, injustice, the sinful behavior of others, or adversities common to life. Instead, reactive thoughts along the lines of "he should" or "he shouldn't" or "how dare he" invariably take center stage in our minds and immediately precede expressions of sinful anger.

James 4:2–3 describes the futile attempts of angry people to get what they want. "Ye lust, and have not: ye kill, and desire to have, and cannot obtain: ye fight and war, yet ye have not, because ye ask not. Ye ask, and receive not, because ye ask amiss, that ye may consume it upon your lusts." When we are angry, we want life on our own terms, without inconveniences, disappointments, or suffering of any kind. We are like those whom James described, who passionately wanted their own way, even to the point of circumventing God's will, or sinning, in order to get it. Any time we have to sin in order to get what we want, we indulge our selfish demands and reject the Word of God. Rather than seeing God in every situation of life and waiting patiently for Him to work on our behalf, we often ignore Him completely and focus only on what we want and the fact that we want it now. How often we act like Martha who came to Jesus asking Him to make Mary get up and help! When we are angry, we do not want what Jesus wants, nor do we have any intention of giving up our desires for His. What we want is for Him to side with us and essentially cater to our selfish demands. When He is not manipulated or bullied into giving us what we ask for, we are all the more agitated or discouraged.

The Root of Anger

Angry behavior reveals our desire to govern our own lives on our own terms, rather than submit to God and live our lives on His terms. At its root, anger is a desire to exalt and worship self and is a refusal to yield to the authority and lordship of Christ. This is why James goes on to address angry people as spiritual adulterers who think and behave in the same way the world does. He says, "Ye adulterers and adulteresses, know ye not that the friendship of the world is enmity with God? Whosoever therefore will be a friend of the world is the enemy of God" (*James 4:4*). We become spiritually unfaithful when we pursue our own interests rather than God's and depend on ourselves to decide what must be done about a difficult situation, what should or should not happen, or how others are to behave or not to behave. Rather than pray, "Thy will be done, on earth as it is in heaven," we are more likely to pray, "Give me this day what I desperately want."

An elderly Christian who had lived her life struggling to overcome anger was walking down the street, sorrowfully pondering the failure of her efforts to contain her explosive anger. Now in the closing years of her life, she was becoming increasingly aware of how her quick temper had caused so many heartaches in her life, had destroyed so many relationships, and had left her a sad and lonely old woman. As she walked along the sidewalk, she came upon two little boys, one of them crying as if his heart would break and the other standing next to him in unconcerned silence. The woman felt compelled to ask the unperturbed child, "What's the matter with your friend?" "Oh nothing," the boy replied. "He just wanted to have his own way." The old woman quietly turned away and continued her walk, pondering what she had just heard. In a few moments, she sighed as she thought to herself, "That is just the matter with me and has been for over seventy years. I have been trying to have my own way and crying because I couldn't have it."

The moment we give our desires over to the Lord and our heart's greatest desire is to be governed by Christ, we remove the fuel that keeps the coals of anger burning. Anger cannot coexist with trust in God's loving shepherding care or with fervent love for God and others. It fizzles out and dies when there is no self-interest or sinful desires to keep it smoldering. The more we understand and believe the love God has for us as His own dear children, the easier it is to confidently entrust Him with our lives and lose our desires in His. Without a mature knowledge of Christ's loving and immensely gracious character, we have a very difficult time believing His will is more blessed and desirable than our own. Yet the more we know of Christ's love for us, and the more we comprehend how much He forgives and extends to us both grace and mercy, the more we understand how to respond to life's irritations and disappointments; and we delight to do so.

Paul expressed this to the Colossian Christians by saying, "Put on therefore, as the elect of God, holy and beloved, bowels of mercies, kindness, humbleness of mind, meekness, longsuffering; Forbearing one another, and forgiving one another, if any man have a quarrel against any: even as Christ forgave you, so also do ye. And above all these things put on charity, which is the bond of perfectness [maturity]. And let the peace of God rule in your hearts, to the which also ye are called in one body; and be ye thankful" (*Colossians 3:12–15*).

As a Man Thinks...

Perhaps you are beginning to recognize that the battlefield in which this war against anger is fought is actually the mind, and the only offensive weapon God has given to win it is the Word of God. In God's Word, we find the truth that sets us free from enslaving sin the moment we believe and appropriate it into our lives. We can be certain of this—none of an author's concocted strategies are going to conquer anyone's anger (which is why this book centers on what God has said rather than what other authors have said). God provides clear instructions about what works and what does not. Paul reminds us, "For though we walk [live] in the flesh [a human body prone to sin], we do not war after the flesh: For the weapons of our warfare are not carnal [like the world's], but mighty [powerful] through God to the pulling down of strongholds [hidden places where sin gets a vice-like grip in our lives]; Casting down imaginations [human reasoning], and every high thing that exalteth itself against the knowledge of God, and bringing into captivity every thought to the obedience of Christ" (*2 Corinthians 10:3–5*). Stop and really ponder these words and their meaning. Notice the great importance God places on bringing *every thought* under subjection to Christ. What we choose to think about and what we conclude in our minds has a powerful impact on what we will do and how it will affect our life, for good or for bad.

Our mind is more than a physical organ called the brain. The human mind includes the immaterial part of man that seeks to understand by processing thoughts into a rational order and then drawing conclusions and acting upon them. Our thoughts influence and produce behavior, yet our behavior also influences and produces thoughts. One feeds upon the other. The foundation of our core beliefs is formed as we engage our minds in drawing conclusions about God, others, ourselves, and the world in which we live. If that foundation is faulty, our future choices and actions will be faulty as well.

Then, the more we make poor choices that reinforce false beliefs, the more we are prompted to make even more poor choices until we become imprisoned by the bars, or beliefs, of our own making. We must replace every wrong belief with God's truth, in order for us to experience the freedom and joy of being set free from all that would enslave us and rob us of the joy God wants us to have as His children. Miraculous change comes only as we are "transformed by the renewing of our minds" (*Romans 12:2*).

Notice the passages in *Ephesians 2:2* where Paul reminds the new believers how they used to behave before they were saved. "Wherein in time past ye walked [conducted your life] according to the course of this world, according to the prince of the power of the air, the spirit that now worketh in the children of disobedience." Before these believers were given new life in Christ, their conduct was openly defiant against the laws of God. Like Satan, they exhibited their self-will and rebellion in the ways in which they lived. In the following passage, Paul goes on to say that before we were saved by God's grace, *all of us* exhibited the traits of those who are controlled by their sinful nature. And what are the outward traits of those who have not been saved? We read in *verse 3*, "Among whom also we all had our conversation [behavior] in times past in the lusts [selfish desires] of the flesh [human nature], and of the mind; and were by nature the children of wrath, even as others." Before we were saved, we acted and thought as those who are in rebellion toward God act and think—but notice how Paul characterizes the actions and thoughts of the unsaved. He tells us they are naturally *children of wrath*. Anger, or wrath, is an integral part of their character affecting not only their actions, but their innermost *thoughts* as well.

Those who have been saved by God's grace are to be known as children of light who walk in love—not children of wrath who walk in darkness. The child of God, in contrast to the child of this world, is able to win the war against the flesh by exercising his new life in Christ and bringing *every thought* into obedience to Christ according to *2 Corinthians 10:3–5*. We do not need to be slaves to the selfish demands and desires of our old human nature. As children of light we are to loathe our self-centered and hateful thoughts and pray as David, "Let the words of my mouth, and the meditation of my heart, be acceptable in thy sight, O LORD, my strength, and my redeemer" (*Psalm 19:14*). Only when the thoughts and desires of our hearts are brought under subjection to Christ do we become victorious over sinful anger.

How we think has a profound impact on how we act and react to things that thwart our will—whether it be the immature behavior of children, the failures and selfish acts of other people, daily adversities, difficult problems, interruptions, rejection, loss, or personal failures. To the degree our thoughts are brought into submission to Christ, our outward life will reflect the nature of our heavenly Father rather than the nature of Satan and his followers. What we think about reveals who we are and what we will become, for the Bible tells us, "As a man thinketh in his heart, so is he" (*Proverbs 23:7*).

What We Believe Determines Our Behavior

It is hard for us to imagine Satan having access to heaven, where even now he delights to stand before God in order to accuse believers living on earth. Job certainly was not aware of the conversation that took place between God and Satan when the evil one targeted him for accusation and predicted that Job would become angry at God and curse Him if Job lost all that God had blessed him with. Satan said to God, "But put forth thine hand now, and touch all that he hath, and he will curse thee to thy face" (*Job 1:11*). The book of Job opens with a description of Job's character—he was described as one who was spiritually mature, honest, and steadfast in his moral principles, someone who feared God and hated evil. Because Satan believed that Job was upright in his character and devoted to God merely because God had blessed him so abundantly, God gave Satan permission to take all that Job had.

In one day, Job lost all his wealth, almost all his servants, and all of his grown children. He was the victim of thieves who stole his goods, of murderers who killed his servants, and of a tornado that killed his children. Yet in his excruciating grief, he did not become angry at God, nor did he curse God or others. Instead, he responded to his trials with grief and quiet acceptance, and worshipped God. The Scriptures say, "Then Job arose, and rent his mantle, and shaved his head, and fell down upon the ground, and worshipped, and said, Naked came I out of my mother's womb, and naked shall I return thither; the LORD gave, and the LORD hath taken away; blessed be the name of the LORD. In all this Job sinned not, nor charged God foolishly" (*Job 1:20–22*).

What amazing faith! Yet notice that it was faith grounded in what Job believed to be true about God. Job did not understand why God had allowed such loss and devastation, but he did know that God is good and just and worthy of his trust. He had hope in the promises of God and was convinced, even in the face of such horrors, that God had a righteous plan he did not understand. It was what Job firmly believed that caused Job to respond the way he did. Still, Satan was not satisfied and told God, "But put forth thine hand now, and touch his bone and his flesh, and he will curse thee to thy face" (*Job 2:5*). God then gave Satan permission to destroy Job's health.

When people lose their home to some natural disaster, they will often comfort themselves by saying, "At least we have our health and each other." But Job did not have the comfort of children gathering around him in his time of sorrow and did not have physical strength or health for which to be thankful. Making matters even worse, Job's wife became angry and scorned him by saying, "Dost thou still retain thine integrity? Curse God, and die. But he [Job] said unto her, Thou speakest as one of the foolish women speaketh. What? shall we receive good at the hand of God, and shall we not receive evil? In all this did not Job sin with his lips" (*Job 2:9–10*). Even with the added loss of his health and loss of a loving wife who might have offered him understanding and support, Job did not become angry or curse God.

But Why?

Repeatedly Job professed his faith to his three friends who tried to blame and condemn him. Job told them, "For I know that my redeemer liveth, and that he shall stand at the latter day upon the earth: And though after my skin worms destroy this body, yet in my flesh shall I see God: Whom I shall see for myself, and mine eyes shall behold, and not another; though my reins be consumed within me" (*Job 19:25–27*). Eternal things were as real to Job as the tangible things he could see. He understood that the trials of this life have eternal significance and do not happen to a believer without purpose. It was this understanding that determined the way he responded to his suffering. He could not answer the question, "Why?" and he could not convince others that God had a purpose other than punishment for sin. Yet he remained unshakable in his belief that God's ways are perfect and require submission. Not only did this belief have a profound effect on his behavior, it ultimately won the approval of God Who blessed him with twice as much as he had had before.

A Life with No Regrets

Joseph was another amazing person, considering the way he reacted to numerous injustices throughout his life. We see no evidence of anger or bitterness toward his brothers for selling him into slavery in a foreign country. He harbored no grudge toward the woman who falsely accused him of rape, though it landed him in prison. He did not become enraged when those he helped forgot about him or when his brothers finally showed up years later to ask for food. This behavior was not the result of some quirk in Joseph's personality or superhuman quality. It was the result of what Joseph firmly believed about God's character and the surety of God's promises. He simply kept on serving God, kept on doing what was right, and kept on trusting God to work everything out in His own time. And God did, for God *always* rewards those who put their confidence in Him, rather than insist on having their own way. When the events in Joseph's life suddenly put him in the second highest position in Egypt, he continued to trust God and rely on Him.

The end of Joseph's story is a joy to read because it has such a happy and satisfying ending. On the other hand, the account of Joseph's angry brothers shows they missed their opportunity to live for God and experience the reward that relying on Him brings. Their life story was not one of triumph or courage in the face of perplexity. While Joseph was free from inner turmoil, though he lived in prison, his brothers were enslaved in guilt and bitterness, though they lived in freedom. Even to the end, they worried that Joseph was going to exact revenge for what they had done to him. What they believed and what Joseph believed made the difference in how they behaved in the circumstances that were allowed in each of their lives. Examine closely the many spiritual truths found in Joseph's reassurance to his brothers. He told them, "Now therefore be not grieved, nor angry with yourselves, that ye sold me hither: for God did send me before you to preserve life" (*Genesis 45:5*). Years later he was still reassuring them. "And Joseph said unto them, Fear not; for am I in the place of God? But as for you, ye thought evil against me; but God meant it unto good, to bring to pass as it is this day, to save much people alive. Now therefore fear ye not; I will nourish you, and your little ones. And he comforted them, and spake kindly unto them" (*Genesis 50:19–21*).

Life with the "Other Woman"

Hannah was yet another believer who faced a tremendous challenge that would have produced enormous bitterness and anger in most women. Though many married women have had the unhappy experience of discovering the "other woman", Hannah actually lived with the "other woman" in her husband's life. The Bible describes her predicament by telling us that Hannah had no children, while Peninnah, her husband's other wife, had many children. Peninnah was Hannah's adversary who provoked her relentlessly, with the specific purpose of making her feel distressed about her inability to have children and of tormenting her with painful words. Hannah's one consolation was that her husband Elkanah loved her and did his best to compensate for her lack of children. Of course, this did not exactly make her life with Peninnah any easier. Rather, it made Peninnah all the more bitter and cruel.

The Scriptures do not record Hannah's fighting or being angry toward Peninnah; but instead, we are told of her continual grief and tears over the matter. One year, as the family made its yearly trek to Shiloh to give offerings to the Lord, Peninnah made it a point to antagonize Hannah over the fact that she had no children to bring with her, the implication being that God had cursed her. This again caused Hannah to grieve, so much so that she wept alone and did not eat. Yet even in the face of this cruelty, we do not see that Hannah retaliated in anger or foolishly refused to have anything to do with God. Instead, she went to the temple and knelt to pray and pour her heart out to the Lord. As she prayed silently, she was so intense in her pleas to God that her mouth moved, though she did not pray out loud. Eli the priest observed Hannah, and jumping to conclusions, presumed she was drunk. He immediately approached her and accusingly asked, "How long wilt thou be drunken? put away thy wine from thee" (*1 Samuel 1:14*). Most of us might have responded to Eli's false accusation with indignant disgust and anger. Instead, Hannah replied with due respect for the office of priest by saying, "No, my lord, I am a woman of a sorrowful spirit: I have drunk neither wine nor strong drink, but have poured out my soul before the LORD. Count not thine handmaid for a daughter of Belial: for out of the abundance of my complaint and grief have I spoken hitherto" (*1 Samuel 1:15–16*).

Hannah, far from being cursed by God, was blessed with faith and a tender heart toward the Lord. What Hannah believed about God is evident by the way she responded to her trial, the way she reacted toward those who treated her unjustly, and the manner she chose to resolve the problem that confronted her. In the crucible of her trials, her character rose to the surface and shined brightly. Before the year was out, Hannah gave birth to Samuel who would become one of God's most faithful servants and prophets. As a testimony to Hannah's faith and love for God, she dedicated Samuel to the Lord and brought him back to Shiloh to serve in the temple even as a child. Hannah gave birth to five more children in coming years and openly gave glory to God for His gift to her. Hannah's prayer of thanksgiving became so well known to young Jewish women that years later, Mary, the mother of our Lord, quoted from it when rejoicing over the coming birth of Jesus.

In All of Eternity, Will It Matter?

It is fun to see from the beginning to the end of so many Bible stories that have been recorded for our benefit and instruction. How easily we can see the right course of action for those who live between the pages of our Bible! Yet how difficult it is for us to see how to apply the same reality to our own daily trials and irritations. Reading accounts of those who acted wisely and exercised great faith is rewarding and delightful. But it is rather sad to read accounts of people who were oblivious to the significance of their sinful choices and unconvinced that trusting God with the difficult circumstances of life brings untold blessing. The Israelites in the wilderness seem so foolish complaining about God's provision and angrily challenging Moses' leadership. The contention that caused Euodias and Syntyche to quarrel seems truly petty from our perspective. Rachel's demanding Jacob to give her children or Eliab's anger toward his brother David when he asked about Goliath makes us shake our heads in wonder. From our vantage point, their anger certainly looks irrational and trivial. But have you ever stopped to consider how irrational *our* lack of faith and *our* anger will look when our lives are viewed from the beginning to the end?

Most of the things we become angry about are forgotten in a matter of hours. Certainly, in all of eternity, very little that bothers us today will matter at all. In order to prolong anger, we have to keep stoking the fire with continual thoughts of disdain and discontent. But suppose we followed the pattern of believers who chose not to become angry over life's heartaches and disappointments, but chose the path of loving and forgiving others and trusting God instead? If we really believe God sees and weighs every action, and we *really* believe we can confidently commit ourselves and our situations to a God Who judges righteously, does it make sense to be angry at those who cause us grief? If we really believe that God wants to bless us as we live for Him and we *really* believe that we have everything we need at this very moment to do everything He wants us to do, does it make sense for us to be angry at what we do not have? If we really believe that heaven is our home and this life is a mere moment in eternity in which we can demonstrate our love and faith in God, does it make sense for us to pout when trials and difficulties come our way? What if we followed the instructions God gave us and learned how to resolve problems in righteous ways in a spirit of love and forgiveness rather than in a spirit of hate and retaliation?

Quite certainly, our attitude and actions *will* reveal what we really believe and whether we want to live our own way, or God's way, to please ourselves, or to please the one Who gave His all for us. Anger does begin with the way we think, what we believe in our hearts, and what desires motivate us. Paul describes the way we need to think in order to display the gracious character of Christ. He tells us to adopt the same mindset as Christ Who humbled Himself to the point of committing His reputation and life completely to God. His was a mindset wholly surrendered to doing God's will, willing to suffer and die in the place of wicked sinners who did not deserve His sacrifice, let alone His love. Paul tells us, "Let nothing be done through strife or vainglory; but in lowliness of mind let each esteem other better than themselves. Look not every man on his own things, but every man also on the things of others" (*Philippians 2:3–4*). How do we think right thoughts? "Commit thy works unto the Lord, and thy thoughts shall be established" (*Proverbs 16:3*). Or in other words, obey God's Word. "But seek ye first the kingdom of God, and his righteousness; and all these things shall be added unto you" (*Matthew 6:33*).

Guard Your Heart

Solomon understood the role the heart plays in all matters of life and passionately warned his children, "Keep [guard] thy heart with all diligence; for out of it are the issues of life" (*Proverbs 4:23*). Solomon was saying what Jesus would later say—that every action, thought, and word comes out of the heart. Solomon wanted his children to deliberately and carefully guard everything that was allowed to reside there. When there is no guard at a gate, anyone and anything enters at will. But with an alert guard in place, nothing is allowed to enter that would pose an eventual threat. Solomon's exhortation cautioned his children not to let anything enter the mind that would threaten to overturn what was good and true by God's standard.

Choices and actions do indeed originate within our hearts where our innermost passions and beliefs dwell. To "keep" our heart is to guard the door of our heart in order to protect us from harm. It is to use vigilant caution, refusing entrance to any thought or desire or misconception that would enter our minds and turn our desires away from Christ, and our beliefs away from the truth of His Word. Every thought must be brought into subjection to Christ in order to win this war (*2 Corinthians 10:5*). A guard is put in place in order to defend and protect something of value from being destroyed or attacked. My friend, your heart is your most valuable possession, for whatever fills your heart controls you. The enemy who has declared war against you wants to destroy you; and he knows that if he gains entrance to your heart, he will win strategic advantage. Therefore, keep your heart with all diligence, for out of it are the issues of life.

THE ANATOMY
OF AN
Angry Man

CHAPTER FOUR

We often can learn more by observing someone who has dealt with life's problems in all the wrong ways than all the right ways. Watching someone suffer the consequences of foolish choices tends to stir within us a desire to avoid his mistakes. Our observation makes us more alert to dangers in our own way of thinking and reacting, and in so doing, prepares us to experience success rather than a repetition of the foolish man's failure. It also has a way of illuminating our own failures in such a way that we are more motivated to correct ourselves and confidently submit to God's discipline and work in our lives. Quite often, the difference between success and failure is not how many mistakes one makes, but how one deals with the mistakes one has made.

The Bible records many accounts of people who miserably failed, along with accounts of people who succeeded in spite of the worst calamities and terribly human flaws in their character. The decisions and motives of both believers and unbelievers alike are recorded for our benefit and make us see how God works in and through the lives of people just like us, no matter what particular experiences are involved. The Bible provides us with many "behind the scenes" facts and clues that help us discern beliefs and motives that prompted actions and produced certain consequences. By carefully observing the cause and effect elements in Bible accounts, we are more thoroughly prepared to avoid that which is destructive and pursue that which brings joy and blessing.

Perhaps no other Bible character better illustrates the way underlying desires and beliefs incite anger and lead to certain sorrow than Saul, Israel's first king. Saul's story provides readers with a case history depicting the way unchecked anger progresses into utter self-destruction. In it we can observe the full spectrum of anger's silent beginning and disastrous tumultuous ending. Like seeds that fall from a dying weed, anger grows unseen and takes root long before it is seen or becomes a threat to nearby plants.

Anger's Unseen Beginning

A weed gets its strength from roots that lie below the surface of the earth. Unless the weed is pulled along with the roots, it will always manage to return bigger and stronger than before. In a similar way, anger is fed by desires and beliefs that lie below the surface of a life, unseen; and unless these are uprooted, anger only comes back stronger and bigger than before. Saul was a man who looked good on the outside but had a heart that provided just the right soil in which anger could take root and grow. As we examine Saul's life, pay close attention to the way Saul saw problems, himself, God, and others. Watch the way his heart was revealed by the way he responded to difficulties and disappointments.

We are introduced to Saul in the ninth chapter of *1 Samuel* as the exceptionally tall, handsome son of a wealthy father who lived in Israel. Samuel, the prophet of God, met with Saul and told him he had been set apart by God to be Israel's first king. This greatly unnerved Saul who humbly replied, "Am not I a Benjamite, of the smallest of the tribes of Israel? and my family the least of all the families of the tribe of Benjamin? wherefore then speakest thou so to me?" (*1 Samuel 9:21*) Samuel assured Saul that God Himself had chosen him and further explained the instructions God had for him and the way God's Spirit would enable him to fulfill his appointed task. After anointing Saul privately, Samuel later presented him to the people as the king they had asked for. Those whose hearts God had touched rejoiced and submitted themselves to the new king. But those who rejected God and were rebellious to His Word despised Saul and refused to acknowledge him. Even so, the Bible tells us that Saul humbly held his peace and did not seek retaliation nor become angry with them.

By chapter eleven of *1 Samuel*, Saul had begun to see himself as the leader of God's people, ready to intervene on their behalf. When messengers came to tell Saul that the Ammonites were threatening to attack the town of Jabesh-gilead, the Bible tells us the Spirit of God came upon Saul as soon as he heard it, and "his anger was kindled greatly" (*verse 6*). This is a clear description of anger that is not only righteous but also a result of being filled with God's Spirit. It was anger aroused on behalf of others who were being overpowered by evil people and was motivated by the same injustice that incited God to be angry with them. Saul had been given authority by God to judge and punish evil and therefore was in a position to deal judicially with the Ammonite's evil. Immediately Saul summoned the men of Israel to help those who lived in Jabesh-gilead and organized them into an army that successfully attacked the Ammonites and rescued the people. When the battle was over, the men who had willingly joined Saul in battle asked him to execute those who refused to acknowledge his leadership or fight. Saul, wanting to extend mercy, refused to exercise his authority in revenge and said, "There shall not a man be put to death this day; for today the LORD hath wrought salvation in Israel" (*verse 13*). Notice that Saul was humble, dependent on God, obedient to God, and merciful. Saul gave God His rightful place and praised Him for what He had done—not what Saul had done.

The Downward Spiral Begins

Immediately following this victory in battle, Samuel gathered the people together and publicly anointed Saul the king of Israel. Samuel then warned them, "If ye will fear the LORD, and serve him, and obey his voice, and not rebel against the commandment of the LORD, then shall both ye and also the king that reigneth over you continue following the LORD your God: But if ye will not obey the voice of the LORD, but rebel against the commandment of the LORD, then shall the hand of the LORD be against you, as it was against your fathers" (*1 Samuel 12:14–15*). During the next two years of Saul's reign as king, he further established his leadership over the people and was prepared to deal with Israel's enemies. When the Philistine army gathered to attack Israel, Saul summoned his army to battle. They came with enthusiasm but quickly hid in fear when they saw the great number of Philistines that were prepared for war with their gleaming chariots and armored horses, their grand display of military might, and their superior weaponry. Saul, meanwhile, was no less afraid as he made his way to Gilgal to wait for Samuel seven days as he had been instructed to do.

When Samuel did not come immediately on the seventh day, Saul impatiently took matters into his own hands and decided to conduct the sacrifice to God himself and fulfill the role of the priest. No sooner had he done this than Samuel arrived and asked him what he had done. Saul evaded personal responsibility for his disobedience by rationalizing and explained that he was afraid because his men were abandoning him and he thought making a sacrifice to God would protect him from the Philistines. Samuel then told Saul that he had acted foolishly by not obeying the command of God. Because of his pride and disobedience, Samuel explained, God would bring an end to Saul's reign and raise up a man that would be after God's own heart, who would have a desire to obey and follow God's Word.

The effect this announcement had on Saul was not immediately apparent. No sooner had Samuel departed than Saul organized his men and began to engage in battle with the Philistines. In contrast to the approach of his father, Jonathan professed his faith in God and relied on Him for victory in the battle. He fought in a different location than his father and inspired the men who joined him with his faith in God's power. He told them, "It may be that the LORD will work for us: for there is no restraint to the LORD to save by many or by few" (1 Samuel 14:6). The Scriptures tell us that Israel overthrew the superior Philistine army and won the victory because "the LORD saved Israel that day" (verse 23) and fought for them. Military might is no match for the power of God.

Foolish and Impulsive

Meanwhile, Saul foolishly commanded the men who were with him not to eat anything until he told them to stop fighting, under penalty of death. Instead of eating or sleeping that night, the men were compelled to engage in a final attack, leaving them dangerously faint and exceedingly hungry by morning. Jonathan, not being present when his father gave the command, stopped to eat honey and drink water in order to strengthen himself for battle. Later, when Saul learned what Jonathan had done, he reacted in anger and ordered him put to death. If the people had not intervened on behalf of Jonathan and rehearsed what he had done in battle, Saul would have executed his own son for no other reason than to save face and prove his authority and might. His harsh sentence was ordered to satisfy his outrage, not for the benefit of Jonathan. Forgiveness and mercy were no longer a part of Saul's character. Instead, self-centered resentment and cruelty replaced the sacrificial love that should characterize a father. Saul was quickly becoming an angry man.

Self-willed and Disobedient

No doubt Samuel's pronouncement had begun to trouble Saul, who was already feeling threatened and humiliated. Still, he maintained his stubborn refusal to willingly give up his position or yield himself to God's work in his life. Instead of responding to Samuel's correction with humility or becoming motivated to examine his own heart or seek repentance from God in any way, Saul took offense and began to show the effects of his resistance to God's judgment in his anger and fear. Even when God gave him an opportunity to demonstrate repentance and obedience to His Word, Saul proceeded to do things his own way. The command God gave Saul was to completely destroy the Amalekites and everything they owned because they hated God's people and were wicked and cruel. God gave Israel the victory over the Amalekites; but instead of following God's instructions exactly, Saul leaned on his own understanding and did what seemed right to him. In his covetousness and self-will, Saul spared the king and reserved the best of the spoils for himself. Saul's pride was beginning to surface in other ways. Following the victory in battle, he went to Carmel in order to build a monument in his own honor, taking credit for the victory God had given. Saul's arrogance and self-sufficiency was becoming more deeply ingrained in his character.

When Samuel arrived in Carmel and once again began to question Saul, he justified his actions, rationalizing that he intended to offer God sacrifices from the spoils of victory. He arrogantly insisted that he had obeyed the commandment of God and proceeded to blame the people for the decision. (Shifting blame and insisting the actions of others are responsible for one's bad temper is a common false assumption of those who are angry.) Samuel understood the condition of Saul's heart and said to him, "When thou wast little in thine own sight, wast thou not made the head of the tribes of Israel, and the LORD anointed thee king over Israel?" (*1 Samuel 15:17*) Samuel did not engage in an argument with proud Saul; instead, he went straight to the heart of the matter and attempted to show Saul the connection between humility and blessing and between pride and judgment. Saul, however, had his mind made up before Samuel began to speak and refused to listen to the message. Again he insisted that he had obeyed God, and again he blamed the people for wanting to spare the animals for sacrifice to God.

Stubborn and Rebellious

The words that Samuel spoke next have been repeated over and over again to others who have rationalized sin by thinking God can be appeased by sacrificial giving. They are penetrating words that continue to warn all who, like Saul, imagine that God will overlook disobedience and self-will. Samuel asks, "Hath the LORD as great delight in burnt offerings and sacrifices, as in obeying the voice of the LORD? Behold, to obey is better than sacrifice, and to hearken than the fat of rams. For rebellion is as the sin of witchcraft, and stubbornness is as iniquity and idolatry. Because thou hast rejected the word of the LORD, he hath also rejected thee from being king" (*1 Samuel 15:22–23*). Saul's behavior revealed whom he really worshipped above all else. It was not God, but himself that he loved. Samuel wanted Saul to understand that God is concerned with our motives and wants our hearts, our devotion, and our obedience most of all. Sacrificial giving is no substitute for loving God and does not magically win God's favor.

Samuel made a rather surprising comparison between stubbornness, rebellion, witchcraft, and idolatry—very serious and destructive sins. At first glance, one might wonder what rebellion, witchcraft, and idolatry have in common. Their common denominator is a heart desire to exalt one's own authority and will above God and His authority and will. It is an attitude that says, in effect, "I will do what I want and what I believe is best for me." An idolater replaces love for God with a greater love for something else. Those involved in seeking supernatural power from the spirit world of Satan attempt to circumvent God's power in a backhanded effort to acquire power for themselves. Those who rebel against God's authority reject God and attempt to replace His authority with their own will. All overthrow Christ and place self on the throne of one's heart instead. We find in the sin of rebellion that very same drive to please one's self that is found in the roots of idolatry, witchcraft… and anger.

Not surprisingly, Saul responded to Samuel's direct appeal with worldly sorrow rather than genuine repentance. He confessed his sin to Samuel enough to tell him what he thought Samuel wanted to hear, perhaps to "get him off his back." He did not admit to anything in order to be right with God, but rather to manipulate God into giving him what he wanted. Almost in the same breath that Saul confessed his sin, he pled with Samuel to honor him by publicly leading a sacrifice and worship to God. Saul was more concerned with the way people would see him than the way God saw him. He was satisfied with an outward show that made him look good to those who followed him, even while his heart remained centered on self-exaltation rather than worship for God. Samuel did lead the sacrifice and worship, for the sake of the people, then left Saul, never to visit with him or confront him again. Sadly, Saul had driven away the one person who loved him enough to speak to him truthfully and warn him with a broken heart.

Resentful and Bitter

In the next chapter, God told Samuel to stop mourning for Saul and to visit the home of David in order to anoint him king. This immediately raised a concern in Samuel's mind because he believed Saul would kill him if he heard about it. God provided Samuel with an appropriate way to conduct his mission. But notice to what degree Saul's anger had progressed. That which was very subtle and hard to detect was now more obvious: Saul's anger had progressed to the point that Samuel feared for his life if he should displease him. Saul was not only angry but also volatile and unpredictable. Anger had now become a weapon to intimidate and force others to comply with his will. Little did he realize that God is not intimidated or controlled by anyone. Without Saul's knowledge, Samuel privately anointed David king in the presence of his family and then quietly slipped away; for he knew that God, in His own time and way, would bring David to the throne in place of Saul. And he knew that God in His own time would humble Saul and bring down the haughty self-will of a king who refused to humble himself. "Better is a poor and a wise child," the Bible warns, "than an old and foolish king, who will no more be admonished" (*Ecclesiastes 4:13*).

God revealed Himself as the righteous ruler of the world whose judgment cannot be thwarted or manipulated by men when He said in *Psalm 75:5–7*, "Lift not up your horn on high: speak not with a stiff neck. For promotion cometh neither from the east, nor from the west, nor from the south. But God is the judge; he putteth down one, and setteth up another." David recognized this spiritual truth and took comfort in knowing he could commit his case to Him Who judges righteously. Knowing God sees and judges all that men do brings great peace and joy to the heart of a trusting believer. But to those who can only see people thwarting their aspirations and getting in their way, there is agony of spirit and despair. It is God Who works in unseen ways and causes one to be promoted and one to be demoted, often for reasons that are beyond our understanding. God has the prerogative to use the basest of men or men after his own heart in ways that He chooses for His glory. David the shepherd boy understood that it is God, our Good Shepherd, Who manages our lives and leads us in ways that are good and right. It is God Who takes care of all our needs at exactly the right time and exactly the right way, and He Who gives those who are His sheep the confidence and security to rest in His care. Asaph sang, "He chose David also his servant, and took him from the sheepfolds: From following the ewes great with young he brought him to feed Jacob his people, and Israel his inheritance. So he [God] fed them according to the integrity of his heart; and guided them by the skillfulness of his hands" (*Psalm 78:70–72*).

Powerless and Alone

The Bible tells us that the Spirit of the Lord came upon David for service while at the same time He departed from Saul. Essentially, Saul was no longer the anointed king of Israel. He may have retained a title and human methods of intimidation, but he had no power from God. Rather than accept God's sovereign authority and right to choose whomever He wanted to do whatever He wanted done,

Saul who was blinded by his pride, refused to repent and allow God to use him in the position of His own choosing. To bring about His sovereign plan, God allowed an evil spirit to trouble unrepentant Saul. Thus Saul began to experience the pangs of depression, anxiety, bitterness, and paranoia that are so often associated with relentless anger and unforgiveness. In *Matthew 18:34–35* we are told that God turns people who refuse to forgive from their heart over to the tormenter. Other passages in which we are told that God turns people over to Satan for chastisement are found in *Acts 5:3*, *1 Corinthians 5:1–5*, and *1 Timothy 1:18–20*. Yet perhaps the most serious of all consequences is the barrier that a spirit of unforgiveness puts between a child of God and his heavenly Father whenever he prays. Our Lord warns, "For if ye forgive men their trespasses, your heavenly Father will also forgive you: But if ye forgive not men their trespasses, neither will your Father forgive your trespasses" (*Matthew 6:14–15*).

Tormented and Afraid

In order to provide Saul with a measure of relief when he was tormented, Saul's servants suggested that he allow them to seek out someone who could skillfully play the soothing melodies of the harp during his times of distress. After Saul enthusiastically accepted this idea, a servant suggested they enlist the help of David who played well and was also of impeccable character and blessed of God. Not seeing the way the hand of God was working in this solution, Saul unwittingly commanded his messengers to find David and bring him to be his armor bearer and personal musician. David's music was so effective that Saul and his servants loved him. At this point, David's presence was not a threat to Saul's objectives; but rather, the arrangement catered to his desires in a way that pleased him. So David divided his time between playing for Saul and keeping his father's sheep.

Not long after Saul had enlisted David's services, David returned home for a time to help with his father's flocks. During this visit, his father asked him to deliver some food and to check on his older brothers who were engaged in a standoff with the Philistines. In the Bible account of the story of Goliath, David recognized the problem facing Israel's army and in stunning boldness professed his belief that God would give a victory to the man who would defeat Goliath in the power of the Lord. This news eventually reached Saul who sent for David and heard for himself his willingness to accept the challenge to fight with Goliath. As David faced heavily-armed Goliath with his shepherd's sling, David said to him, "Thou comest to me with a sword, and with a spear, and with a shield: but I come to thee in the name of the LORD of hosts, the God of the armies of Israel, whom thou hast defied" (*1 Samuel 17:45*). In contrast to Saul's fear, David stood confident in his firm belief that the battle was the Lord's and that the cause for which he fought was just and right. He faced the giant without fear and ultimately cut off his head, to the horror of the proud Philistine army. This gave immense delight to the people of Israel and to the king and made David an instant celebrity. Saul then took David into his house permanently and would no longer let him return to help with his father's sheep.

What Saul did not yet see, Jonathan his son was beginning to comprehend—that David's victories and rise in prominence was in the providence of God, for David was destined by God to become king. In sharp contrast to the prideful refusal of Saul to relinquish his position, Jonathan loved David and gladly removed his own princely robe as the heir to his father's throne and gave it to David. Jonathan's desire was God's will and God's glory, not his own will and his own glory. He was content to serve God in any way God chose. Meanwhile, unbeknown to Saul, David was quickly rising in popularity as a result of his victory, his faith, and his wise behavior. When the women met Saul and honored him with singing and dancing, Saul was pleased; but his pleasure quickly turned to anger when he heard them sing about Saul slaying his thousands and David slaying his ten thousands. Immediately Saul's jealousy and fear fueled his wrath; and he began to silently resent David's goodness and accomplishment, regarding it with contempt rather than thankfulness or respect. From that day forward, the Bible says Saul eyed David suspiciously and feared he would one day displace him.

Jealous and Hateful

Those who are consumed with anger cannot rejoice with those who rejoice, or smile with sincere joy when others are promoted or blessed in ways they secretly covet. Such a person is discontent with God's provisions and dealings in his own life and craves instead what he believes will bring him honor and satisfaction. Anger demands the benefits others possess, regardless of whether they are merited or earned and regardless of whether God chooses to withhold them for one's good or for His glory. Anger often belittles the accomplishments and blessings of others in an effort to raise questions about the motives and worthiness of those who prosper. Such anger is appeased and satisfied only when others are ranked in a lower position and is enraged when others are recognized and honored.

In stark contrast, one whose heart's desire is to be like Christ will respond to trials and disappointments as David did, and will pray as he prayed at a time when Saul cruelly persecuted him without cause. "It is good for me that I have been afflicted; that I might learn thy statutes. The law of thy mouth is better unto me than thousands of gold and silver. Thy hands have made me and fashioned me: give me understanding, that I may learn thy commandments. They that fear thee will be glad when they see me; because I have hoped in thy word. I know, O LORD, that thy judgments are right, and that thou in faithfulness hast afflicted me. Let, I pray thee, thy merciful kindness be for my comfort, according to thy word unto thy servant. Let thy tender mercies come unto me, that I may live; for thy law is my delight. Let the proud be ashamed; for they dealt perversely with me without a cause; but I will meditate in thy precepts. Let those that fear thee turn unto me, and those that have known thy testimonies. Let my heart be sound in thy statutes; that I be not ashamed" (*Psalm 119:71–80*).

Rather than enjoy David's song, Saul bristled with indignation to hear him express his faith in God. Saul's suspicions and fears rapidly turned into hatred as his thoughts became silently consumed with self-pity, envy, and resentment. Whereas David's music once soothed and comforted him, now it only irritated him further. (Those who love and fear God love God's music; those who harbor ill feelings and resentment toward God hate it.) Saul sat and listened to the melodies of the harp with his javelin in his hand, more consumed than ever with his hatred of David. When he could hide his malice no longer, he hurled the spear at David with the intent of killing him. Twice David avoided Saul's deadly aim, making Saul all the more afraid of him as he recognized God was protecting David as He once protected him.

Vengeful and Malicious

Because Saul could no longer tolerate David's presence, he assigned him a place in the military, hoping he would be killed in battle. However, what Saul meant for evil, God used for David's good. David excelled as a warrior and as a leader and continued to win the admiration of those he humbly served. The stumbling blocks Saul hoped would destroy David served only as stepping-stones in his continued assent toward the throne. David was wisely humbling himself under the mighty hand of God; and as a result, God would one day exalt him. Far from being thwarted by Saul's efforts to stop David's rise to power, God's plan continued and David prospered as he conducted himself with godly integrity and wisdom and learned crucial lessons in preparation for his coming coronation.

Anger now clouded Saul's ability to reason objectively or to see the unfolding events as a blessing for God's people and a plan in perfect harmony with God's gracious and merciful character. All he could see was his own loss and his own sorrow; for his view of life and eternity was shortsighted, self-centered, and void of spiritual understanding. He saw no good purpose in David's accomplishments and could not bring himself to be thankful for his integrity or godliness. He saw his own loss as devastating and his sorrow as justification for hating others, rather than a call to repent of his self-will and pride. In his mind, David was the direct cause of his troubles, not his own sinful attitude and refusal to believe God and walk with Him in humility and obedience. Saul had drifted far away from humble dependence on God's Word and a zeal for the cause of God and the welfare of His people that he displayed in earlier years. Now he could not see beyond his own pain, his own desires, and his own disappointments to consider the way his sin was destroying others and bringing a reproach on the work of God. At this point, anger had become a part of Saul's personality and character, a habit that controlled him even as his own jealousy and hatred controlled him.

The more David accepted everything that happened in his life as the will of God and depended on God to work out every injustice and calamity for His glory, the more Saul loathed David and plotted to destroy him. Saul still wanted to appear as a benevolent and good king to win the favor of the people, yet inwardly he had every intention of thwarting God and destroying David. Saul came up with a plan that he hoped would lead to David's death by offering David his daughter in marriage if he would kill one hundred Philistines as his dowry. David humbly accepted the offer; but rather than being killed himself, he returned having killed two hundred Philistines. Saul's plot backfired and ended with the marriage of his daughter to David, his secret enemy. The Bible says, "Saul was yet the more afraid of David; and Saul became David's enemy continually" (*1 Samuel 18:29*). Guilt always causes those who are angry to secretly fear God's judgment or chastisement. And fear brings torment, according to *1 John 4:18*, being unable to rest in the love and mercy of God.

Saul's unchecked anger could no longer be concealed but gave way to open contempt as he voiced his condemnation of David and ordered his servants to kill David. As is often the case, anger fuels a desire to enlist the support of others. Angry people commonly exaggerate, distort the truth, leave out facts, outright lie, and paint the object of their anger in the most unfavorable light possible in order to win sympathy and appear righteous in their contention. An angry person will not only hate those who displease them but also despise those who disagree or treat the object of their wrath with love and mercy. More often than not, those who dare to confront an angry man or woman become objects of contempt. Those who join the angry man's unjust cause, however, will be lavishly praised and rewarded.

Divisive and Unreasonable

Once an angry person begins to enlist supporters, those who take the angry person's offense are divided from those who in good conscience cannot. In Saul's case, Jonathan his son recognized his father's foolishness and unjust hatred of David and made several appeals on David's behalf. With predictable precision, Saul lashed out at his son and condemned his godly behavior as foolish. On one occasion, however, Saul chose to dissuade his son with a deceitful show of supposed agreement. Outwardly, Saul made Jonathan believe he had reconsidered and would no longer seek to kill David. Yet in his heart he continued to seethe, until once again, he hurled his javelin at David in an effort to kill him.

David began to see that neither he nor Jonathan could reason with unreasonable Saul. The Bible tells believers, "If it be possible, as much as lieth in you, live peaceably with all men" (*Romans 12:18*). David had done just that but now was forced to accept the fact that it was not possible to live peaceably with one who was so consumed and controlled with anger and hatred. He sadly came to realize that Saul would not cease in his attempts to murder him; and therefore, David was forced to flee. That night his wife put pillows in the bed and told Saul's messengers that David was ill. When Saul heard this, he ordered his messengers to return and bring David to him, in the bed if necessary, so he could slay him. When they returned to David's house, they discovered the pillows under the blankets of the bed and reported to Saul that David had fled.

Infuriated, Saul began what would turn into years of chasing David, threatening him, plotting against him, and being consumed with hatred for him. He would angrily accuse his own son and blast him with profanity for his refusal to turn against David, and stoop so low as to coldly order the death of all the priests of Nob because they innocently gave David food and helped him. He drove David into the wilderness, forcing him to hide in caves and flee for his life, and eventually caused him to leave the country altogether. Yet in all of this, David continued to put his trust in God and prospered still.

Twice David was in a position to kill Saul and was encouraged by his men to take advantage of the situation to avenge himself. David rested instead on a sovereign God Who alone had the right to decide when and how Saul would be punished and when he would die. Unlike Saul, David viewed injustice from God's perspective, trusting that God would use it for good in ways he could not then understand, and would in time judge it. Saul's malice would not prevail against David as it served only to drive David closer to the Lord and more dependent than ever on His sustaining grace and protection. When those who are persecuted flee to God for protection, the poison darts that are hurled by others cannot destroy them. David learned this precious truth in the classroom of terrible injustice and would later recall God's faithfulness and sing praises for His loving protection.

David expressed his joy in God's care when he wrote, "From the end of the earth will I cry unto thee, when my heart is overwhelmed: lead me to the rock that is higher than I. For thou hast been a shelter for me, and a strong tower from the enemy. I will abide in thy tabernacle for ever: I will trust in the covert of thy wings. Selah. For thou, O God, hast heard my vows: thou hast given me the heritage of those that fear thy name. Thou wilt prolong the king's life: and his years as many generations. He shall abide before God for ever: O prepare mercy and truth, which may preserve him. So will I sing praise unto thy name for ever, that I may daily perform my vows" (*Psalm 61:2–8*).

Saul had rejected God's Word and God's ways and therefore had nowhere to run for comfort or protection. He was a man who professed to believe in God, but a man who nevertheless had abandoned God, and therefore became a man who was abandoned by God to his own devices. Jeremiah the prophet warned people much like Saul by proclaiming, "Thine own wickedness shall correct thee, and thy backslidings shall reprove thee: know therefore and see that it is an evil thing and bitter, that thou hast forsaken the LORD thy God, and that my fear is not in thee, saith the Lord GOD of hosts" (*Jeremiah 2:19*). By Saul's own admission on several occasions, he knew that David was the rightful heir to the throne and the one that Samuel foretold would be given the kingdom by God Himself. He admitted David's behavior was righteous and his own sinful, yet he would not humble himself to accept God's providential dealings in his life or give up his determination to retain his throne and ultimately his own will. Position was everything to Saul: God's Word and God's will meant nothing unless it served his own purpose and personal aspirations.

Desperate and Depressed

Because Saul had estranged himself from God, God ignored him and left him to cope in his own strength. When the Philistines once again gathered themselves to engage in war with Israel, Saul became deeply afraid. He could no longer seek the help of Samuel, for Samuel had died. And he could no longer appeal to God, for God's back was turned to him. He was not willing to repent of his sin or to give up his throne to his enemy, the man whom God had anointed king. So in Saul's desperation, he turned to a woman who used sorcery, still presumptuously using every means in his power, no matter how wicked and sinful, to manipulate and obtain what he wanted. To Saul's dismay and the sorceress's surprise, God intervened with one last message to Saul given by Samuel himself. It was not a new message but the one Saul had heard many times before and rejected. But this time, Saul listened, because God also told him he had rejected God's Word for the last time and would die the next day.

Imagine how Saul must have trembled when he heard the words of Samuel. "Wherefore then dost thou ask of me, seeing the LORD is departed from thee, and is become thine enemy? And the LORD hath done to him, as he spake by me: for the LORD hath rent the kingdom out of thine hand, and given it to thy neighbour, even to David: Because thou obeyedst not the voice of the LORD, nor executedst his fierce wrath upon Amalek, therefore hath the LORD done this thing unto thee this day. Moreover the LORD will also deliver Israel with thee into the hand of the Philistines: and tomorrow shall thou and thy sons be with me: the LORD also shall deliver the host of Israel into the hand of the Philistines" (*1 Samuel 28:16–19*).

It is not surprising that Saul fell to the ground and became weak with fear. He had imagined he could ignore God and maintain his own way. He might have been able to convince himself that he could do what he wanted and sin with impunity—but not now. Saul had lived without a fear of God or fear that God would hold him responsible for his choices, and had unleashed his anger and selfish will on the very people God loved and protected as His own. And now, he knew he would face God within twenty-four hours and be required to stand before Him and give an account of his life. Furthermore, there was no way to change the final destiny he had brought upon himself. Suddenly, in the face of death, all the things he wanted and had fought for did not seem important; but his opportunity to live for something other than himself was over. He had chosen to please himself as his goal in life, rather than to please God; and this goal had reaped for him exactly what God had warned it would. Saul could not conquer his anger because Saul refused to wholeheartedly obey God's Word. His anger did not bring about satisfaction or joy. It did not work the righteousness of God, and indeed anger never does. In the end, it always brings sorrow and loss—sometimes for eternity.

Self-destructive and Defiant to the End

Perhaps Saul entertained the hope that he could defy death or escape the chastisement of God. The Bible does not say. What we do know is that Saul pulled himself together and went into battle, rather than cowardly refusing to lead his army or bring dishonor on himself in the eyes of the people. Saul did die in battle, as God had predicted, along with three of his sons. But he did not die an honorable death; for even in the end, Saul sought to control his fate. The Bible tells us that Saul was mortally wounded in the battle; and rather than be captured or humiliated by the enemy, he commanded his armor bearer to kill him. When his armor bearer refused, Saul took his sword and used it to take his own life. Only the people of Jabesh-gilead, who had been loved and protected by Saul before he became proud and arrogant, risked their lives to retrieve the beheaded bodies of Saul and his sons and give them an honorable burial befitting one who had been king. Yet ironically, Saul, being dead, was not present to enjoy this honor.

Anger destroys the one who harbors it; yet sadly, it also destroys others who are affected by it. Saul's anger led to the deaths of his three sons. It alienated him from his own children and from those who loved him. But most importantly, it alienated him from God and made fellowship with Him impossible. You cannot keep a tight fist clinched around anger and love God or others at the same time. It is impossible. You must turn against anger, or anger will cause God and others to turn away from you. James warns us that God resists the proud—or is *opposed* to the proud—but gives grace to the humble (*James 4:6*). You have only two choices. You can repent and take sides against your anger, humble yourself under the discipline of God, and experience God's grace. Or, you can do as Saul and refuse to believe God will hold you accountable for your anger, refuse to repent, make excuses, blame others, believe you are justified, rationalize, minimize, condemn those who confront you, accuse God of mistreating you, threaten those who expose you, destroy those who oppose you, and retaliate with vengeance against those who hurt you. If you choose to do this, however, know that you also choose the same fate as Saul; for God will become your enemy, and you will find yourself as alone and miserable as he.

THE WAY WE LOOK at God

CHAPTER FIVE

God's Sovereign Nature

How would you expect someone to act who received numerous death threats, was falsely accused, imprisoned as a result, and then forgotten by friends and family? Would you imagine such a person calmly responding to these emotionally wrenching events without anger or malice toward anyone and without doubting God's love or good purpose in allowing it? Considering the terrible circumstances he was in, the apostle Paul's letter to the Philippians was astounding: it was written after his being falsely accused, imprisoned, and largely abandoned by his friends. Therefore, we would expect his letter to be filled with heart-wrenching descriptions of his personal sorrow, grief, anger, and fear; but instead, we read of his confidence in Christ, his joy, his love for God, and his concern for other believers. Paul's letter was not a "put on" worded in such a way that he would be exalted as a super Christian or would elicit the sympathy of others. Rather, from start to finish, he wrote with deliberate purpose in order to convey a message of hope and encouragement to those who would read it.

The key to understanding why Paul reacted in the highly unusual way he did can be found in many of his statements, but perhaps none sum it up better than the one found in *Philippians 1:21*: "For to me to live is Christ, and to die is gain." What distinguishes Paul from so many others who cannot make this same claim about themselves are the vastly different goals and desires he had for his life, as well as the beliefs he held regarding God's character and the purpose for all that happened to him. Paul took God at His word; therefore, he confidently believed everything that the Scriptures reveal about Him. As we read through the little book of Philippians, we are able to observe many of Paul's expressed desires and beliefs. It is not hard to see that it is what he believed and what he desired that enabled him to confidently commit himself to the care and love of God with the calm assurance that no evil—not even evil like he experienced—happens to a believer without purpose or plan.

Accepted, Forgiven, and Beloved

Very few Christians are called to endure imprisonment as Paul did, yet all of us experience the effects of living in a world filled with selfish people who inflict hardship upon us in varying degrees. If we believe that these daily irritations or other types of difficulties occur without God's permission or involvement in any way, we are not likely to give much thought or concern to the way we respond to them. The less we are aware of God's presence and involvement in our lives, the more likely it is that we will react in anger and be concerned only with the irritation that has displeased us. Then again, if we *do* believe there is nothing that happens in this world—big or small—that escapes God's attention, we may just as easily react in anger that is directed toward God, *unless* we also believe that God is just, good, loving, merciful, and righteous. How we interpret God's involvement in our lives, what we believe about His character, and how we believe He regards us personally, make a world of difference in the way we respond to personal failures, the failures of others, or events that bring difficulty or sorrow into our lives.

Paul's letter to the Philippian believers begins as many of his letters do with a greeting of grace and peace from God our Father, and from the Lord Jesus Christ. It is a greeting meant to encourage and strengthen believers by calling to remembrance the significance and blessing of God's grace and God's peace. It reminds us that no human can hope to approach God on the basis of his own works, his own discipline, his own righteousness, or his own sacrifices. Believers are accepted in the beloved *only* on the basis of God's wonderful grace and have forgiveness and peace with God *only* by the blood of Christ that was shed for our sins. This gives great hope and reassurance to believers who might be tempted to doubt God's love when they have failed or when trials come into their lives. It is precious to know, beyond any doubt, that there is no condemnation to those who are in Christ Jesus, for He has taken our condemnation upon Himself and has been punished on the cross for our sins, in our place. God's wrath was poured out on Christ so that we who have put our trust in Him might be forgiven, accepted, and beloved of God. What marvelous grace—what a price that was paid for our peace!

To Know Him Is to Love Him

Paul's letters to all the churches are filled with expressions of his love for God and God's love for him. He told us in *Romans 8:37–39* that he was persuaded, *absolutely convinced*, that nothing is able to separate us from the love of God that we have in Christ Jesus. In *Philippians 3:10*, he described the passion he had to know Christ; for the more he learned about him, the more he grew to love him and the more he desired to know Him more intimately still. He quoted David when he said, "I believed, and therefore have I spoken" (*Psalm 116:10; 2 Corinthians 4:13*). It is what Paul believed and what David believed that prompted them to speak about the Lord and tell others what they knew, no matter what the cost. Paul's greatest delight was to know and serve Christ. *Herein was Paul's source of strength and overcoming power in the face of any difficulty or disappointment.*

Paul knew and believed God's Word. Therefore, Paul knew and believed God is good and had a good purpose for *everything* that happened to him. He experienced joy as he cooperated with the way God was leading and working in and through his life, because he was confident in God's promises and purposes. Paul's absolute confidence in the reality of God's love and forgiveness made it possible for him to place his trust in Him. He knew God was for him, not against him. He knew God loved and accepted him on the basis of his faith in Christ. He knew God was present with him and governed his life, and he knew God had a good purpose in allowing whatever difficult experiences came his way in any given day. Furthermore, he was absolutely convinced that God would never forsake him nor withdraw His mercy or His providential care. So when provocation came, Paul saw it in the context of God's love and sovereign will for him—and this made all the difference in the world in how he responded.

Anger is the typical first reaction of an *immature* self-focused believer who is faced with a trial. Turning to God for strength, wisdom, and deliverance is the typical first reaction of a mature believer whose life is focused on Christ. Rather than rebel against life's trials, whether big or small, mature believers submit to them— even as they aggressively work to resolve them. (Submission is not passivity.) Paul wrote to believers who were very likely upset and troubled by the cruel injustice they knew he was enduring. It was not enough for them to know that God was not caught by surprise and that He permitted the injustices to happen; for that would have only led to more confusion, if not despair. They had to know, as Paul explained to them, that there was a worthy purpose behind his suffering, one that he was gladly willing to suffer and die for. Paul also listed many of the good results God had brought out of the suffering so that these believers could get a clearer picture of God's masterful use of events that Satan had designed for evil and destruction.

Paul told them, "But I would ye should understand, brethren, that the things which happened unto me have fallen out rather unto the furtherance of the gospel; So that my bonds in Christ are manifest in all the palace and in all other places; And many of the brethren in the Lord, waxing confident by my bonds, are much more bold to speak the word without fear" (*Philippians 1:12–14*). Notice that Paul's focus was not on his suffering but on the things that gave him his greatest delight—believers boldly explaining the gospel message and lost sinners gladly hearing it. Had Paul been unconcerned with the salvation of the lost, uninterested in the work of Christ on earth, oblivious to the realities of eternity, and ignorant of God's righteous and loving character, he would not have responded with joy at being imprisoned falsely. He would not have viewed it as an opportunity, nor would he have been motivated to submit to God in order that his experience be used to accomplish eternal good. Rather, he would have acted like any other human who lacks spiritual understanding—he would have become angry.

Mistreated by Brethren

It was not simply the imprisonment orchestrated by unbelievers that tried Paul's patience—it was also the mistreatment he received from fellow believers. Paul explained to the Philippians that Epaphroditus, his faithful partner in ministry, had become ill and almost died because he worked himself so hard in order to make up for the Philippians' lack of care for him. Paul told them about this because they had heard that Epaphroditus had been ill, and Paul wanted them to understand that Epaphroditus labored out of love for the Lord and for the young Philippian believers. Paul also lamented that he had no mature believer who was available to care for the spiritual needs of the Philippians other than young Timothy, whom he was sending to them.

The great apostle Paul could have been bitter and resentful that so few cared about contributing to his support in light of the many sacrifices he had made on their behalf. He could have resented the fact that he had so few to help him in ministry, who would love the new believers individually and share the work and burdens of caring for them. He might have grieved that his was a lonely responsibility with few who could understand his activities, priorities, or the choices he was making. Yet he talked of his difficulties without malice or concern, explaining that he knew his God would supply all his needs according to His riches in glory, and that he could do all things through Christ Who strengthened him. It was not just that Paul believed God would compensate for whatever the believers failed to supply. More importantly, he understood that he was involved in the ongoing growth and development of new believers and would naturally encounter many difficulties as a result. This was something he both expected and accepted as part of his work and ministry.

Paul had the mind set of a loving mother who knows that in the course of raising children, she will be required to change many diapers, settle innumerable childish disputes, calm many childish fears, and endure many immature choices. It is the joy of seeing children grow into maturity that makes every inconvenience, every childhood battle, and any expense that is encountered in the process well worth it. Paul did not talk about his difficulties in order to win sympathy for himself or to cause others to feel guilty, but rather out of concern that the believers would grow in their understanding and faith so that they would reap the benefits of giving. Paul told them, "Not because I desire a gift: but I desire fruit that may abound to your account" (*Philippians 4:17*). Again, we can see that Paul's attitude and reactions stemmed from what he believed and desired. He was not living to please himself, but living to please God and help others.

At the very outset of his letter, Paul described his confidence that, "he [Christ] which hath begun a good work in you will perform [finish] it" (*Philippians 1:6*). He told of his earnest desire and prayer that the Philippians' love for the Lord and for one another would grow, that their knowledge of Christ would also grow, and that they would become discerning and wise as a result. Then further into his letter, he assured them of something else he firmly believed to be true—"it is God which worketh in you both to will and to do of his good pleasure" (*Philippians 2:13*). Paul recognized that no life experience happens apart from God's greater work of disciplining and training all of His children so that they might grow up into spiritual adulthood and experience the joys and privileges of maturity.

We Are a Work in Progress

A young Christian is much like the child who does not yet realize how important the father's restraints and discipline are to his future happiness. For much of his youth, he obeys because he fears his father's chastisement or because he wants to please his father; but as he grows into adulthood, he begins to understand the reasons behind a loving father's ways. Maturity changes the way a child regards a father's discipline, but it also changes the way a child sees many other things. Ask most first graders if they are looking forward to being married someday, and they will likely shriek with horror at the very thought. But wait ten years to ask the question again, and suddenly marriage will not seem like such a bad idea after all. Little children do not normally jump with glee when bedtime comes; and if they are given a choice, most of them would rather have recess all day than study math. It is not until a child matures and develops the understanding of a responsible adult that he begins to take pleasure in the very things that used to be so distasteful.

Our Christian growth follows a similar pattern. As long as we remain children in our understanding, we will tend to act the way any child does when he is subjected to things he does not like: we will become angry. However, as we mature and look back on our spiritual infancy, we will laugh at the way we acted, just the way adults laugh and groan over ways they behaved when they were children. The process of growing into maturity is not always pleasant, and the shortsighted tendencies of youth often make it difficult to see the temporary pain of growth in a broader perspective. Just as we assure our children that they will be glad for parental discipline when they are adults, so our heavenly Father assures us that He has our best interest at heart and subjects us to discipline so that we will have long-term joy later. "For they [earthly parents] verily for a few days chastened us after their own pleasure; but he for our profit, that we might be partakers of his holiness. Now no chastening for the present seemeth to be joyous, but grievous: nevertheless afterward it yieldeth the peaceable fruit of righteousness unto them which are exercised thereby" (*Hebrews 12:10–11*).

Peter exhorted young believers, "Wherefore let them that suffer according to the will of God commit the keeping of their souls to him in well doing, as unto a faithful Creator" (*1 Peter 4:19*). Peter does not attempt to minimize the pain of any suffering or imply that it is not sometimes extremely difficult. What he does is encourage those who suffer to look forward to the coming joy of maturity and future rewards and to commit themselves to a wise and loving heavenly Father Who is faithful to finish the work He began. Every believer is a creation of God who is unfinished and under construction until the day he enters heaven.

Shepherds Are Sheep Too

Paul saw himself as part of God's construction crew working under the direction and supervision of Christ, and saw Christ as the master architect and builder Who alone is able to orchestrate all the necessary tasks into completion. So when Paul was confronted with the immaturity and foolish choices of growing believers, he did not react in anger as a child, but as a mature parent who day after day endures his child's immaturity and patiently guides and teaches, disciplines, and loves his children. He understood, too, that he himself was still growing and maturing in Christ and that he too was God's creation, still under construction. Instead of childishly demanding that God and others keep his daily life free from disappointments and hardships, he accepted them, submitted to the process of learning how to respond to them as Christ would, and looked forward to the rewards he was confident awaited him as a result.

Paul understood both his present maturity as a leader and his ongoing quest to know and become more like Christ in the future. Thus he could say, "Not as though I had already attained, either were already perfect [mature]: but I follow after, if that I may apprehend that for which also I am apprehended of Christ Jesus. Brethren, I count not myself to have apprehended: but this one thing I do, forgetting those things which are behind, and reaching forth unto those things which are before, I press toward the mark for the prize of the high calling of God in Christ Jesus. Let us therefore, as many as be perfect [mature], be thus minded: and if in any thing ye be otherwise minded, God shall reveal even this unto you" (*Philippians 3:12–15*).

Paul understood the sovereign work of God in every believer's life, not as a theological curiosity to debate with the scholars, but as a simple fact that governed his daily life. He understood that his decisions and choices were subject to God's intervention, and he was happy to have it so. We see how Paul revealed this belief in the way he told believers of his plans. He prefaced many statements with, "by the will of God," "if the Lord will," or "if the Lord permit" (*Romans 1:10; 1 Corinthians 4:19; 16:7*). Our problem is that we do not see God in the little events that cause us difficulty, nor do we like to anticipate *any* disruption to our plans. We do not wish to yield our will to God for any redirection of His making, particularly if it comes in the form of an interruption caused by sinful people who thwart our will or a trial that causes us great inconvenience. Our lack of understanding and awareness of God's presence and work *every* minute of our lives sometimes causes us to behave like spoiled children who pout and angrily complain when they do not get their own way.

In contrast to our own spiritual blindness, Paul's constant awareness of God's presence and work in his life made him alert to the possibility that God could choose whether or not to grant him his desire in the way he would like. Rather than their being an annoyance and disappointment, Paul joyfully accepted diversions and changes to his plans as God's divine guidance and will, knowing it was far superior to his own, even if he did not always understand why—and even if it required sacrifice and hardship. Paul did not attempt to circumvent God's will or interpret God's instructions in a way that would accommodate his wishes. He saw God as a loving and wise Shepherd of the soul, worthy of his trust and adoration, every moment of the day. As a result, he followed closely to the Savior, not wishing to stray from Him or imagining he knew a better route to green pastures. Paul did not see God involved in *some* activities, but in *every* human activity. In fact, Paul recognized the utter impossibility of his being able to move so much as a baby finger apart from the enabling will of God. He stated this belief in his address to the men of Athens, "For in him [Christ] we live, and move, and have our being" (*Acts 17:28*).

Guided by That Unseen Hand

Truly, though we reason and devise our plans in our hearts, it is God Who ultimately works unseen to direct (and redirect) our steps (*Proverbs 16:9*). This truth will either annoy you or comfort you, depending on whether or not you believe God's ways are better than your own, and depending on whether or not you desire to have the right to govern your own life, or desire God to govern and direct your life instead. In order to put your trust in God's wise management of your life and obey Him, you must believe, as David, that the Lord is good and "righteous in all His ways" (*Psalm 145:17*). Otherwise, you will come to find that you are fighting a battle you cannot win with a God that loves you enough to deal with your foolish and spiritually childish behavior. Unless it changes, it will only bring loss and regret in the end.

When trials and irritations come, as doubtless they will, you will either react in anger because you are displeased, or you will react in submission to God, knowing that whatever difficulty or injustice you face is allowed by God and intended to produce maturity in you as well as in others, and is ultimately for the glory of God. The more you grow in your faith, in your knowledge of Christ, and in your knowledge of God's character and His unseen work in the affairs of men, and the more you understand and believe that God truly knows you, loves you, and delights in blessing you, the more you will be able to learn how to respond to irritations and trials with acceptance rather than with anger. Habits of anger are learned over time, but so are habits of faith.

David put his trust in God, even when cruel and unreasonable men were ruthlessly persecuting him. Unlike Saul, he accepted God's work in his life and believed he would one day see the goodness of the Lord in this life on earth (*Psalm 27:13*). David slept in peace rather than fear because he believed God was awake and never stopped watching over him (*Psalm 4:8*). David waited on God to work out the circumstances of his life as He chose and refused to retaliate or respond with hatred or bitterness, because he firmly believed God would judge the sins of others in His own way and time. Like Christ, he learned to commit himself to Him Who judges righteously and looked to God for deliverance. David's confidence was rooted in his knowledge of God, his desire to obey and follow God, and his firm belief that everything God has revealed about Himself in the Scriptures is absolute truth that one can rest his life upon. As a result, God marvelously delivered David, blessed him, sustained him, and honored him.

Just as every person acts consistently with that which he truly believes and desires in his heart, so David responded consistently with those things that he believed and desired. If you pay close attention to David's statements recorded throughout the Psalms, you will hear him declare his faith and his desire to walk with God according to God's ways. The way David saw God was crucial in the way David responded to the promises of God and God's work in his life. As you study the life of David, you will begin to see the underground root system (beliefs and desires) that in turn produced his extraordinary outward behavior, which ultimately resulted in eternal rewards and blessings.

The Foundations of Peace

Psalm 145 provides a good example of the underlying beliefs that silenced David's anger and produced humility and praise to God instead. The statements David makes throughout the song are meant to teach us about God's wonderful character and mighty power and to give us a proper understanding and view of God. All of the following declarations are found in *Psalm 145*.

- God's greatness is unfathomable.

- God is the King of the entire universe.

- God is worthy of praise.

- God's acts are mighty and wonderful.

- God's greatness is beyond man's comprehension.

- God is good.

- God is righteous.

- The Lord is gracious.

- The Lord is full of compassion.

- The Lord is slow to become angry.

- The Lord is very merciful.

- The Lord is good to all.

- God's tender mercy is seen in His management of all His creation.

- God's kingdom is glorious.

- God's kingdom is everlasting.

- The Lord upholds His children when they fall.

- The Lord encourages those who become discouraged.

- The entire creation depends on God to feed them.

- God satisfies the righteous desire of every living thing.

- The Lord is holy (pure, without fault) in everything He does.

- The Lord fulfills the desires of those who fear Him.

- The Lord hears the cries of His children when they pray.

- The Lord delivers those who rely on Him.

- The Lord sustains and delivers from destruction all those who love Him.

Paul exhorts us, "Having therefore these promises, dearly beloved, let us cleanse ourselves from all filthiness of the flesh [human nature] and spirit, perfecting holiness in the fear of God"(*2 Corinthians 7:1*). To be holy is to be set apart for God's use as opposed to being set apart for the world's use or for our own sinful pursuit of pleasure. To be in the fear of God is to be aware that God sees and weighs everything we do and deals with us accordingly. It means we reverence and love God so much that we will flee from anything that would bring a reproach upon our Savior or grieve His heart. This is the way we are to live our lives on this earth and the only way we will experience God's enabling power and joy.

We have looked at the way a mature believer views the sovereign nature of God and have considered how he regards the irritating circumstances in his life. Now let's take a moment to consider how guilt, unbelief, and fear affect the way one sees God and responds to irritations.

Guilt and Anger

Adam and Eve lived on the most beautiful piece of property in the entire world. They enjoyed perfect weather, spectacular views, marital harmony, and a personal friendship with God that allowed them to walk their garden path with Him and talk with Him face to face each afternoon. God's loving provision for their care and enjoyment was abundantly evident in everything He had made for them and in every last detail of their created bodies and environment. Adam and Eve lacked nothing. So when Satan addressed Eve, together with

Adam, and suggested that God had been less than truthful or fair with them, one would think they would have scoffed at his words and immediately removed themselves from his presence. But they did not. Instead, Eve listened as the serpent accused God of lying and keeping something good from them. He twisted God's words just enough to give them a different slant and make them appear unclear. Satan reinterpreted what God had said and why He said it in such a way that Eve distrusted God's motives and became emboldened to disobey His command. And of course, this led to the exact disastrous results God had warned them would occur.

Satan's methods have not changed. He continues to relentlessly work to distort the way we see God. He delights in painting God as a cruel and unreasonable slave master Who takes pleasure in the suffering of people. The last thing he wants us to know is that God's love is immeasurable, His mercy beyond our capacity to comprehend, and His goodness overwhelming. He wants us to question God's love and motives. He twists the Scriptures just enough to mislead us and cast suspicion on what God has said. He hates the Word of God and does everything he can to keep us from examining it closely, depending on it, or understanding it. Because the truth of God's Word is the only offensive weapon that exposes Satan's lies and defeats him, he works to keep us from it. And if he cannot keep us from it, he works to obscure its meaning. This not only clouds our judgment but also produces despair, confusion, anger, and fear.

The Path to Victory

Immediately after Adam and Eve disobeyed God and sinned, they experienced for the first time an immediate sense of guilt and fear, which prompted them to cover themselves rather than to expose themselves to the gaze of the Lord. Instead of meeting the Lord with their usual joy and enthusiasm when they heard Him walking in the garden, they hid themselves from His presence. When God called for them, Adam answered that he was afraid. Instead of immediately accepting responsibility for their sins, Adam and Eve attempted to shift the blame and rationalize their disobedience.

This same response whenever people sin has repeated itself down through the ages right up to the present time. Sinful disobedience produces guilt, followed by attempts to cover up the sin. The sinning person no longer enjoys God's presence and fellowship, but instead, fears God's judgment, rationalizes his behavior, and blames something or someone else other than himself for what he did.

Whenever God confronts a sinner with His truth, the sinner is given only one option that will remove guilt, cover the sin, restore fellowship, dispel fear, and produce honest transparency—he must cease blaming anything or anyone for the failure, acknowledge the sin, put his trust in God's covering in order to remove guilt, accept God's loving provision, and seek God's forgiveness, so that fellowship with God will again be possible. Any response other than repentance toward God and acceptance of His grace is inadequate and insufficient for the removal of sin's stain upon the heart of man. Without the cleansing power of God's sacrifice, sin incrementally destroys one's ability to recognize what is true and fills a life with spiritual darkness that cannot coexist with peace and joy.

God graciously provided a sacrifice for Adam and Eve's sin and promised to one day send a Redeemer, God's own Son, Who would be born into the world in order to give the ultimate sacrifice and pay the penalty of sin once and for all. Adam and Eve stepped forward into the light of God's presence and bowed themselves to God's will and discipline in their lives. By acknowledging their guilt and helplessness and putting their trust in God's provision for their sin, they were able to experience restored fellowship with God, though from that point, they would commune with God "from a distance" unknown to them before they sinned. In the Epistle of *1 John*, we are told, "If we say that we have fellowship with him, and walk in darkness, we lie, and do not the truth; But if we walk in the light, as he is in the light, we have fellowship one with another, and the blood of Jesus Christ his Son cleanseth us from all sin" (*1 John* 1:6–7). One cannot continue hiding from God in the darkness and at the same time experience freedom from the effects of guilt and sin or know the joy that fills a heart when fellowship is restored with God.

God impressed upon Adam and Eve the seriousness of sin's consequences by showing them that the atonement for sin required the shedding of innocent blood in order to provide a substitution for sin's punishment—the innocent for the guilty. God instituted a system of offering a sacrificial lamb as a token of one's faith in the coming Redeemer Who would one day offer Himself as a sacrifice for sin, once and for all. In order to approach God, Adam and Eve and those born after them would have to come to God His way, solely on the basis of faith in God's provision. Sinners in the Old Testament received forgiveness of sin and redemption the same way sinners in the New Testament now do—through faith. Whereas those who lived before the coming of Christ looked forward to the cross, those who live after the coming of Christ look back to the cross. Both, however, must depend on God's sacrifice alone for the forgiveness of sin and may not obtain forgiveness in any other way than by God's grace, through faith alone.

Anger Follows Disobedience

Some time after Adam and Eve were banished from the garden, Eve gave birth to two sons. Cain, the oldest son, grew up to be a farmer while Abel, the younger son, grew up to be a shepherd. Cain and Abel were well aware of God's requirement that a lamb be brought as an offering to God before one could approach God or have His favor. At some point, Cain must have become resentful that he was required to purchase a lamb from his brother in order to present an acceptable offering to God. Perhaps he reasoned that an offering from his own labors in the field was just as good since it represented his own sacrifice and hard work. At the appointed time and place where man came to meet with God, Abel brought the required lamb, while Cain brought the best of the fruit that he had grown from the ground.

Instead of winning the praise of God as Cain had imagined it would, his gift was utterly rejected. At the same time, Cain observed that his brother's offering to God was accepted. Rather than changing his behavior and complying with God's requirement, Cain reacted in bitterness and anger. In fact, the Bible describes Cain's response as *very* angry. Because he was outraged that he could not come to God on his own terms and in his own way, his face took on the tightened and downcast look of someone who is angry and at the same time deeply depressed. In a merciful appeal, God came to Cain and asked him *why* he was angry and *why* his countenance betrayed his depression. Notice that God drew Cain's attention to the reason, or motivation, for his anger. (Remember—what makes anger sinful is what motivates it and how it is expressed.) God's question gave Cain an opportunity to examine his motives and alter his behavior, but Cain was not interested in examining himself. He was interested only in accusing and blaming someone else.

After asking Cain why he was angry, the Lord reminded him that his offering would be accepted just as His brother's was if he would "do well" or in other words, obey God's Word and bring the required sacrifice. God warned, however, that should he rebel and choose to disobey this requirement, sin was crouching at his door like a lion, waiting to devour him. Notice that God offered Cain a choice. He could choose to deal with the real issue of disobedience and do what was right, or he could choose to disobey God, in which case he was in danger of being destroyed by his own sin. Cain's anger was not the result of some uncontrollable emotion that was compelling him to act against his will, but rather, it was the result of Cain's perception of his problem and the way he interpreted both his brother's obedience and God's refusal of his own offering. Cain made a deliberate choice to ignore what God said in order to maintain what he believed was justifiable anger.

Had Cain dealt with the cause of his anger and chosen a righteous resolution, his anger would have melted. Instead, it escalated until it grew into an explosion of fury. Like others who are confronted with sin and refuse to repent, he became defensive and angry when told he was wrong. Cain viewed Abel as the cause of his guilt and anger, not his own self-will and disobedience toward God. So he seethed in his jealousy and resentment until they consumed him and ultimately energized him to murder his brother in a field.

God's Mercy Revealed and Refused

After Abel's death, God once again confronted Cain with a question designed to provoke a confession. But again, Cain reacted in anger and defensiveness rather than humble repentance. His anger and guilt had only grown greater and filled him with all the more arrogance and spite. God then asked him point blank what he had done, and revealed that He knew Cain had killed his brother. At this point, Cain was caught and could not escape God's judgment. Yet even then, he expressed only sorrow for his own punishment, not sorrow for his own sin. Unlike his mother and father who repented and were restored in fellowship with God, Cain merely accepted his merciful punishment with resentful resignation and then was banished from the presence of the Lord. Cain's guilt remained because Cain refused to come to God in repentance and humility and refused to put his trust in God's mercy and God's method of removing the guilt of sin.

Guilt is to our inner life what pain is to our physical life—it is a flashing signal that indicates something is wrong and needs to be taken care of. Physical pain prompts us to seek medical help, take medicine, or change our course of action to prevent further injury and find relief. Guilt that results when we become aware that we have sinned against God or others is designed to alert us of our need to seek God's help and receive the relief that comes from being forgiven. An absence of physical pain, or distress caused by guilt, leaves us not only unaware of a problem that could be harmful or fatal but also without motivation to deal with it thoroughly and immediately. True guilt prompts us to take responsibility for our sin and come to a place of repentance so that we will seek and receive God's forgiveness on the basis of Christ's sacrifice for our sins.

The ultimate purpose of guilt is to bring us into a right relationship with God and others, not to drive a wedge between the Lord and ourselves. We will come to God in faith as Abel did, when we recognize our ways are wrong and His ways are right. When we see Him as He is, we will run to Him, not away from Him as Cain did. David understood this and exclaimed, "For thou, Lord, art good, and ready to forgive; and plenteous in mercy unto all them that call upon thee" (*Psalm 86:5*). Anger melts when we see God in His infinite goodness and mercy, ready to forgive and cleanse us from sin the moment we will come to Him in agreement and confess it (*1 John 1:9*).

When guilt is taken care of God's way, fellowship with Christ is restored and peace and joy replace anger and remorse. On the other hand, when people choose to continue in their sin and refuse God's provision for guilt resolution, they are left to deal with their misery alone and have no hope of receiving God's peace. Refusing, like Cain, to confess and forsake sin results in misery in many forms; but one of the most common ways it is expressed is through anger that is directed at others or toward God. Such an angry person does not see God's gracious provision, mercy, or love. He sees God only as he wants to see Him—as unfair, unloving, rejecting, and condemning.

Fellowship Restored; Anger Dissolved

In an attempt to appease and escape internal misery, people will often deny that they are guilty of anything or that they are angry, and will instead blame others for their misery, drown out their guilt and anger with activity, excuse it, dull its pain with drugs or alcohol, or even inflict punishment or pain on oneself or others. Interestingly enough, people still attempt to deal with guilt as Cain did by offering God a variety of altruistic acts that give the appearance of righteousness. But all of these methods of managing guilt only add to guilt's torment—they can never take it away. No amount of therapy, mood-management drugs, or self-sacrificial acts of benevolence will replace the nagging inner turmoil of guilt that robs a life of joy and peace. Man can ignore God and use his own methods to dull the pain, but they can never cure the disease. Yet praise be to our wonderful loving God Who has made a way for us to enjoy restored fellowship with Him!

Just as Cain and Abel were allowed to come into God's holy presence if they would by faith bring the proper sacrifice that made atonement for sin, so we are granted full fellowship with God when we come into His presence by faith, trusting in the Lamb that He has provided. Cain and Abel's lamb represented the coming Christ Who would one day offer Himself a sacrifice for sin once and for all. The *only* acceptable lamb we can bring to God is the Lamb of God Who alone is able to take away the sin of the world. We do this by faith, just as those who lived before the cross brought their lamb by faith. "Therefore being justified by faith, we have peace with God through our Lord Jesus Christ:...For if, when we were enemies, we were reconciled to God by the death of his Son; much more, being reconciled, we shall be saved by his life" (*Romans 5:1, 10*). God has made us in such a way that only repentance toward Him removes the ravages of guilt caused by sin. "For he hath made him to be sin for us, who knew no sin; that we might be made the righteousness of God in him" (*2 Corinthians 5:21*).

When we learn to respond to guilt by repenting of our sin and humbly seeking God's forgiveness, we not only grow in our faith and walk with Christ, but we develop a much greater understanding of God's love and grace. When we begin to apply God's truths to the problem of guilt, we begin to experience the freedom and joy that is found as we see God's greatness, forgiveness, and compassion in contrast to our own frailty. This is the practical reality of fearing God as the Scriptures teach. "But there is forgiveness with thee, that thou mayest be feared" (*Psalm 130:4*). There is only one thing that prevents those who struggle with guilt and anger from coming to Christ as God has directed—a refusal to submit to God or give up one's cherished sin. In the Gospel of John we are told, "And this is the condemnation, that light is come into the world, and men loved darkness rather than light, because their deeds were evil. For every one that doeth evil hateth the light, neither cometh to the light, lest his deeds should be reproved. But he that doeth truth cometh to the light, that his deeds may be made manifest, that they are wrought in God" (John 3:19–21). Cain would not come to God on God's terms because Cain would not deal with his sin.

When guilt is left unresolved, it brings torment that results in anger, defensiveness, defiance, and selfish pursuit. Lashing out at others, having a "short fuse," and being irritable or intolerant are just a few of guilt's consequences. Sin must be dealt with on God's terms before anger can be successfully conquered. The purpose of guilt is to drive us to the throne of God so we can experience restoration of fellowship and find in Him the strength and help we so desperately need. Guilt confronts us with our need for repentance and points us to the only One Who is able to meet our need and satisfy our longing for relief. When we begin to comprehend God's love and delight in bringing us to Himself and covering us with His own righteousness, our soul finds rest and encouragement. The marvelous love and forgiveness of God becomes our focus, not our sin. It is as if a great light comes on in our minds and fills us with such love and appreciation for God that we want to sing and find others to love as a result.

False Guilt

There are other reasons other than sin against God why a person might experience the effects of guilt. Guilt's effects are torturous to those with an overly sensitive conscience, to those who tend to blame themselves for the sins and failures of others, or to those who accept blame for violating the judgments of man, not God. People who have been excessively abused by others sometimes accept their abuser's accusations out of fear and intimidation. Others learn to accept blame in an effort to please another person or win approval. Still others become so introspective and morbid in their thinking that they imagine they are the cause of whatever goes wrong around them. Accepting blame does not bring relief from false guilt. Guilt can only be resolved by recognizing it as a false accusation against one's self that has no biblical basis, and by rejecting it.

Finally, guilt is a tormenting slave master to those who lack sufficient faith to confidently believe and accept God's forgiveness when they come to Him for it. Fear and doubt short-circuit the joy of forgiveness or the realization that joy is found in God's righteousness, not our own. Rather than build their faith by saturating themselves in the knowledge of God's Word (Faith comes by hearing and hearing by the Word of God—*Romans 10:17*), they often work to make themselves feel righteous by their own efforts and strength. They want to *feel* righteous and acceptable to God in an effort to assure themselves they are forgiven. Instead of looking to God's Word and relying upon His truths for assurance, they look inside themselves for evidence that they are righteous and acceptable. This is a dangerous dead end that produces constant anger and unhappiness, not reassurance or faith.

Torments of Perfectionism

A person who fails to understand God's grace and imputed righteousness often strives to achieve (by his own efforts, determination, and will power) the highest degree of goodness or holiness he possibly can. Such behavior is a form of perfectionism that leads to an obsessive drive to excel to such a degree that one does not experience the pain of human failure, weakness, or sin. Perfectionism is a subtle effort to *feel* oneself to be righteous on the basis of one's own self-denial, discipline, or moral excellence. Perfectionism may also be a means of managing guilt for real, unconfessed sin as a substitute for repentance.

Perfectionists tend to set standards for themselves and others that God Himself does not demand. When they or others do not live up to the rigid expectations they develop, perfectionists typically become angry, irritable, and agitated. Their fear is that failure makes them unacceptable to God; whereas, exact observances of God's law make them acceptable, thereby eliciting His divine favor. This error in their understanding makes admitting fault or weakness extremely painful. Not only do they avoid admitting failure, they turn their focus on finding fault in others in an effort to bolster their own sagging ego.

Because perfection can never be attained by human effort, the perfectionist develops a short fuse and tends to be constantly irritated with both himself and others. A perfectionist has a hard time just humbly and thankfully being whatever God allows him to be, accepting failures, limitation, and growth as part of his humanity. He fails to understand God's sanctifying work in his life and his responsibility simply to walk with God and grow in grace. As a result, he fails to see God's progressive work in the lives of other believers as well, and tends to focus on what others appear to be outwardly—not on what God is doing to correct and draw them to Himself or how God is slowly conforming them to His own image.

The only antidote to guilt is repentance and faith in God's promise to forgive and cleanse from sin. The only antidote to *false guilt* and perfectionism is two-fold: a right understanding of God's expectations, grace, and provision; and a rejection of man's demands and unbiblical pronouncements.

Fear and Anger

Fear and anger are common emotions that are often experienced simultaneously. Suppose, for instance, that a child was suddenly grabbed from a playground and thrown into a van as his mother watched in horror. She would naturally experience great fear and at the same time, great anger toward the person who would do such an evil thing. This emotion would not be sinful in any way. Rather, a mother caught in a situation such as this would be expressing her natural, God-given capacity to comprehend both danger and injustice and respond with appropriate action. These two powerful emotions would immediately energize her in such a way that she would be both physically and emotionally prepared to respond with passionate and aggressive actions. She would not be content to stand still and meekly call to the man who was grabbing her child; she would shout as loudly as she could and run toward the van as fast as her body would propel her in an effort to do anything in her power to intervene.

We would not commend a mother who did *not* respond with appropriate emotion when her child was snatched from her. If she displayed no fear for her child's safety and no anger toward her child's kidnapper, we would wonder if she truly loved and cared for her child or if she lacked the capacity to reason and understand the significance of such an event. However, suppose she not only alerted people around her to call the police but also opened the door and rescued her child before the van could speed off with the child inside. Suppose a police officer was able to intercept the van and arrest the driver for attempted kidnapping. Would we commend the mother if she then drew a gun from her purse and fatally shot the man as he was being placed in the police car? Perhaps we would have a sense of sorrow for her, but we would certainly *not* commend her in the least. She was not using the gun for self-protection, but as a weapon of angry revenge.

Again, it is not the emotion by itself that is wrong, but the reason behind the emotion and the way it is expressed that make it righteous or sinful. Fear and anger do not in any way justify murder— or any other sinful words or actions. One's anger and fear must have a just cause *and* be handled in a just way. This mother would be acting responsibly and righteously if she did everything in her power to testify in court and bring this man to justice. It would be honorable for her to warn others so that they would not become victims of his evil deeds, and it would be wise for her to insist that he stay in jail so that the innocent in society would be protected. This would not be a sinful expression of fear but a wise expression of appropriate caution toward a very real threat. Vengeance, however, that is expressed for the purpose of venting one's outrage and resentment is not necessary for the purposes of justice and is forbidden by God.

Fear Can Be a Blessing or a Curse

Fear is a natural, God-given response to a threatening, or potentially threatening, situation. The ability to quickly assess danger and appropriately respond is a skill that is developed as we mature and learn about the environment in which we live.

Many things determine how we learn to assess a potential threat. Our past experiences with threatening situations remain in our memory and greatly influence our reactions toward new situations that we perceive as threatening. What we have learned about the experiences of others also influences the way we react to our own circumstances that we believe are similar. Our reactions are also influenced by the varied facts we know (or think we know) about the situation at hand. Our accuracy in assessing our particular limitations and skills plays a big role in the way we respond to threatening situations, as well as the way we individually perceive life's difficulties or potential suffering. However, the *greatest* factor in determining how we will respond to fearful events or potential fear is our concept of God's role in world events and in our own personal lives, and the degree of confidence we have in God's shepherding care of His children. What we specifically believe about God's goodness and character and how confident we are in God's intentions and promises have a profound effect on the way we will face life's difficulties, failures, and potential tragedies.

When any of these various factors, including how we see God, are inaccurate or deficient, fear can cease to be a helpful function and instead become an impediment to daily living. Reasonable fear that aids in a quick and accurate response for the purpose of survival and safety is much different than fear that develops as a result of doubting God's faithfulness. Helpful fear can be quickly transformed into needless and sinful worry or paralyzing anxiety if our view of God's faithfulness and character is in any way immature or faulty. When this occurs, the child of God typically begins a spiral of distrust, fearful anticipation, or frantic attempts to make sure nothing bad happens to him. This frame of mind may lead to his having additional fears of rejection or abandonment by God, or his thinking may become so intense that he becomes hyper-vigilant and prone to anxiety and anger. Whatever the particular outcome, fear is a terrible torment, whether or not the fears have a legitimate basis or are admittedly unfounded.

Anger and Fear Can Be Controlled

Contrary to what we often believe, the emotions of fear and anger do not mysteriously overtake us and force us to spontaneously explode against our will. Anger and fear are not experienced apart from a perception of impending loss or threat. In the life of a believer, his perception of loss or threat is considerably altered as he grasps and applies the reality of God's presence and overruling power. Although those who struggle with anger may believe that they cannot control their angry outbursts, the fact remains that fear and anger are the result of perceptions that *can* be changed *and* controlled. How one interprets any given event will determine how he responds to it. First comes the perception, and then springs the emotion, followed by a response that is believed to be appropriate. Neither the perception nor the response occurs without being preceded by deliberate cognitive assessment that reflects a person's beliefs and desires.

Suppose a young husband was late coming home from work. Because he neglected to call home to warn his wife, she waited expectantly at the time he usually walked in the door. Dinner became cold, and the minutes turned into hours, as the young wife mentally rehearsed all the terrible possibilities that might be causing her husband's delay. Before long, she was filled with dread every time the phone rang and feared he may have been involved in a serious car accident. She began calling local hospitals and the highway patrol, tension rising in her voice as she anxiously pondered what she should do next. Then suddenly, she heard her husband's car pull into the driveway and quickly threw open the door to see that indeed her husband was safely home. As he sheepishly walked toward the door, however, her great relief gave way to explosive anger; and she began belting out a tirade of angry words between sobs and threats. She continued to relentlessly pelt him with rebuke and became even more outraged when he became defensive and irritated with her behavior. Believing she was perfectly justified in her anger, she began hurling objects at him and ordered him to sleep in his car.

As she slammed the door and bolted tight the locks, the young man was doubtless thinking to himself, "What happened?" He could not understand why his wife would act so irrational or why she would not let him explain what had happened. This in turn caused him to believe he was being unjustly treated, because he had assumed his secretary had called to tell his wife that his meeting with the boss would run late. Thus he began to fume, rehearsing all the ways that his wife's behavior was unreasonable and unjust and his without offense. He was outraged, but at the same time, filled with fear that his wife might reject him completely. When he noticed the neighbors' open windows, he was filled with humiliation and became even more irate. Instead of walking away or enduring what he believed to be a direct hit to his manhood, he wheeled around and began pounding on the door, threatening to call the police if she did not open it immediately. In spite, she turned off all the lights and went to bed, while he, not wanting to let her have the last word, smashed a window and proceeded to unlock the door to come in. And then a police car drove into the driveway...

Perceptions Matter

This kind of scenario occurs thousands of times in any given minute all across our country. It would be nice to think that it did not happen in the homes of Christians, but indeed it does. In order to discern more clearly how perceptions affect behavior, let's examine what took place in the minds of this husband and wife as their story unfolded.

Because it was not the first time this husband had been late, his wife assumed he was ignoring her wish that he call and let her know if he were running late. Although she never talked about it or was aware that it still influenced her, she had vague memories of her own father coming home late and her mother pacing the floor, and finally of her father packing his things and leaving in order to be with another woman. Secretly, she harbored fear that her own husband might be involved with another woman, or that he stayed at work late because he did not want to be with her. So when the minutes started ticking away past the time he should be home, she was filled with fear, not just that he might have been delayed by a car accident, but that his delay was connected in some way to a lack of love for her. Thus she perceived that her security and safety were in danger—the perfect condition that can instantly turn fear into an angry explosion.

Fear and anger both have the capacity to produce enormous tension, and both do change our body chemistry in such a way that we become alert and physically ready to either fight or run from whatever we believe is a threat to our safety or survival. The more our perceptions of a potential threat consume our thought processes, the more our emotional and physical energy build in preparation for action. In this husband and wife scenario, the wife's mind became fully engaged as she rehearsed all the possibilities as to why her husband might be late. As a result, she became both physically and emotionally alert and prepared to act.

There Is Always More to the Story

By the time the car finally pulled into the driveway, the wife's emotions were in high gear and the stage was set for a dramatic display of emotion. She experienced relief as soon as she realized her husband was safe; yet at the same time, fear and anger arose in proportion to the tension that had been building in response to her thoughts and interpretations. Yelling became a release for the built-up tension of fear and anger. At that particular moment, she would not have agreed that she could stop the tirade at any time—although she could have with sufficient motivation to do so. She chose not to bring her emotions under control because she was in the habit of venting them in hurtful and sinful ways, and because she believed her anger was justified. Therefore she found it quite easy to say whatever came to her mind, no matter how hurtful or incendiary.

What this wife wanted was reassurance that she was loved; and to have that reassurance, she believed her husband needed to express his sorrow and more or less agree that she was "entitled" to vent her displeasure in the way she was doing. When her husband reacted with annoyance instead, she further interpreted it to mean he was insensitive to her distress and was not at all willing to accept responsibility for his offense. From there, the dispute snowballed as husband and wife continued reacting toward each other's anger, each believing the other was guilty and unreasonable and themselves reasonable and virtuous.

Now let's consider the thoughts going through the husband's mind as he drove home and then encountered his wife. As he looked at his watch, he sighed, thinking about his wife waiting patiently for him at home. His one consolation was that his secretary was willing to call his wife, because he was delayed in a meeting. For once, he thought to himself, he had remembered to let his wife know he would be late— but still, he knew she would be disappointed that the meeting went so long. As he pulled into the driveway and saw his wife standing in the doorway, he smiled and looked forward to relaxing with her for the rest of the evening. As he walked toward the house, however, he realized she was not smiling, but rather had her arms folded and her lips tightened into a familiar look of furor. Before he could question her, she exploded in a barrage of ugly words that cut into his heart like a sword.

"This is outrageous," he thought to himself, "and I don't have to take this kind of abuse!" Though he did not talk about it and did not consider it important enough to think much about, he dreaded any confrontation out of fear that it would end in personal rejection and heartache. He had been fired from two jobs for irresponsible behavior and still did not sense that his new job was secure. So his wife's malicious words rang in his ears, re-opening tender wounds, until he believed he could stand it no longer. In retaliation for the hurtful things she was saying, he began to throw burning darts of his own, deliberately choosing statements he knew would hurt his wife in a personal way. Because he was tired, on edge after a tense meeting with his boss, and in no mood to be greeted by a tearful, angry wife, he felt justified in his vengeance and believed she deserved his angry words and threats, just as she believed he deserved hers.

When the husband suddenly became aware that the neighbors were doubtless hearing the entire fight, he became embarrassed as he sensed his guilt; but he quickly reassured himself by blaming his wife for it. As his wife slammed the door and turned off the lights, he felt helpless, embarrassed, misjudged, and full of hatred—enough so that he was further emboldened to threaten his wife in an effort to satisfy his resentment, and was determined to get into the house to prove he would not be forced out. The last thing on his mind was resolving the problems he was facing by talking to his wife. As he smashed the window and reached inside the door to open it, he felt a surge of satisfaction. He was already focused on barreling upstairs to grab his wife and teach her a lesson—he would show her how it feels to be abused and mistreated…he would teach her a lesson she would not forget…

Bombs Ready to Explode

Sometimes a police officer is called in time to interrupt escalating violence—sometimes no one is summoned to help. For some, a fight like this typically ends when one or both parties exhaust the energy of their anger and begin to communicate more constructively. Others continue their threats and ugly words until one or the other leaves, giving both enough time to regain a sense of reality and look at the perceived offense more objectively—though some never come back and end up severing the relationship completely. Yet for others, the fight ends only when the weaker of the two is bruised and bleeding and sufficiently terrified to appease the vengeance of the other. Explosive anger is a dangerous and destructive power, but all the more so when fear is added to the mix.

It would not be unusual in the least for two people to behave in this way if they did not know the Lord, had never heard the gospel, and were never exposed to the treasures of God's Word and God's ways—people whom the apostle Paul described as being by nature, the children of wrath. Yet it is extremely disappointing to see two professing believers, who ought to be displaying the love of God, so consumed in fighting for their perceived rights that they express their anger and fear in shamefully wicked and hateful ways. Even more disappointing is the way they are able to justify their sin, blame it on the other party, and self-righteously presume that God pities them and understandingly overlooks their spirit of hate and anger. They do not see God as the answer to their problems, nor their problems as an opportunity to see God's power at work in their lives. They have the blinded mind set of immature believers who fail to comprehend the power of God's love and His available power to transform their character.

At the Root of Fear

Fear always involves our human tendency to want to lean on our own understanding, or wisdom, rather than on the written Word of God. It manifests itself in believers who remain immature spiritually and neglect their responsibility to know God from the Scripture. This is why John tells us, "Herein is our love made perfect, that we may have boldness in the day of judgment: because as he is, so are we in this world. There is no fear in love; but perfect [mature] love casteth out fear: because fear hath torment. He that feareth is not made perfect in love" (*1 John 4:17–18*).

The person who is characterized by fearfulness and anger has not developed a clear understanding of God's love or nature and has not yet come to comprehend the way God's love changes our relationship to Him and His response toward us. Without an unwavering confidence in the promises and character of God, one cannot possibly face the trials and uncertainties of this life without apprehension. Everything about God invites a person to trust Him and delight in His love and care for every aspect of his existence.

Fear, in the most concise biblical sense, is the decisional incapacity to take God at His Word, or at face value. In this context, it is a form of unbelief. This is a universal problem among all human beings and is one of the most common ways the sin nature expresses itself. The first emotional response after Adam sinned was a sense of guilt and fear. Almost without exception, the first comment made to a person when God or an angel approached him was, "Fear not." The human response to the presence of God tends to initially be one of fear.

The Scriptures presume that a growing Christian will develop the peace of mind and boldness of spirit that is to characterize one who is growing in the knowledge of God and learning to trust Him in every area of his life. "For God hath not given us the spirit of fear; but of power, and of love, and of a sound mind" (*2 Timothy 1:7*). Spiritual maturity is marked by boldness and a lack of fear, together with a spirit of love. David declared, "The Lord is my light and my salvation; whom shall I fear? The Lord is the strength of my life; of whom shall I be afraid?" (*Psalm 27:1*) "In God I will praise his word, in God I have put my trust; I will not fear what flesh can do unto me" (*Psalm 56:4*). In contrast, the Scriptures use the word *fearful* to describe the ungodly that do not know God. In fact, the very first characteristic of the lost used in the horrendous list of sinful character traits in *Revelation 21:8* is *fearful.*

One who is consumed with fear and anger loses his ability to think with discernment and begins to make life-changing decisions on the basis of emotions. "I'm afraid that if I discipline my children they won't love me." "I'm afraid that if I object to my husband cheating on me that he will beat me." "I'm afraid if I tell my daughter not to date this boy that she will run away and get pregnant." "I'm afraid that if I tell the truth I won't be believed." "I'm afraid that if I don't lie for the boss I'll get fired." And so on, and so on.

Paul faced numerous fears and trials and tells us, "Our flesh had no rest, but we were troubled on every side; without were fightings, within were fears." At the same time, his reasonable and normal human fears were put in the context of his confidence in God's sovereign control and his recognition that God gives appropriate deliverance and comfort in every trial. So in the same passage Paul also exclaims, "I am exceeding joyful in all our tribulation." Then he goes on to describe how God had specifically comforted them (*2 Corinthians 7:4–7*).

The Connection between Unbelief and Anger

Matthew 6 provides a description of the two major problems that lead to needless anxiety. The first is a life that is centered on the treasures found in this world, while at the same time clinging to the belief that one loves God. This is a divided focus on God and treasures (money) and only leads to inner turmoil. God tells us our great treasure is to be Himself and that He alone is to be the object of our highest affections (*Genesis 15:1; Psalm 73:25–26; Colossians 3:1*). When our priorities are right, we are able to rest confidently in God's care and purpose for our lives. The second problem addressed in *Matthew 6* is the problem of unbelief and its connection to anger and anxiety. When we refuse to believe God's Word, we are left to our own imaginations and the false notion that we control our own destiny and must somehow protect our own selves.

With both problems, we attempt to save our own lives or preserve our own way of living; and in doing so, we end up losing our lives, or forfeiting the only life worth living. Fear leads us to believe we must defend and fight for our own protection. When self-preservation consumes our thoughts and actions, our entire life focus becomes ourselves. This self-preservation is a recipe for anger and contention, particularly when efforts to find security and reassurance fail. When our hearts are filled with doubts and fears, we become irritable, fretful, and overly sensitive.

Psalm 78 provides an overview of those who died in the wilderness, fretting against the Lord, refusing to see His love or care for them. Israel's unbelief and doubt made them fretful, angry, and defiant. Throughout their life, they leveled unreasonable charges against

God, doubting His mercy and refusing to believe He had their best interest in mind. We see them angry with God, angry with Moses, and angry at one another. When they tried to take matters into their own hands and protect themselves in their own way, life became more miserable. The very thing unbelieving Israel was rejecting— faith in God's love and trust in God's ways—was the very thing that would have produced the peace and contentment that had the power to dispel both their fear and anger.

Fears that fuel anger include fear of God's rejection, fear of God's judgment, fear with regard to one's salvation, fear of loss, fear of death, fear of man, fear of suffering, fear of failure, and fear of loneliness. The answer to the fear of rejection is found in *Luke 12:32*. The answer to the fear of not having needs met is found in *Matthew 6*. The fear of trials and suffering is answered in *Matthew 8:24–27*. The fear of the future is answered in *John 14:1–2*. The fear of damnation is answered in *John 5:24*. The fear of persecution is answered in *Matthew 10:14*. And the fear of being perplexed is answered in *Matthew 28:5*. If any fears are left besides these, they are covered in *Philippians 4*, "Be careful [anxious] for nothing."

Fears that lead to expressions of frustration and sinful anger can be traced to an inaccurate understanding of God's character and an insufficient knowledge of God's Word. The only other possibility would be a blatant refusal to believe what God has said about Himself and a refusal to appropriate the provisions He has made to deliver us from every fear. The antidote to fear is faith in God's shepherding care and love. David testified, "I sought the Lord and he heard me, and delivered me from all my fears" (*Psalm 34:4*). Paul also understood the connection between joy and confidence in God's love. He stated, "Now the God of hope fill you with all joy and peace in believing, that ye may abound in hope, through the power of the Holy Ghost" (*Romans 15:13*). A growing faith in God's love results when we grow in our understanding of God's love for us. "We love him, because He first loved us" (*1 John 4:19*). And a mature understanding of God's love, the Bible tells us, dispels fear.

THE WAY WE LOOK *at Others*

CHAPTER SIX

Take a moment to think about the last occasion in which you can remember experiencing or expressing anger. Chances are, it involved someone who displeased you in some way. Can you recall the last time tears filled your eyes or the last time you felt as though your emotions had taken a direct hit? It is quite likely that people were involved in whatever touched your heart enough to make you cry or make you sad. The fact is, people have a tremendous capacity to bring both joy and sorrow into our lives, especially if they are people we love.

We love to be loved by people; but oh, how we hate to be rejected, despised, or scorned by them. In a perfect world, everyone would love us all of the time and no one would ever treat us with contempt or disrespect. People would be perpetually kind, merciful to our faults and failures, sensitive to our needs and desires, and tirelessly attentive to our thoughts and ideas. They would be quick to forgive us, slow to correct us, and have an endless supply of patience and encouragement. Above all, they would do exactly what we want them to do all of the time, without fail. But…this is not a perfect world. It is a world filled with people who are by nature sinful and selfish. It is a world in which we are far more concerned with how we are treated than how we treat others; and because of this, it is a world filled with conflict and disappointment.

As much as we long for an ideal environment complete with exceptionally loving people, the reality is, we live in a world of sinful people of which *we too* are a part. Our world is so characterized by a love of self rather than a love for others that even our most noble acts of kindness tend to have a tinge of self-interest in them. When we do give and love, we expect to be loved in return and often react quite indignantly when our expectations are not fulfilled or our acts of kindness are not appreciated. We tend to give in order to get and do not continue loving or giving if our love is not reciprocated. From a purely human point of view, we believe an investment of love and kindness ought to yield dividends, preferably in greater proportion to what was invested. When it does not, it seems perfectly just to withdraw the investment completely and invest elsewhere. The law of the world is, "Do unto others as others have done unto you," or, "before they do it unto you."

When people believe they deserve to be treated in a particular way, they also believe they have a "right" to respond in anger when their expectations are not met. Spend some time watching a group of children at play, and you will doubtless observe them retaliating in anger whenever they believe they have been wronged or slighted in the smallest way. "I hit him because he hit me first!" is a line parents and teachers hear on a regular basis. It would be nice if children outgrew the "he hit me first" mentality; but sadly, children tend to learn more adult ways of expressing the same thing. The adult version is, "If you had (or had not) _____, I wouldn't have had to _____." Or in other words, "It's not my fault that I treated you so sinfully; it's really yours." At its core, this is the same rationale that keeps inner-city gangs shooting at each other and insures a never-ending supply of wars between nations, races, social classes…and family members. Quite simply, though we may call it justifiable anger, God calls it "hatred" and "revenge."

What may seem perfectly reasonable to our way of thinking is, in reality, raw hatred, no matter how well we justify it or disguise it in righteous trappings or prefer to call it "extreme dislike." And why do we typically hate? Because the object of our hatred does not love us or treat us in the way we believe he should. Very rarely do we hate the sin committed against God, which would be righteous hatred. Rather, we hate the sin committed against ourselves, and we hate the person who committed it. When the smallest shred of hatred enters our hearts, we tend to forego restraint and, in some way, hurt whomever and whatever we believe has hurt us. If only for a moment, we see such a person as our enemy, not as a fellow believer, not as an enemy of righteousness or an enemy of God. We tend to disassociate ourselves from one who has wronged us in some way, rather than approach him as a fellow sinner or beloved Christian brother or sister entangled in sin.

God has a better way! Be forewarned, however—God's ways bear no resemblance whatsoever to our human ways.

Love and Hate

We love to read Scriptures that reassure us, "God is love." We are comforted to hear that God is ready to forgive, merciful, longsuffering, gentle, patient, and kind. These are all things that we *long* to hear, in fact, what our hearts *delight* to hear. We also enjoy hearing passages of Scripture that tell us to love one another (especially when those we want to love us hear it too). The average unbeliever likes to hear these things too, and would not object to displaying these sentiments on a plaque in their home any more than a believing Christian would. However, this is as far as the world's "let's just get along" philosophy and God's commands to believers bear any resemblance to each other. As we get more specific, they dramatically divide into two opposite ways of living.

The Lord instructs us to "Love your enemies, bless them that curse you, do good to them that hate you, and pray for them which despitefully use you, and persecute you" (*Matthew 5:44*). As if that is not mind-boggling enough, He also tells us by what standard we are to treat others. "Therefore all things whatsoever ye would that men should do to you, do ye even so to them: for this is the law and the prophets" (*Matthew 7:12*). But that is not all—Christ commands believers to be willing to forgive a repentant person 490 times in one day, *for the same sin*, and to initiate reconciliation even when the other person's offense causes broken fellowship (*Matthew 18:15, 22*). But God does not stop there. He commands us to set aside our own comfort and take the time and effort to appeal to a sinning believer, plainly (and lovingly) addressing sin that is threatening to destroy him (*Galatians 6:1*).

Perhaps you are thinking, "Surely there is a limit somewhere to how long a Christian is to treat a hateful person with love and kindness." It may surprise you to learn that there is not a limit, if you believe "Charity [love] never faileth," or that it "endures" all things (*1 Corinthians 13:7–8*). Even though a Christian may need to separate himself from a wicked, hateful person, or confront the sins of a hateful person, he is not to do so motivated by hatred, but by love.

Have you gotten the idea yet that *this is impossible* in and of our own selves? Are you wondering why God would instruct us to behave so radically different than the world when these kinds of reactions are in such direct opposition to our natural human nature? This kind of behavior makes no sense at all—unless you understand that we have described the nature of Christ, which can only be duplicated in the hearts of those who have put their trust in Christ and received Him as their Savior from sin.

Achieving the Impossible

We do not simply emulate Christ; we are to *become* like Christ. Believers are given the indwelling Holy Spirit in order to accomplish this. He teaches, comforts, guides, and corrects Christians in the process. We are given the Word of God, which is powerful enough to transform the mind of a believer, changing what we think and desire, and how we behave. Peter gives us wonderful news when he reminds us, "Whereby are given unto us [believers] exceeding great and precious promises: that by these ye might be partakers of the divine nature, having escaped the corruption that is in the world through lust" (*2 Peter 1:4*). The character of a believer is transformed as he learns and conforms to the Word of God and as he depends upon Christ for the power to apply it in his life.

The one quality that characterizes a true believer most is his capacity to love others as Christ loves others. At the same time, the unmistakable mark of an *unbeliever* is an unwillingness and inability to love believers or those who do not love him in the way he desires. John reveals that this was the reason Cain murdered Abel, and what made him so distinctly different from his brother. He says, "For this is the message that ye heard from the beginning, that we should love one another. Not as Cain, who was of that wicked one, and slew his brother. And wherefore slew he him? Because his own works were evil, and his brother's righteous...We know that we have passed from death unto life, because we love the brethren. He that loveth not his brother abideth in death. Whosoever hateth his brother is a murderer: and ye know that no murderer hath eternal life abiding in him" (*1 John 3:11–12, 14–15*).

Biblical love is not merely a description of feeling, attachment, or devotion. Love is a word describing deliberate choices of action. Love does not take—it gives. Love does not tear down—it builds up. In other words, love behaves in very specific, predictable ways and is summed up and defined well in the following passage of Scripture: "Love worketh no ill to his neighbor: therefore love is the fulfilling of the law" (*Romans 13:10*). The one law by which we can judge any action or decision we make is this: is it loving?

Never mind what he or she did or said to you. Was your response loving? Did it reflect the way Christ responded to those who wronged Him? (See *1 Peter 2:18–23*.) Or did it emulate the way someone once wrongfully treated you? Responding to one who wrongs you with the kind of love and kindness that God commands does not in any way lessen an offender's sin against you or the fact that God will hold him responsible for his sin and deal with it. Yet his sin does not excuse your sinful manner, nor does it free you from God's command that you respond with love, humility, patience, and mercy, rather than anger and hatred. Remember that God will hold you responsible for your sinful reaction just as He will hold your offender responsible for his or her sinful action toward you. The proof of your relationship with Christ is this: how you treat those who have been hateful or adversarial toward you, not how you treat those who have loved and honored you. Our Lord has said, "For if ye love them which love you, what reward have ye? Do not even the publicans the same?" (*Matthew 5:46*).

When our words and actions hurt or destroy another person, they are not acts of love but acts of resentment and hatred. Hatred retaliates and hurts those who hurt us, and it will not overlook fault, nor will it refrain from returning an attack with malicious words or deeds. When we respond to another person's sin with cutting and hurtful actions and words, we emulate the devil, not our heavenly Father. We provoke the one we ought to be treating with kindness to hate the Lord we claim to represent and to rebel and hate us also. The Bible tells us, "Hatred stirreth up strifes: but love covereth all sins" (*Proverbs 10:12*). "See that none render evil for evil unto any man; but ever follow that which is good, both among yourselves, and to all men" (*1 Thessalonians 5:15*).

Loving the Unlovable

Dear believer, if you are truly born of God, you *can* obey God's command to love even the unlovable. Acts of love are to be a choice we make in response to God's love for us and in obedience to His commands to us, not in response to an emotional feeling that must overtake us in order to motivate us to love others. God never commanded us to have emotional feelings. These may or may not be present at times when we simply step out in faith and obey the command to love. Christ commands all believers to love others in the same way we would love Him if He were bodily present with us, and He promises He will one day reveal the motives of our hearts and reward all those who have sincerely loved others on His behalf. When we look into the face of our brother or sister in Christ, we are to see *Him*. When we look into the eyes of an unsaved sinner, we are to see a poor condemned sinner for whom Christ died and who could have been us. How foolish for us to think that an unbeliever has the capacity to love the way God enables believers to love!

Consider the chilling warning Paul gives to believers who mistreat and hold grudges against other believers. "That no man go beyond and defraud [oppress] his brother in any matter: because that the Lord is the avenger of all such, as we also have forewarned you and testified. For God hath not called us unto uncleanness, but unto holiness. He therefore that despiseth, despiseth not man, but God, who hath also given unto us his holy Spirit. But as touching brotherly love ye need not that I write unto you: for ye yourselves are taught of God to love one another" (*1 Thessalonians 4:6–9*).

We cannot possibly sin against others with impunity, for God considers such mistreatment as mistreatment against Himself. He *will* respond. Remember that God will treat us the way we treat others. "For with what judgment ye judge, ye shall be judged: and with what measure ye mete, it shall be measured to you again" (*Matthew 7:2*). "For he shall have judgment without mercy, that hath shewed no mercy; and mercy rejoiceth against judgment" (*James 2:13*). "For if ye forgive men their trespasses, your heavenly Father will also forgive you: But if ye forgive not men their trespasses, neither will your Father forgive your trespasses" (*Matthew 6:14–15*).

Reacting toward others in anger and malice can become an enslaving habit with far- reaching consequences. It is an incredibly destructive habit that *will* exact a price and cause much pain and sorrow as time unfolds. Anger is like a tornado that leaves a path of destruction wherever it touches down. No true believer who deals with others in anger is able to escape God's chastisement. Those who harbor anger and resentment in their hearts are like those who would harbor a nest of baby rattlesnakes under their bed. The creatures will not remain babies for long but will grow, until one day, they will sink their venomous teeth into their target with deadly results.

God's Antidote

God mercifully provides a three-part antidote to the deadly poison of hatred, malicious words, and resentful actions. Paul instructs us, "That ye put off concerning the former conversation [behavior] the old man, which is corrupt according to the deceitful lusts [selfish desires]; And be renewed in the spirit of your mind; And that ye put on the new man, which after God is created in righteousness and true holiness" (*Ephesians 4:22–24*).

- Put off the sinful ways that come naturally to our human nature.

- Change our minds to reflect the mind of Christ.

- Put on the qualities that emulate Christ and are the specific righteous counterpart to our sinful ways.

Again, in *Colossians 3:8 and 12–14* we are taught, "But now ye also put off all these; anger, wrath, malice, blasphemy, filthy communication out of your mouth…Put on therefore, as the elect of God, holy and beloved, bowels of mercies, kindness, humbleness of mind, meekness, longsuffering; Forbearing one another, and forgiving one another, if any man have a quarrel against any: even as Christ forgave you, so also do ye. And above all these things put on charity, which is the bond of perfectness [maturity]."

- Mercy conquers harshness.

- Kindness conquers malice.

- Humility conquers pride.

- Longsuffering and forbearance conquer impatience.

- Forgiveness conquers bitterness, and most important of all—

- Love conquers hate.

All our attempts to stop hating or resenting are futile unless there is a genuine decision to love others as Christ loves us. Love is what conquers hate, not merely a desire to stop hurting or hating. Jesus told us that it is our love for one another that captures the attention of an unbelieving world and identifies us as followers of Him (*John 13:35*). It is our love that demonstrates the difference between good and evil in the presence of an unbelieving world that cannot comprehend the love of God. Just as our heavenly Father is kind unto the unthankful and to the evil, so we are to be kind to those who make themselves our enemies; and we are to do good to them and speak well of them (Matthew 5:44–48). The children of this world angrily hate those who they believe hate them, but we are not to be like them—we are to be like Christ Who is our example.

If you are having a difficult time loving others, examine your understanding of God's love for you and the basis of that love. As you study the Scriptures, ask God to give you understanding so that you will better comprehend the wonder of His love so freely given to us on the basis of His character alone, not because we deserve it or are lovable in the least. The more we know about our Lord and Savior and the more we comprehend the depths of our sinful nature, the more we will marvel at His love for us and be able to respond with love for others. John tells us, "Herein is love, not that we loved God, but that he loved us, and sent his Son to be the propitiation for our sins. Beloved, if God so loved us, we ought also to love one another" (*1 John 4:10–11*).

It is a believer's love for others, not his talent, zeal, or labor for Christ, that marks him as one who truly loves God. John warns us,

"If a man say, I love God, and hateth his brother, he is a liar: for he that loveth not his brother whom he hath seen, how can he love God whom he hath not seen? And this commandment have we from him, That he who loveth God love his brother also" (*1 John 4:20–21*). "And the King shall answer and say unto them, Verily I say unto you, Inasmuch as ye have done it unto one of the least of these my brethren [least important], ye have done it unto me" (*Matthew 25:40*).

The way we all wish we could be loved is the way God Himself loves us, and the way believers *can* learn to love others if they choose to do so by the grace and strength of God! Remember that God Himself teaches the believer to love others. He will help you!

Jealousy and Anger

Anger and destruction are the inseparable companions of envy. Cain murdered Abel because he was jealous of Abel's relationship with God (*Genesis 4:4–8*). Rachel was jealous of Leah (*Genesis 30:1*) and Leah of Rachel (*Genesis 30:15*), causing family turmoil right up to Rachel's death. Jacob's brothers-in-law were jealous of the prosperity of Jacob (*Genesis 31:1*) and enraged their father against him. Joseph's brothers envied the attention their father gave their younger brother (*Genesis 37:4–11*) until they could not speak peaceably at all to Joseph and ultimately sold him into slavery. Even those of godly reputation mar their lives and ministry with the sin of jealousy. Miriam and Aaron were envious of Moses' leadership and God-given authority (*Numbers 12:1–10*). Saul was so envious of David that it consumed his life until he vowed to kill David (*1 Samuel 20:31*). The Bible tells us that the priests who plotted the crucifixion of Jesus did so because they were jealous of Him (*Matthew 27:18; John 11:47*).

The Bible identifies envy as being the direct cause of much anger and cruelty. In fact, the Bible uses the word <u>cruel</u> in connection with envy numerous times. "Wrath is cruel, and anger is outrageous; but who is able to stand before envy?" (*Proverbs 27:4*) Envy is so treacherous that the Bible makes note of the fact that one cannot resolve it apart from repentance and submission to God. One cannot reason with it, appease it, or compromise enough to make it go away. It burns with very little fuel and can flare up suddenly without provocation of any sort. "Jealousy is cruel as the grave: the coals thereof are coals of fire, which hath a most vehement flame" (*Song of Solomon 8:6*). The various types of cruelties associated with envy and anger are endless, but all invariably result in much sorrow and grief to whoever is involved.

Jealousy is seldom a huge problem between people who have little to do with one another on a daily basis. The less contact and interaction one has with another and the less dependency one has upon another, the less likely it will be for jealousy to become a dividing issue. However, the more people's lives interconnect with one another, the more both parties become vulnerable to interpersonal relationship problems that stem from jealousy. As a general rule, the closer the relationship, the greater the potential for jealousy of every sort to flourish. Almost every incident of jealousy recorded in the Bible involves family members or close friends and associates—and for good reason: family members tend to be an integral part of our lives. (Count the number of family members in the list provided above.)

Jealousy is typically motivated by one of two things:

- The fear that someone might take something of great value or take something that is perceived as a crucial need

- Resentment that someone possesses something that another person desires, particularly if that other person believes he deserves it as much or more than he who possesses it

Both of these motivations are rooted in discontent with God's provisions and distrust in what God has allowed or might allow. Those who are fearful are generally unaccustomed to resting in the shepherding care of the Lord Jesus Christ and have a tendency to struggle more with jealousy in one form or another. It is a problem that is closely related to their dependence upon people and circumstances to give them a sense of security, identity, and purpose. Relationships that are based upon need rather than biblical love are almost always guarded with such extreme hyper vigilance that they become hotbeds for unfounded jealousy. This occurs in part because fear drives the human imagination to perceive a threat when no threat is present.

Following is a list of common things people often fear being taken away by others:

- One's position, job, title, or authority
- One's success or present affluence
- A desired promotion
- The esteem of others, popularity, or the respect and attention of others
- The exclusive love of one person
- The love of a child

Following is a list of common things people often covet that others possess:

- Children, family, spouse, heritage
- Status, wealth, popularity, education
- Beauty, intelligence, talent, health
- Possessions, privileges, gifts, honors
- Joy, confidence, personality, knowledge
- Ministry opportunities, privileges, authority (In Christian circles)

Portrait of a Jealous Heart

Jacob traveled far from home as a young man and took a job with a rancher who became his father-in-law. He agreed to work fourteen years in exchange for his two daughters and six years in exchange for cattle. During this twenty-year period, Laban changed Jacob's wages ten times, each time trying to get the greater advantage over Jacob. Though it appeared that Jacob was merely experiencing common family problems, God provides us with "behind the scenes" information so that we can examine and learn the significance behind Jacob's experience.

First, we can see the unmistakable hand of God in His allowing and providentially overruling the events that took place in Jacob's life. Second, we can see how God was using each event to transform his character and place Jacob exactly where he needed to be in relation to God's greater plan. The Scriptures tell us that God saw what Laban was doing to Jacob and intervened in such a way that Jacob was blessed in spite of Laban's trickery and manipulation. Every effort Laban made to get an advantage over Jacob and keep him dependent on him failed *because God made it fail*. The family recognized and admitted that God blessed both Laban and Jacob's flocks for Jacob's sake but that God ultimately removed riches from Laban and gave wealth to Jacob.

Rachel's brothers, meanwhile, took their father's offense, and not understanding all the facts, began to resent Jacob's prosperity. When Jacob overheard them talking (not a coincidence), he realized they believed he had taken away that which was their father's (and ultimately theirs). He heard them tell each other that he had gotten all his glory by taking it from their father. At this point, the Lord spoke to Jacob and told him to leave the home of his father-in-law and return to his family and home. God was working behind the scenes, preparing Jacob and his family for changes that were to take place. Because God knew exactly what He was doing, every incident fell into place at exactly the right time, exactly as God planned.

Notice that the brothers became angry as their jealousy grew. They feared Jacob taking what they wanted for themselves and began to see him as a threat, rather than a hired hand working under them.

Their position in the family was at stake, as well as their wealth. What they did not recognize was that God had given them all that they had and that it was God who was changing Jacob's position and theirs. God was moving in the events that were transpiring for a specific purpose and goal, but all they could see was their own personal loss.

Look Behind the Scenes

The Scriptures tell us, "The LORD killeth, and maketh alive: he bringeth down to the grave, and bringeth up. The LORD maketh poor, and maketh rich: he bringeth low, and lifteth up. He raiseth up the poor out of the dust, lifteth up the beggar from the dunghill, to set them among princes, and to make them inherit the throne of glory: for the pillars of the earth are the LORD'S, and he hath set the world upon them. He will keep the feet of his saints, and the wicked shall be silent in darkness; for by strength shall no man prevail" (*1 Samuel 2:6–9*).

King Saul became consumed in jealousy as he recognized David to be God's choice for the throne. He desperately wanted to cling to the position he had become accustomed to and refused to humbly step down. He wanted to maintain the adoration of the people, the authority he enjoyed, and the benefits of being king. The thought of losing it was unthinkable to him because he loved his position far more than he loved God. As he plotted and worked to thwart David's growing popularity and finally became determined to kill him, his efforts only backfired on him. The more his efforts failed, the more his fear and jealousy flared until they caused him to become what we might label in our society today as a paranoid schizophrenic.

David would become king because God anointed him to be king, and nothing Saul could do would thwart God's plan or prevent God from governing as He saw fit. Solomon, David's son, would one day write, "A sound heart is the life of the flesh: but envy the rottenness of the bones" (*Proverbs 14:30*). Envy destroys from the inside out. It eats at one's heart until it poisons a person's thoughts and enslaves his very personality. Envy robs its victim of sleep, peace, and joy. It may seethe below the surface for a time, but it eventually erupts into malicious words and cruelty. Envy is destructive, not only because it leads to greater sins and a loss of joy, but also because it is so often excused, denied, and covered up, even when it surfaces in vengeance and wreaks havoc in a life.

The prodigal son's older brother was also touched with jealousy and became angry and bitter toward his younger brother, as well as his kind and loving father. Perhaps he too had become accustomed to his exclusive place in the family and was not looking forward to sharing his father's love with his brother, now that he had returned home. Or perhaps he feared his father would be too generous and would help his brother with the money he stood to inherit.

His understanding was blinded to the point where he believed his resentment, jealousy, and anger were a legitimate irritation, not sinful or destructive emotions. The young man saw only what he wanted to see and ignored the unseen hand of God that was working in his brother's heart, working in his father's life, and even working to accomplish good in his own life. His fear and jealousy only made him miserable and kept him from marveling at God's providential dealings in their lives. It made no difference whatsoever in God's greater purposes and plan. Like a wise parent who ignores his child's whining, God continues to work in the lives of his children in ways of His own choosing.

The Pharisees that plotted against Jesus and planned his death believed they had the power to control history—but they did not. Their envy moved them to hate the very Messiah they professed to be seeking and blinded them to the destruction they brought upon themselves. The more popular our Lord became and the more the people sought His wisdom and healing, the more they envied Him—and hated him. They feared losing their positions of authority, the esteem of the people, and their privileges in the political hierarchy of their day. It is amazing that the Bible gives us the exact motivation behind their plot to destroy Jesus—envy (*Matthew 27:18*).

This is the madness that envy is capable of producing. However, again, what the Pharisees imagined to be the means of destroying their enemy was the very means God would use to provide the world with a Savior and to ultimately exalt Jesus as Lord of Lords and King of Kings. David understood this when he wrote, "The LORD bringeth the counsel of the heathen to nought: he maketh the devices of the people of none effect" (*Psalm 33:10*). Though the earth rejects Him still, God is now and forever will be the sovereign ruler of heaven and earth. Can you imagine the Pharisees' horror when they discover too late that the One they envied to the point of wanting Him tortured on a Roman cross stands before them as their Judge?

Consider the story of Leah and Rachel—two sisters caught in the wicked tangle of polygamy, enduring the ravages of jealousy within a marriage God never intended to include three. Leah wanted Jacob's love and affection and was jealous of Rachel's favored position. Rachel envied Leah's children and became angry and miserable as a result.

Cosider too, the siblings of Moses—Aaron and Miriam. Miriam was given a ministry and responsibility by God Himself, according to *Micah 6:4*. Had she been content with what God had given to her, she might have left a legacy much different than she did. Even the most mature, wise, and spiritually gifted are not exempt from the sin of envy; for Miriam, God's gifted teacher and singer, fell prey to it. The Scriptures indicate that she became critical and resentful of decisions Moses was making. She envied Moses' authority and relationship with God and began to insist that she and Aaron be given equal authority with Moses. She wanted to be included in the inner circle, not because God appointed her to be there, but because it served her own purpose and catered to her desire to be respected and esteemed. Notice that Moses did not manipulate, fight, yell, or demand that he be honored; yet God stepped in and quickly put Miriam in her place. She was demoted and her future ministry was marred, yet her pride was thoroughly dealt with.

No Good Thing Will He Withhold…

It is a very dangerous thing to want something God has not given, whether it is a position, honor, or possessions. Remember, at this moment in your life, you have exactly what God has permitted you to have. You do not need to fear losing any position that God wishes you to retain, and you do not need to be concerned in the least that God has no rewarding place of service prepared for you. "A man's gift maketh room for him, and bringeth him before great men" (*Proverbs 18:16*).

Be content with what God has given, and you will have great joy. But be forewarned—should you choose to envy what God has given to someone else, or attempt to obtain something God has not given you, not only will you become miserable, but also you will bring upon yourself God's discipline until your pride is crushed. And even if God permits you to have what He has not chosen for you, know this—it will not bring you the joy you imagine it will bring. Enjoyment with no sorrow attached is a gift that God gives when we wait upon Him and receive from Him in His time, rather than when we impatiently grab something for ourselves. Take it and you will be unsatisfied. Receive it and you will be delighted.

Remember, "Promotion cometh neither from the east, nor from the west, nor from the south. But God is the judge; he putteth down one, and setteth up another" (*Psalm 75:6–7*). Lest we think we can predict what and why God does what He does, we are reminded that He also may choose to use the basest of men when it serves His purpose. He uses the wicked, and He sometimes allows good people to suffer for a good cause. God does not always withhold something because He is disciplining us; sometimes He withholds things that are not good for us. Life is a whole lot simpler when we take God at His word and rest in the knowledge that "No good thing will he withhold from them that walk uprightly" (*Psalm 84:11*). Envy cannot survive when we truly believe this promise.

God's ways are truly above our ways, and His ways are past finding out. There is coming a day when God will judge every person, every nation, and every person to whom He delegated authority. As those in heaven patiently wait for that day, so must we on earth wait as well. "The LORD hath prepared his throne in the heavens; and his kingdom ruleth over all…Thy kingdom is an everlasting kingdom, and thy dominion endureth throughout all generations" (*Psalm 103:19; 145:13*).

All that we are, all that we have is in the power of God's hand first of all. We need not fear losing anything, for our lives do not consist of anything we have—including our titles. David recognized this and boldly confessed to God, "Thine, O LORD, is the greatness, and the power, and the glory, and the victory, and the majesty: for all that is in the heaven and in the earth is thine; thine is the kingdom, O LORD, and thou art exalted as head above all. Both riches and honour come of thee, and thou reignest over all; and in thine hand is power and might and in thine hand it is to make great, and to give strength unto all" (*1 Chronicles 29:11–12*).

The Prosperity of the Wicked

We cannot possibly understand all the reasons God moves as He does; but we can know that His judgments are right, holy, and good. We can know He is a faithful Creator that we can trust. Therefore, we can confidently yield to His judgments and learn to keep all that is in our hand open to Him. Our fears and aspirations will not thwart God's work in our lives—but they certainly have the power to make us discontent and envious of others who have what we may secretly desire. Still, God gives to them just as He gives to us, and all the fretting in the world will not change what God does. Let us pray, then, as Isaiah did, "But now, O LORD, thou art our father;

we are the clay, and thou our potter; and we all are the work of thy hand" (*Isaiah 64:8*).

Asaph gave a testimony in song that told of his envy and how God brought him to a place of repentance and submission. He confessed, "I was envious at the foolish, when I saw the prosperity of the wicked" (*Psalm 73:3*). Asaph, like many of us, thought of his envy as his just being hurt or upset at some injustice. How easy it is to compare ourselves more favorably with someone we dislike who is prospering or being honored in ways we do not believe they deserve. Though jealousy may be hidden, the implication is that we believe we deserve what someone else is being given more than he or she deserves the honor. Perhaps we have been unfairly treated, passed up for a promotion, or deprived recognition for legitimate achievement. Though it may be disappointing, it has not escaped the eyes of God, nor is it an exception clause to *Romans 8:28–29*.

As you read Asaph's psalm, you will notice how he became focused on the prosperity of people who are wicked and wondered why those who were righteous sometimes seemed to suffer. His thoughts became so introspective that he said, "When I thought to know this, it was too painful for me." Thankfully, the song ends in triumph, not because Asaph found answers to his questions, but because he turned his attention to the Lord and came into His presence. As he pondered the end of the wicked and the end of the righteous, he began to understand the situation from an eternal perspective. As the Lord drew Him to Himself, he began to put his trust in God's good and sovereign work and recognized how foolish it was for him to fret and complain.

Asaph finished his song by professing something every envious heart needs to profess as well. "Nevertheless I am continually with thee: thou hast holden me by my right hand. Thou shalt guide me with thy counsel, and afterward receive me to glory. Whom have I in heaven but thee? And there is none upon earth that I desire beside thee. My flesh and my heart faileth: but God is the strength of my heart, and my portion for ever. For, lo, they that are far from thee shall perish: thou hast destroyed all them that go a whoring from thee. But it is good for me to draw near to God: I have put my trust in the Lord God, that I may declare all thy works" (*Psalm 73:23–28*).

The antidote to jealousy is a humble willingness to be thankful and content with God's provision, no matter what it might be. Love for others and a willingness to obey God and accept His work, limitations, and ways in our lives are the truths that conquer envy.

Poor Listening and Communication Skills

Many people prefer to talk rather than listen, either because listening requires patience or because listening requires them to engage in a meaningful exchange of information that is difficult for them. There are many reasons why a person may have learned poor listening habits. Sometimes the problem begins in childhood and stems from the particular dynamics of the family in which one was raised. Sometimes it is learned during school-age years when children tend to become confident or withdrawn, depending on their particular experiences of success and failure. Many people are simply gregarious and more impulsive in nature or more naturally attracted to leading. Yet for others, poor listening is primarily a habit that became ingrained in them because listening and communicating require time, and they have not learned to be patient enough to invest the time, or interested in what others have to say enough to listen to them. However the habit is learned, it is one that produces many problems in later years—among which is the problem of drawing inaccurate conclusions and then reacting in anger.

The habit of careless listening, or tuning out what others are saying, leads to surmising, drawing hasty (and often incorrect) conclusions, and reacting impulsively. It causes people to become quick to judge and slow to listen *before they react*. Even when poor listeners are not talking, they may *not* be listening intently in an effort to weigh information carefully or to understand what another person is saying. Sometimes they listen only to be polite or to "earn" the right to do what they really want—talk and be listened to. Their impatience and self-interest make them prone to tuning out in boredom or *thinking ahead* of the person they are listening to in order to begin constructing their own story or defense. They imagine, in error, that keeping themselves quiet when another is talking is the same as listening. It is not!

Just as a failure to learn good listening habits leads to tension and anger, so does the failure to learn good speaking habits. Many people prefer to remain observers in life because it is "safer" and requires no effort. Others decline to speak out because they fear the reactions of others or come to believe they cannot express themselves accurately. Whether the habit is learned as a result of one's experiences, as a result of one's natural inclinations, or because one has not learned to express himself, it is a habit that short-circuits good communication skills and leads to anger. Those who fail to express themselves appropriately tend to tolerate in silence until tension builds to the point where they will suddenly "blow up" in anger.

Drawing Conclusions

People who struggle with anger tend to be opinionated people, whether they are talkative or quiet, and whether they neglect listening or speaking. They have often developed the habit of dogmatically drawing their own conclusions based on their own perceptions and then hanging on to them tenaciously—even when evidence is clearly stacked against them. Many tend to avoid discussing their perceptions or testing them in profitable conversation to insure accuracy because they want to avoid communication. They also often neglect the all-important step of clarifying, questioning, inquiring, and fact-collecting, leading them to make conclusions drawn by little information or by intuition alone. This practice leads them to the habit of surmising instantly without careful investigation of facts, and then repeating conclusions as if they were fact. Unless others capitulate to them, they will often become angry and hateful or attempt to intimidate others into agreeing with them.

Reasoning with angry people who tenaciously refuse to communicate is next to impossible because they lack sufficient self-discipline or self-denial to work at listening patiently and communicating effectively. They are often determined to prove their own way or establish their own superiority or authority over others, rather than humbly listening and exchanging information in order to come to a wise conclusion.

When angry people assume positions of authority, they tend to cut off anyone who will not acquiesce to their point of view without objection or discussion. Many of these leaders view others with differing perspectives as enemies, disloyal associates, or threats to the personal kingdom they are working to establish. Just the opposite is true—those who are willing to engage in discussion without concern for their own position are those who truly want what is best for their leader. Good examples of people like this would be Nathan, the friend who had enough courage to confront King David after he had sinned with Bathsheba, and Hanani, the prophet who confronted Asa after he won a battle with the help of God's enemies. David had enough humility to listen, but Asa became enraged and treated Hanani with contempt and cruelty.

The Dangers of "Yes" Men

Leaders who follow the advice of people who will not challenge them or confront them when they are in error are much like Rehoboam who became king after the death of his father Solomon. Rehoboam rejected the wisdom of those who were older and more experienced than he and chose instead to listen to the young men who professed to be his friends. The Scriptures tell us that God allowed him to have his way because God knew his foolish anger would divide the kingdom according to the prophetic warning He had given years before. Husbands who refuse to listen to the input of their wives often cut themselves off from the very person God desires to use as a contributing partner in the decisions of life. Pastors who feel threatened by deacons or others whom God has added to the church family do the same—as do mothers, teachers, employers, and the like. Leaders who will not listen and communicate with others are prone to be threatened by the input of one under their authority, unless they are secure enough in God's work in their lives and humble enough to see the way God so often works.

People struggling with anger dramatically improve their ability to control sinful reactions when they work at increasing their patience, love, and respect for others' opinions and feelings and learn better communication and listening skills. Simply disciplining oneself to suspend judgment and take the time to understand before one draws a conclusion resolves much anger. The Scriptures have much to say about our words and the necessity of applying ourselves to the art of learning how to use gracious speech. "The heart of the righteous studieth to answer: but the mouth of the wicked poureth out evil things" (*Proverbs 15:28*).

Poor Problem Resolution Skills

People characterized by anger often develop the habit of attacking *people* in supposed self-defense, rather than attacking the *problem*. This sometimes includes attacking and berating themselves or attacking people covertly rather than openly. This sinful practice is the result of failing to confront and work out problems biblically with the means God has provided for us. Working out problems in a godly way requires us to be humble, to be focused on the issue and not ourselves, to be in control of our own spirits, and to be ready to love and forgive. These disciplines do not come naturally to any of us. They must be learned and practiced *deliberately*.

God tells us that Christians are so protected by God that we are never allowed to experience a problem without also being given sufficient strength and God-given grace to deal with the problem righteously. Furthermore, God reminds us that our heavenly Father is faithful—He cannot lie and never fails to do exactly as He has promised. God Himself assures us that He always provides a way to escape when the trials of life assault us. Finally, we are told that while we suffer the same difficulties and trials in this world that others who do not know God suffer, we do not suffer anything without a purpose, and we are always delivered from every affliction in some God-given way (*1 Corinthians 10:13*).

Before we can learn to deal with problems in a way that pleases God and elicits His blessing, we must understand and believe all of these important truths. We read in *1 Corinthians 10:13*, "There hath no temptation [trial] taken you but such as is common to man: but God is faithful, who will not suffer [allow] you to be tempted [tried] above that ye are able; but will with the temptation also make a way to escape, that ye may be able to bear it." Again, the Holy Spirit tells us through David that "The righteous [saved people] cry, and the Lord heareth and delivereth them out of all their troubles…Many are the afflictions of the righteous: but the Lord delivereth him out of them all" (*Psalm 34:17, 19*). God uses specific words to express the emphatic certainty of the truth—*no, will not, will, and all.*

Anger may take the form of mild marital conflict that is irritating but quickly resolved. In these cases, it would be wise for couples to spend time learning effective conflict resolution, which may be all that is needed to bring matters under control. Sometimes, however, conflict may be moderately severe, to the point where family life is disrupted and filled with tension on a regular basis. This level of anger warrants the investment of much time and effort, as well as the involvement of a responsible third party, to bring it under control. But anger that increasingly escalates over time to become violent enough to put family members in physical or emotional danger is serious enough to warrant immediate intervention so it will not become lethal. In these cases, anger and poor problem resolution skills are only a small part of the problem. There are many factors involved that overlap angry behavior.

When we are faced with any kind of trial or problem, our human tendency is to either blow up in anger because we do not like what is happening, run the opposite direction because we do not want to deal with it, clam up out of fear and despair, or attempt to circumvent the trial in an effort to find an easier way to deal with it. None of these methods are righteous and none can be employed without painful consequences. God's way is to acknowledge and confront the problem, seek God's Word for direction in finding the way of escape God has provided, obey the scriptural admonition for dealing with the particular problem, and then wait and trust God to intervene to do what we are powerless to do.

Unforgiveness

A lack of forgiveness toward others shows up in many subtle ways. Those who do not forgive become critical and judgmental toward the flaws and failures they see in others. They are often easily irritated or disgusted by others' sins and demonstrate a low tolerance level for their imperfections. Unforgiveness is commonly manifested as a lack of mercy or patience with people (including children) who do not immediately respond to expectations. People who have difficulty forgiving have difficulty allowing others to be human, to fail, or to grow. They tend to see only what others are at the moment, not what they can become. They are particularly angry when the failures and sins of others affect their plans or expectations in some way, or when others embarrass or inconvenience them. Their focus is on what they want for themselves or what they expect, not on what is edifying to someone else or what will encourage them in the sometimes long process of Christian growth.

Christians who struggle in the area of forgiveness clearly do not comprehend the magnitude of their own sin debt or God's forgiveness for them. They sometimes fail to comprehend the patience God has with our frail human character and our tendency to fail repeatedly. If Christians wrongly imagine that God demands instant perfection from them, they are all the more demanding that those around them exemplify perfect character. Often, it is as though some believe they deserve God's forgiveness and patience, but others do not—that in some way their own sins are more understandable and forgivable than the sins of others.

When we behave in this way, we become like the servant in *Matthew 18* who was forgiven the equivalent of a billion dollars simply because he asked forgiveness and then refused to forgive a neighbor a few dollars when he too begged for mercy. The worst sins people commit against us are trivial when compared to the sins Christ bore on the cross in our place. A lack of forgiveness is really a lack of understanding with regard to God's love and grace that He has extended and does extend to us every day of our lives. Maintaining a spirit of unforgiveness blatantly ignores Christ's suffering on our behalf or His goodness in extending to us His mercy on a daily basis.

We are to forgive, not on the basis of merit, but on the basis of what God, for Christ's sake, has forgiven us. God forgives because of Who He is and who we are in Christ. When we minimize our own sin and magnify the sins of others, we put ourselves in grave spiritual peril. God warns that any refusal to mercifully forgive others from the heart results in torment. He does not tell us exactly what torments He will allow each of us to experience as a result of unforgiveness. However, torment certainly includes depression, anger, anxiety, broken fellowship with Christ, and a barren Christian life. Jesus solemnly reminds us that our heavenly Father does not forgive or restore fellowship to those who do not forgive others. He will show mercy toward us to the degree we show mercy toward those who fail or sin against us.

The Bible warns us in many places that God and God alone has authority to execute justice and vengeance. God *will* punish unrepentant violators by His law and will hold them responsible; therefore, we are not to assume God's prerogative to deal with injustices in ways that go beyond the limits of judicial laws written by man or the ordinances given to the local church. God is justly angry with the wicked every day. Therefore, our fear that God will not justly hold a wicked offender responsible for his crimes is unfounded.

God, unlike man, is perfect in justice and can be trusted to handle offenders with absolute righteousness. No criminal clears the debt he owes to God or makes himself acceptable to God simply because he has paid his debt to society and is free from further judicial penalty. There is yet a court that convenes in heaven where offenders face an all-knowing Judge Who will give a sentence of His own at a time of His own choosing. Knowing this calms the fears of those who are victims of evil, for they see God as He is—perfect, as well as perfectly holy, merciful, and loving.

Bitterness

Bitterness is closely linked to resentment and hatred, developing most often when our reputation is damaged, when pain is inflicted on a loved one or on us, when our expectations are frustrated, and when others do not live up to our desire for them. Bitterness grows out of unresolved anger and hatred. It is much more than a fleeting emotion or momentary irritation—it is a deep-rooted attitude of anger and resentment that is embedded into one's thoughts and words. Bitterness is a subtle germ that wiggles into our life disguised as hurt, disappointment, sorrow, or emotional pain. These emotions seem quite reasonable in times of suffering or when we are treated unjustly. As a result, they are often cultivated and nurtured until they unexpectedly explode into anger, bitterness, and hatred. Rather than bringing relief or comfort, bitterness strikes as a wild tornado that rips and destroys everything in its path.

Bitterness is produced when we respond to difficult or hurtful events in unbiblical and destructive ways. We might respond by smugly and silently ignoring those we resent. Or, we might respond by attacking them with words designed to hurt or express disagreement or contempt. Sometimes we simply do nothing and simmer silently along with those who commiserate with us. When we enjoy "punishing" those who have hurt us, when we long to see them "put in their place" or destroyed in some way, we are actually putting ourselves in the place of God. God alone has the right to punish and judge sin—and He will. We, however, do not like to commit a hurtful incident to God or trust Him to take care of it in His own time and in His own way. We prefer "helping" God out by inflicting pain and punishment of our own.

Bitterness sees only the pain caused by an offense against a loved one or us—not how God could use the offense for good in our lives. Bitterness sees the wrong in others, not the wrong in us. Rather than following the example of Joseph who trusted God to turn around for good that which others intended for evil, bitter people moan as Jacob did and say, "All these things are against me!" *Genesis 42:36* and *50:19–20* are passages that give testimony to these truths. The antidote to bitterness is forgiveness and trust in God's character, purpose, and ultimate justice.

The Real Problem

It is human nature to believe that other people are the direct cause of our anger. We want to believe it is they who need to change, not ourselves. Anger is typically explained away with thoughts such as, "If they would only…," "But they should…," or "If they hadn't…" This thinking prompts determined efforts to control people and circumstances in an attempt to keep ourselves free from anger. In many cases, it leads to sinful attempts to dominate and control people by force. Exerting control over people not only fails to contain anger but also insures increased anger, for no amount of force can change the fact that people and circumstances will *never* be perfect in this world. The mere frailty of human beings absolutely guarantees daily disappointments and irritations because we live in imperfect bodies with imperfect memories, understanding, coordination, motives, maturity, and intelligence. Moreover, we are *all* sinful and self-centered by nature and, without exception, we *all* battle on a daily basis with the effects of sin and our human weakness.

No amount of control exerted over others is able to conquer anger because it is not the world, the people in our world, or the situations in which we find ourselves that are the problem. The problem lies within our own heart. It is our emotion-backed demands and expectations that make us suffer. It is our sinful heart that causes us to react in anger to the sins and failures of others. What needs to change, then, is our heart—not our circumstances; for try as we might, we will never eradicate life's irritations and disappointments. As long as people possess a human nature, we must never expect them (or ourselves) to live so perfectly that they never make a mistake or display self-centeredness. It helps to remember that spiritual growth and maturity are progressive, making even the Christian a work in progress. Expecting people to conform to our wishes in perfect compliance is guaranteed to keep us angry, because quite simply, their acting that way is an impossibility.

In this world, people will selfishly refuse to let you get in front of them on the freeway. You will get stuck behind big semi trucks traveling slowly up an incline when you are late for an appointment. Your children will fight with their siblings, get in trouble at school, leave tools outside to rust, lose things, and break expensive objects. They will put dings on your car door with their bikes, run when they should walk, and play when they should be asleep. Plenty of people will misunderstand you, misquote you, and fail to appreciate you. Your spouse will forget an important date, make mistakes in the checkbook, and disagree with you when you least want a disagreement. There will be days when the phone will ring incessantly and telemarketers will not have a clue how many others have already interrupted your morning. Neighbors will complain about the silliest things and then keep you up all night with their music. They will let their dog romp in your front yard—and leave something for you to clean up. Someone may very likely burglarize your home, smash the windows of your car, or cheat you in a business transaction. You *will* get flat tires, and you *will not* escape the trials and irritations of this life.

So why live as though your happiness depends on none of these things happening? Though you are powerless to control your world in such a way as to eradicate problems and irritations, you are not powerless to change the way you *think* about them. Accepting the inevitable problems of living in an imperfect body in an imperfect world with other imperfect people disengages rage. Learning how

God works in the midst of problems and how He delivers us out of every problem and works everything for our good and His glory dispels anguish. We can live happily together with other sinners in this imperfect world only if we learn how to love our neighbor, how to listen and communicate more effectively, how to resolve problems biblically, and how to forgive and overlook fault. Sure—it is easier to blame people, find fault, and brood about all the things we suffer; but it does not lead to happiness, nor does it conquer anger.

We might be able to discipline ourselves in such a way that we learn to control disgust, irritation, and anger toward others; but discipline alone is powerless to transform the human heart into the loving, forgiving nature of Christ. We are transformed only as we align our thinking with the Bible and obey it. God tells us, "And be not conformed to this world: but be ye transformed by the renewing of your mind" (*Romans 12:2*). "Whereby are given unto us exceeding great and precious promises: that by these ye might be partakers of the divine nature, having escaped the corruption that is in the world through lust" (*2 Peter 1:4*).

THE WAY
WE LOOK
at Ourselves

CHAPTER SEVEN

During the period of time in which Daniel lived, kings in the orient commonly set aside the best-looking, brightest, and healthiest young men who were taken captive out of a conquered territory. From these the king would separate for himself "the cream of the crop," who would then be subjected to emasculation in order to insure their loyalty in the service of the king for the rest of their lives. After undergoing further training in the language and laws of the land, they would become advisors to the king or serve in official capacities that required intelligence and a broad scope of knowledge. It was this barbaric practice that brought Daniel, a Jewish teenager, into Nebuchadnezzar's palace in Babylon where he was assigned to serve the king.

Growing up in Jerusalem as a descendant of King David entitled Daniel to receive an excellent education and provided special privileges and opportunities that would prepare him for future leadership in Judah. He was quite likely very popular in Jerusalem, given his attractive stature, athletic strength, and intelligence. Having been taught the finer points of the Mosaic Law, he would have been respected among the most distinguished scholars of the land. Only the loveliest Jewish girls would have been selected as candidates to be his future wife and among his friends would be the most promising of Judah's young men. No doubt Daniel looked forward to his fast approaching manhood with the same optimistic hopes and dreams that any other teenager would entertain.

It was at this high point in Daniel's young life that Jeremiah the prophet was fervently preaching to the people of Jerusalem, warning them of God's coming judgment if they would not repent of their sins and idolatry. The society in which Daniel grew up was arrogant, spiritually cold, and steeped in pleasure-seeking and pagan idol worship. They wanted nothing to do with Jeremiah and had no desire to obey the Lord or turn from their sinful ways. The Bible does not tell us how Jeremiah's ministry may have influenced Daniel's young life; but it does tell us that, unlike the adults, Daniel and his closest friends grew up to become faithful followers of the Lord and put their trust in Him. Perhaps it was the example of Jeremiah that inspired Daniel to stand steadfast in his faith and loyalty to God.

The Destruction of Hopes and Dreams

It is hard for us to imagine what it must have been like for the children and young people who were living in Jerusalem the day the Babylonian army conquered the city and began pouring through the gates. With flashing swords and spears, they overpowered the men who were armed and trained for war, and killed them. Then the soldiers systematically plundered the houses and herded the people outside the city to be bound in fetters and chains. No pity was shown toward the elderly, the sick, or the very young—they had all become property to be disposed of or used at the whim of their captors. When finally the soldiers had finished killing and looting the city, they set the buildings and houses on fire and left them to burn while the captives watched in stunned horror and disbelief. That was the last scene they would remember of their city and home before being forced to make the long journey on foot to

Babylon. It was not the end of the Babylonians' cruelties or the end of the Jews' sorrows and heartache, but it was certainly the end of life as they had once known it.

Once in Babylon, the people struggled to survive as slaves in a hostile country that regarded them with little more respect than household animals. They were despised, abused, and destitute, without hope and without a means of escape. One would not be surprised if those who had lost so much and seen so much cruelty and hatred became angry and bitter; in fact, it would be quite surprising if they were *not* filled with contempt and anger. Although it was their own sin and stubborn refusal to repent that had caused God to withdraw His hand of protection and allow this horror to come upon them, it would have been easy, in fact, *natural*, to blame the barbaric and murderous Babylonians for all their sorrows.

It is remarkable that this is the point at which we are introduced to a teenage boy who went through all of this and more, yet purposed in his heart to love and obey the Lord and trust Him no matter where his life took him or what events confronted him. Though his former hopes and dreams were crushed and his future among the king's eunuchs was bleak in comparison to the future he had once looked forward to in Jerusalem, Daniel continued to worship God and grew more (not less) devoted to Him. Daniel chose the path of submission and acceptance, though he did not know what twists and turns lay ahead in his life's journey.

Though the Babylonians had the power to kill him or preserve his life, to strip him of everything he owned or destroy everything he loved, they could not destroy Daniel's faith in God or his love for Him. Daniel's identity was not wrapped up in his earthly heritage, his wealth, or in any other temporal thing; therefore, he was not destroyed when these things were destroyed. He was a child of God, with the irrevocable privileges of a child of God, no matter what new identity and name the king of Babylon gave him and no matter what circumstance or trial fell upon him. The Babylonians could maim his body or destroy it altogether—but they could not touch his soul or destroy who he was. The king called him Belteshazzar, after his god, but the King of the Universe called him Daniel, a man greatly beloved of God.

The Pursuit of Happiness

Many times we become angry or despondent when the things we set our hearts upon are withheld or taken from us. Instead of driving us to the feet of our God and causing us to acknowledge that He alone is our life and joy, we often react in sorrow or anger, as though happiness itself is being withheld from us. If we believe our happiness depends on something we must acquire or if we believe we must have someone's affection, respect, or approval in order to be content, we will be driven to live our lives trying to attain these things; and if we cannot, pitying ourselves because of it. If we *do* obtain whatever it is we desire, we will live our lives fearing its loss.

If our image is what gives us satisfaction, we will become distressed or angry if anything threatens to tarnish it. If our sense of accomplishment provides our greatest joy, we will become distressed or angry when anything interferes with our quest for progress. In essence, whatever provides our sense of personal identity, worth, and fulfillment becomes our greatest focus in life and is what ultimately controls and motivates us. It could be a title, possessions, achievements, the love and affection of another person, our physical appearance, health, a particular responsibility, the accomplishments of our children or spouse, or even a ministry given to us by God. The list is endless. We have only to note our reaction when something is threatened or destroyed to determine its place in our heart, for we tend to react in proportion to the significance we place on something.

Loss and difficulty of any kind ought to drive us to confess to the Lord as Asaph did, "Whom have I in heaven but thee? and there is none upon earth that I desire beside thee. My flesh [human efforts] and my heart [human reasoning] faileth: but God is the strength of my heart, **and my portion for ever**" (*Psalm 73:25–26*). If we are living in pursuit of happiness and fulfillment, we will react in anger or distress whenever life becomes unpleasant or our happiness appears to be thwarted or threatened in any way. It is the pursuit of God Himself—not happiness, and certainly not God's gifts—that ultimately produces lasting joy and contentment. If God is our reward, trials are merely rocks to climb on, not impediments to our joy. And if God is our reward, we need not fear losing Him, for it is He who keeps us by His power, not we who keep Him by our power (*1 Peter 1:5*). No earthly joy is permanent or secure; therefore, it is foolish to center one's hopes and expectations on uncertain riches, relationships, or accomplishments.

The Joy of Our Heart

What animates your conversation and causes you to become alert and enthusiastic? What topic makes your eyes light up and your face to shine? What images capture your idle thoughts and what desires cause you to dream? Answer these and you will have a fairly clear picture as to what you are living for and what holds first place in your heart. Perhaps your answer includes some noble venture undertaken self-sacrificially, the welfare of others entrusted to your care, or some good work for God that is profitable and wholesome. While these are certainly not evil in and of themselves, even such good things as these miss the mark and have the potential to become idols of the heart that will steal your affections and keep you from delighting in God Himself.

The prophet Jeremiah preached to those living in Jerusalem who professed to love God but in their hearts delighted most in other things that gave them pleasure. God spoke through Jeremiah as He showed the people that their priorities were wrong and that their affections were set on things that could not satisfy. Again and again, the Lord challenged the people to turn to Him with all their hearts, repent of their sin, and find in Him their greatest joy. "Thus saith the Lord, Let not the wise man glory in his wisdom, neither let the mighty man glory in his might, let not the rich man glory in his riches: But let him that glorieth glory in this, that he understandeth and knoweth me, that I am the LORD which exercise lovingkindness, judgment, and righteousness, in the earth: for in these things I delight, saith the LORD" (*Jeremiah 9:23–24*).

Our knowledge can become obsolete and clouded with age. Our strength can be destroyed by sickness, and our riches can be lost in a moment. None of these things can sustain us in times of sorrow, produce peace of mind, or make us men and women who are able to patiently respond to life's irritations and disappointments without sinful anger and resentment. Knowing God, on the other hand, produces joys and rewards that last for eternity and cannot be touched by any trial or tragedy in this life. Daniel lost many things that were dear to him, but he did not lose what mattered most. He was able to respond with grace and confidence to horrors we cannot even imagine, because he knew God and knew beyond any doubt that he was a beloved child of God. Daniel set his affection on things above, not on things on the earth—and it made all the difference in the world in the way he reacted to disappointment and difficulty on this earth. His example makes Paul's admonition to believers all the more precious to us. "If ye then be risen with Christ, seek those things which are above, where Christ sitteth on the right hand of God. Set your affection on things above, not on things on the earth. For ye are dead, and your life is hid with Christ in God" (*Colossians 3:1–3*).

Seek and Ye Shall Find

Daniel believed his primary purpose was to glorify God with his life, though he lived in the midst of a heathen land surrounded by people who tried his patience, misunderstood his motives, hated his presence, and rejected his God. He found comfort in the promises of God and believed the words of Jeremiah's letter that was written to those who were taken captive in Babylon. He did not look back and mourn for what he had lost, but looked forward and rejoiced in what God would accomplish in the future. As a result, Daniel's life was blessed in remarkable ways and glorifies the Lord yet today as we read his story.

Jeremiah's letter to the Babylonian captives began, "Thus saith the LORD of hosts, the God of Israel, unto all that are carried away captives, whom I have caused to be carried away from Jerusalem unto Babylon" (*Jeremiah 29:4*). Then he exhorted the people not to rebel but to live where they were and continue marrying and bearing children so they would increase in number. The letter urged the people to seek the peace of the foreign city in which they lived and to pray for it, to reject the words of false prophets, and to be comforted in knowing the Lord would bring them again to Jerusalem after seventy years had gone by. Then finally, the Lord reminded them again, "And ye shall seek me, and find me, when ye shall search for me with all your heart. And I will be found of you, saith the LORD" (*Jeremiah 29:13–14*).

God wanted the people to seek *Him*—not freedom, not the destruction of their enemies, and not happiness. In seeking the Lord with all their heart, they would find freedom from bitterness, despair, and anxiety. In seeking the welfare of their enemies, they would be delivered from hatred and anger and be a living testimony of God's power and willingness to forgive all who repent of their sin and believe. In seeking to know and find God Himself rather than temporal happiness, they would find true joy and purpose for living. The Lord Jesus taught the same principle when He said, "Seek ye first the kingdom of God, and his righteousness; and all these things shall be added unto you" (*Matthew 6:33*). It has always been and always will be the believer's union with Christ Himself that opens the windows of heaven and enables him to produce the fruit of the Spirit, which includes joy.

So often, Christians become busy in the work of God, believing their sacrifices and commitments constitute a relationship with God. Many study and learn the Bible, pray and sing, teach and preach, and live exemplary lives of separation from sin. Yet inwardly they know they are going through the motions without any real passion for the Lord Jesus Christ Himself or any heartfelt devotion to knowing Him or applying His Word. Hidden behind closed doors and in the secluded corners of their minds are found the works of the flesh, which include adultery, fornication, lasciviousness [lack of control], hatred, wrath, and envy. They are like husbands and wives who live together peaceably but sleep in separate bedrooms and share no real physical or emotional intimacy. Theirs might look like a good marriage on the surface, but no children will be born, and the marriage is not a satisfying relationship.

The Divine Nature vs. Human Nature

Twice the Scriptures tell us Daniel was a man who had "an excellent spirit." He was described as someone who had knowledge and understanding, someone who was free from a spirit of bitterness or wrath. Daniel was not merely controlling anger and bitterness—he had no anger and bitterness *in his spirit*. Daniel's gentle and patient attitude was not a well-orchestrated act so others would admire him. He was a genuinely godly person whose inward character and wisdom flowed naturally from him whether he was in the palace or in his own home. When our very nature is transformed as Daniel's was, we do not *act* loving and forgiving—we *are* loving and forgiving. This inward change is what Peter described when he said, "Whereby are given unto us exceeding great and precious promises: that by these ye might be partakers of the divine nature, having escaped the corruption that is in the world through lust [selfish desires]" (*2 Peter 1:4*). It is also what we know to be the fruit of the Spirit, described in *Galatians 5:22–24*. "But the fruit of the Spirit is love, joy, peace, longsuffering, gentleness, goodness, faith, meekness [humility], temperance [self-control]: against such there is no law. And they that are Christ's have crucified the flesh with the affections and lusts."

Every believer desires to be filled with the fruit of God's Spirit. We long to be filled with love and joy and know the peace of God. We desire our homes and personal lives to be characterized by patience, longsuffering, gentleness, goodness, faith, and humility. We know a great number of problems would be resolved if we had more self-control and could resist indulging attitudes and habits that get us into trouble. Yet we persist in trying to acquire these things in our own way, by our own strength, rather than acknowledging our total inability to produce them in and of ourselves. Apart from the power of God, we can only produce fake fruit. We can act loving in ideal circumstances; but as soon as something turns against us, the loving façade crumbles and we become what we are—angry and unforgiving.

Our human efforts may be able to imitate an outward show of spiritual fruit, and some individuals with a high level of self-discipline and gifts of persuasion may be able to produce an aura of spiritual fervor and the illusion of spiritual fruit. But no believer can produce by his own efforts the kind of heart-level transformation of character that yields the genuine fruit of God's Spirit spontaneously. We produce spiritual fruit as a by-product only when we abide in Christ. If we do not abide in Christ, we can only imitate and act the part. This practice will lead to guilt, irritability, anger, and despair. No one can live a Spirit-filled life by his own strength and willpower.

We can get rid of worldly clothing and ungodly entertainment and pray three times a day—but so do our Islamic neighbors. We can throw out the cigarettes and alcohol and attend our local church every time it meets—but so do our Mormon neighbors. We might be able to do good works and give large sums of money to the church—but so do our Catholic neighbors. We can knock on doors and zealously witness to others—but so do Jehovah's Witnesses. We can do any of these things in the power of our human efforts, just like people who have never trusted Christ or been born again; but we cannot be like Christ apart from a relationship with Christ. Jesus said, "Abide in me, and I in you. As the branch cannot bear fruit of itself, except it abide in the vine; no more can ye, except ye abide in me" (John 15:4).

Under Pressure and Persecuted

The evidence of genuine change can best be seen in the way we behave when we are under pressure or when we are being persecuted. Those who love people who love them are not at all unusual. Even the ungodly can do this. It is those who love their enemies and are kind to them that display the character of Christ (*Matthew 5:44–48*). James reminds us, "If any man among you seem to be religious, and bridleth not his tongue, but deceiveth his own heart, this man's religion is vain" (*James 1:26*). The best place to observe the level of control we have over our tongue is not at church, but in the home where we are most comfortable being ourselves.

In the years preceding the earthly ministry of our Lord, the Romans, who had no problem making a public show of their power and dominance, crucified thousands of Jews for little or no reason. This barbaric practice infuriated the Jewish people who complied with Rome in order to preserve their lives, but inwardly hated those who governed them. Roman soldiers became accustomed to hearing the scathing outpouring of verbal hatred that was vented at them by those who were being crucified. Certainly, they understood the anger and wrath that naturally arises in one who cannot fight back in any way or defend himself from humiliation and torture.

One day, however, something very different occurred as the Romans scourged and mocked, then tortured and hanged the Lord Jesus on a cross at Calvary. This man did not swear or threaten or spew out hate or bitterness (*1 Peter 2:21–23*). Even more amazing, He prayed and said, "Father, forgive them, for they know not what they do." Our Lord's response was so astounding and His love so apparent, that it prompted one Roman soldier to exclaim, "Surely, this was the Son of God."

Years later, Rome devised yet another means to satisfy their thirst for violence by torturing those who were called Christians. These Christians were torn apart by lions for sport, impaled on poles and set on fire to light the city, beheaded, burned, and publicly humiliated and hanged. Yet incredibly, the Christians displayed the patience and love of Christ and were so filled with peace and courage that many observers marveled and became convinced something supernatural had changed the inner character of these believers. Rather than destroy Christianity, the testimony of its dying martyrs fanned the sparks into flames that spread the gospel fire throughout the world.

The world still watches as Christians undergo persecution and are treated unjustly, but do they observe anything supernatural about our character? Are they convinced by the way we respond to our enemies that something miraculous has taken place in our lives? Do they see love or hate in our eyes? Can it be said that we respond in the same way Christ did? If we cannot respond graciously when we are treated rudely or suffer the slightest inconvenience unjustly, how will the world see Christ in us and what miraculous change in our character will they find irresistibly attractive? And if Christian parents treat their children with the same impatience and contempt that characterizes the world, how shall their children see Christ or desire His involvement in their lives?

The world recognizes those who love Christ by the way they follow His example and love one another. Jesus said, "By this shall all men know that ye are my disciples, if ye have love one to another" (*John 13:35*). Perhaps one reason we see so little supernatural transformation among professing believers is that so few Christians seek to know or love the Lord with all their heart. It seems that even believers have become lovers of pleasures more than lovers of God (*2 Timothy 3:4*). They, as others, pursue happiness and the American dream with zeal, while their Bibles sit on counters and shelves only to be carted off to church every now and then. Perhaps this explains why few display the genuine fruit of God's Spirit in their lives and few overcome the downward pull of the flesh. It seems that only a small minority say as Jeremiah, "Thy words were found and I did eat them; and thy word was unto me the joy and rejoicing of mine heart: for I am called by thy name, O LORD God of hosts" (*Jeremiah 15:16*).

Beloved of God

Our hearts are touched when someone we highly esteem tenderly addresses us by name. Words that are personal in nature, that reveal a sincere interest and convey an attitude of love and respect, evoke within us a sense of joy and comfort; for God has implanted in our nature the capacity to love and be loved. We might imagine then how significant it must have been to Daniel when he heard the angels deliver a message from God addressing him as "greatly beloved" of God. The Bible records three different times when a heavenly messenger used this phrase to convey the very personal and tender love of the Lord to Daniel (*Daniel 9:23, 10:11, 10:19*). We are not told Daniel's reaction, but perhaps he was struck with the thought that the Almighty Creator God *knows* me. Not only that, but He *loves me*. And as if that is not mind boggling enough, He *loves me greatly*. I suspect Daniel must have pondered those precious words over and over again in his mind, enjoying the comfort and delight of their message. We cannot help but marvel ourselves, especially considering the fact that no other person in the Bible was spoken to in this way so repeatedly.

Love is a powerful force. It melts the hardest heart and makes it sing. It instills courage that will face the fiercest foe undaunted. It comforts and calms our deepest fears and has power to strengthen us in the worst of life's calamities. It makes life worth living and separation at death most bitter. It can motivate the most lethargic into action and tame the wildest nature. Love can make us willing to forgive the most wicked sins, endure the most difficult hardship, and make it a joy to sacrifice our own pleasure in order to please the object of our care. Love always produces a willingness to give, a desire to nurture, the ability to face obstacles, and a delight in knowing and understanding those we love. Most importantly, love conquers hatred, which is the very root from which anger springs.

The power of love produces more than we can list or imagine, for it is the most basic essence of Who God is and what God accomplishes in the hearts of those who put their trust in Him. Is it any wonder, then, why Paul earnestly prayed that new Christians would become grounded in an understanding of Christ's love for them, in order that they be filled with all the character qualities of God. Notice the order in Paul's prayer, and in particular, the order of the action words. "That Christ may **dwell** in your hearts by faith; that ye, being **rooted and grounded** in love, May be able to **comprehend** with all saints what is the breadth, and length, and depth, and height; And to **know** the love of Christ, which **passeth** knowledge, that ye might **be filled** with all the fullness of God" (*Ephesians 3:17–19*).

Rooted and Grounded in Love

As we continue our study of anger in light of the Scriptures, we cannot omit the evidence that anger resides most often in hearts that are not only filled with fear and lack of love for others, but most significantly, not rooted and grounded in a secure comprehension of God's love. Anger tends to plague those who doubt the love of God, who struggle to believe He knows, loves, and forgives them personally. As we study those in the Bible who confidently rested in God's shepherding care in spite of trial and disappointment, we will notice that their level of peace reflected their level of confidence in the love of God. We love Him, the Scriptures tell us, because He first loved us (*1 John 4:19*). As we grow in our understanding of God's love for us, we grow in our love for God and consequently, our love for others.

Jude exhorted believers in the close of his letter to keep themselves in the love of God, "looking for the mercy of our Lord Jesus Christ unto eternal life" (*Jude 21*). Like Paul and others, Jude understood the crucial impact an awareness and understanding of God's love and mercy has on the believers. David, too, exclaimed that it is the awareness of God's remarkable love that causes believers to put their trust in His care. He said, "How excellent is thy lovingkindness, O God! therefore the children of men put their trust under the shadow of thy wings" (*Psalm 36:7*). David found the Word of God sweeter than the words spoken by a loved one because it conveyed the love of God to him. He told the Lord, "How sweet are thy words unto my taste! yea, sweeter than honey to my mouth!" (*Psalm 119:103*)

Many believers imagine themselves to be on the sidelines, able to watch but not able to play, as other believers enjoy the delights of God's love. Sometimes this mindset is the result of a refusal to repent of sin, in which case such people have good cause to fear God's judgment and correction. They will only know the joy of God's salvation when they repent and confess their sin! Yet many Christians sit on the sidelines needlessly and yearn to be included, not realizing they *are* included and can join their teammates any time they wish. No child of God is rejected or considered inferior—all are accepted and invited to enjoy the blessings of God's loving care.

We cannot please God apart from faith, for taking God at His Word and believing He is exactly what He says He is, and that He is a faithful rewarder of all who seek Him, glorifies Him and delights Him as nothing else can. This means, *every child* is given the means to please and glorify God equally, no matter what his talent or ability (*Hebrews 11:6*).

Listen carefully to the words of Paul in the opening of his letter to the Ephesian Christians. "Blessed be the God and Father of our Lord Jesus Christ, who hath blessed us with all spiritual blessings in heavenly places in Christ: according as he hath chosen us in him before the foundation of the world, that we should be holy and without blame before him in love: Having predestined us unto the adoption of children by Jesus Christ to himself, according to the good pleasure of his will, To the praise of the glory of his grace, wherein he hath made us accepted in the beloved. In whom we have redemption through his blood, the forgiveness of sins, according to the riches of his grace" (*Ephesians 1:3–7*). Notice that every adopted child of God is accepted on the basis of his trust in Christ's sacrifice—not on the basis of his own merit. It is the blood of Christ applied that enables us to stand before Him holy, without blame, loved, forgiven, and accepted—not our perfection or lack thereof. Now *that's* something to sing about!

Transformed by Love

The more we understand the height and depth of God's grace and love, the more our hearts are transformed by its power. This is why Paul constantly makes a connection between the knowledge of Christ and peace, and why he calls our attention to our position in Christ as the basis for our loving behavior toward others. We find the recipe for conquering anger in the following list of qualities that he tells us to deliberately cultivate in our lives. "Put on therefore, as the elect of God, holy and beloved, bowels of mercies, kindness, humbleness of mind, meekness, longsuffering: Forbearing one another, and forgiving one another, if any man have a quarrel against any: even as Christ forgave you, so also do ye. And above all these things put on charity [love], which is the bond of perfectness [maturity]" (*Colossians 3:12–14*).

Daniel is not the only believer referred to as the beloved of God—if you are a believer, you are the beloved of God as well. John tells us, "Behold what manner of love the Father hath bestowed upon us, that we should be called the sons of God: therefore the world knoweth us not, because it knew him not. Beloved, now are we the sons of God, and it doth not yet appear what we shall be: but we know that, when he shall appear, we shall be like him; for we shall see him as he is. And every man that hath this hope in him purifieth himself, even as he is pure" (*1 John 3:1–3*).

Dependence on Christ = Peace

Just before the children of Israel took possession of the land that God had promised them, He cautioned the people, telling them to beware that they did not forget the commandments they had learned, or the fact that it was by God's power that they were miraculously sustained in the desert. He reminded them that they were made to be completely dependent upon God so that they would know that man does not live by bread alone, but by every word that proceeds out of the mouth of the Lord.

The Lord then described for the people the beauty and fruitfulness of the land and houses they were about to inherit and reminded them to be thankful and to remember that God gave these to them. Lastly, the Lord warned them never to imagine that they could accomplish or acquire anything apart from Him. He told them not to "say in thine heart, My power and the might of mine hand hath gotten me this wealth. But thou shalt remember the LORD thy God: for it is **he that giveth thee power to get wealth**, that he may establish his covenant which he sware unto thy fathers, as it is this day" (*Deuteronomy 8:17–18*).

It is easy for us to forget the reality of God's presence because we cannot feel, see, or hear Him with our sense of touch, sight, or hearing. By faith, we comprehend that He is present and active in our lives. We cannot see the oxygen in the air or the air that we breathe, but we *can see* the definite effects of its presence or absence. Though we cannot see God, we *can* see the evidence of His work all around us every day. This is what the Scripture is referring to that tells us, "Now faith is the substance of things hoped for, the evidence of things not seen" (*Hebrews 11:1*). Yet even when we acknowledge the fact that God is the author and sustaining power of the entire universe, we tend to forget He is also the author of our personal existence and sustenance.

Though we may not understand it or acknowledge it, God is presently sustaining our lives, giving us the ability to take our next breath and do whatever it is we are doing. At any moment, He can intervene and change our plans or simply withdraw His hand of protection. He is the author of our abilities, our limitations, our inherited characteristics, and anything that makes us uniquely us. Though He gives us the freedom and responsibility to make choices, He, and not we, controls the outcome. James corrected believers who were living and making plans without regard to the fact that they were only allowed to do so by God's decree. He told them, "For that ye ought to say, If the Lord will, we shall live, and do this, or that" (*James 4:15*).

We tend to become increasingly more careless and self-assured as we lose our awareness that God is present, observing and weighing everything we say, do, or think. Forgetting that He is actively involved in the affairs of our lives blinds us to the reality that He cannot be ignored or defied without consequence. The more we imagine ourselves to be the master of our fate rather than God, the more we tend to forget that God uses people and circumstances to accomplish what He will in our lives. We know that whatever God does is good and right and just, yet we often fail to connect the events of our everyday lives as the good and just work of God. We complain when our lives do not turn out the way we had planned, as if nothing but fate or people got in our way.

Complaining about our circumstances or the difficulties caused by people or problems is really complaining about God's work in our lives. So, though God holds offenders responsible for their sin, He also wants us to recognize that He uses the offenses of others to accomplish what He will. We see this in Christ's statement to the disciples: "Then said he unto the disciples, It is impossible but that offences will come: but woe unto him, through whom they come!" (*Luke 17:1*) So then, the offender is responsible for his sin and will be dealt with by God, but we are responsible for the way we choose to respond to the offense and will be dealt with by God as well.

When trials and difficulties present themselves each day, we ought to recognize the fact that God is present, overseeing these events and allowing them. Our immediate human reaction may be to become angry, but the immediate reaction God wants us to learn is thankfulness. Perhaps you are thinking, "You've got to be kidding!" No, actually, I am not, and neither is God when he tells us, "In everything give thanks: for this is the will of God in Christ Jesus concerning you" (*1 Thessalonians 5:18*). This seems preposterous to us only because we zero in on the difficulty or offense, rather than the outcome that God wants to bring about because of it. No matter what happens, the believer can give thanks for whatever good outcome God wishes to bring about because of it. This kind of thankfulness is not designed to make us passive, but to produce appropriate acceptance, dependence on Christ, and habits of godly problem solving.

When we fail to learn how dependent we are on Christ, we become like ancient Israel who tried to compartmentalize God into a space of time reserved for Him on a certain day. Because they lived as though He was completely uninvolved in their daily lives, rather than their consulting with Him or acknowledging His presence, they took up the reins of their own lives and proceeded to depend on themselves alone for direction. Not only did they become proud and self-willed, but also they soon became angry and vindictive. Everything unpleasant that happened to them brought discontentment, an accusation, justification, and retaliation. They regarded the faults and failures of others as the reason they suffered, and their own good character qualities as the reason they prospered. This led them to regard with contempt and disdain others who were less successful or who were annoying. Before long, they had completely replaced God's wisdom with their own and presumed that their talents and wealth rightfully belonged to them for the purpose of providing their own enjoyment.

These were like the wealthy man Jesus told us about, who prospered and built bigger barns for his goods, unaware that God was about to end his life and make him give an account of what he had done with all God had given to him. "And he said, This will I do: I will pull down my barns, and build greater; and there will I bestow all my fruits and my goods. And I will say to my soul, Soul, thou hast much goods laid up for many years; take thine ease, eat, drink, and be merry. But God said unto him, Thou fool, this night thy soul shall be required of thee: then whose shall those things be, which thou hast provided? So is he that layeth up treasure for himself, and is not rich toward God" (*Luke 12:18–21*).

Compare this attitude to the mindset of Daniel when he sought God's help and was given the ability to interpret the king's dream. Daniel praised God and said, "He giveth wisdom unto the wise, and knowledge to them that know understanding: He revealeth the deep and secret things: he knoweth what is in the darkness, and the light dwelleth with him. I thank thee, and praise thee, O thou God of my fathers, who hast given me wisdom and might, and hast made known unto me now what we desired of thee: for thou hast now made known unto us the king's matter" (*Daniel 2:21–23*).

Earlier in the book of Daniel, we read that it was God Who brought Daniel into favor with the prince of the eunuchs and God Who gave Daniel and his three friends their knowledge, wisdom, and learning skills (*Daniel 1:9, 17*). The fact that Daniel acknowledged this revealed his faith and understanding. So when a huge crisis arose, he immediately responded by seeking God's help, rather than by expressing anger or dismay. Put yourself in Daniel's place and imagine how you might have acted when soldiers appeared to inform you that you, your friends, and all the wise men of the city were to be slain by order of the king. This event did not take God by surprise at all—in fact, God had not only prepared Daniel but also some key circumstances that would change the outcome of this event.

Because Daniel and Arioch, the soldier, knew one another by name, Arioch allowed Daniel to ask him why the decree was given so hastily. Arioch explained that the king had had a dream and asked the wise men to interpret it but that he could not remember the dream. Therefore he demanded that they first tell him the dream and then interpret it. When the wise men replied that this was an impossible demand, the king became furious and commanded them all to be destroyed, including Daniel. Upon hearing this, Daniel asked to see the king and requested the king give him time, after which he would show him his dream and the interpretation. Time being granted him, Daniel immediately went home and asked his believing companions to pray for God's mercy and for the information the king sought so they would not be destroyed.

That night, God revealed the dream and the interpretation to Daniel, who immediately awoke and praised the Lord for His intervention and mercy. When Daniel was led into the king's presence, he was given the opportunity to speak. He explained that no person could show the king what he wanted to know, but that there is a God in heaven who could and had made known the dream and the interpretation. Daniel refused to share God's glory but told the king, "This secret is not revealed to me for any wisdom that I have more than any living, but for their sakes that shall make known the interpretation to the king, and that thou mightest know the thoughts of thy heart" (*Daniel 2:27*). As Daniel conveyed the message of the dream he began, "Thou, O king, art a king of kings: for the God of heaven hath given thee a kingdom, power, and strength, and glory" (*Daniel 2:37*). When the explanation was finished, the king fell on his face in reverence to Daniel and said, "Of a truth it is, that your God is a God of gods, and a Lord of kings, and a revealer of secrets, seeing thou couldst reveal this secret" (*Daniel 2:47*). Then the king promoted Daniel, gave him many gifts, and appointed Daniel and his three friends to be chief governors in the land.

It all seems so easy when we read about it in the Bible, but we forget that Daniel did not know how the crisis would turn out. He had no idea what God was doing or what He wanted to accomplish. He simply knew that God could be trusted and that He was aware of all that had happened. He understood that Nebuchadnezzar possessed no power or authority that God did not give him and that a higher authority than he was overruling him. Nebuchadnezzar, on the other hand, had a short memory and a hot temper that God was going to deal with. It seems that he went without a pause from praising the God of heaven to setting up a golden idol for the people to worship. Such is the outcome when one is sorry but not willing to turn from his own ways in repentance.

Dependence on Self = Anger

When Nebuchadnezzar was told that Shadrach, Meshach, and Abednego refused to bow to his idol, he flew off into a rage and commanded them to be brought to him. After threatening them and telling them they would be thrown into a burning furnace if they did not obey, he arrogantly mocked and said, "And who is that God that shall deliver you out of my hands?" (*Daniel 3:15*) Obviously the king still did not grasp the fact that he was accountable to Almighty God, believer or unbeliever, and that he had no power but that which was given to him. Daniel's three friends humbly replied that indeed their God could deliver them; but if He should choose not to, they still would not bow to the idol. Again, these three believers did not know the outcome, but they did know in whose hand their lives were held.

Nebuchadnezzar's pride was overturned once more when God chose to preserve the lives of his three servants. Again Nebuchadnezzar praised God and made a decree that no one in the entire nation would be permitted to speak against the God of Shadrach, Meshach, and Abednego. While he admitted that no other God could deliver the way God had, he did not renounce his own gods or confess that they were nothing. Nebuchadnezzar acknowledged God's existence and superior power, but he had not yet submitted himself to Him or made Him *his* God. God, however, was at work in his life in a most remarkable and merciful way.

Some time later, because Nebuchadnezzar once again wanted the interpretation of a disturbing dream, he called for Daniel. This time, Daniel became very troubled as God revealed its meaning. The Bible tells us he sat speechless for an hour before he began to carefully explain. The tree that the king had dreamed about represented the king himself, Daniel explained. It would be cut down, though the stump would remain. Then Daniel gave the reason this would happen—that the living would know that the Most High rules in the kingdom of men and gives it to whomever He chooses and sets over it the basest of men. God wanted the king, as well as you and me, to know that Nebuchadnezzar was not given the kingdom because God saw something good in him, but because he served God's purpose.

You would think that after all that had happened, the king would be humbled; but he stubbornly refused to repent of his pride. Twelve months passed and the incident was all but forgotten. As the king walked in his palace, he began to speak, "Is not this great Babylon, that I have built for the house of the kingdom by the might of my power, and for the honour of my majesty?" (*Daniel 4:30*) (Note the *I* and *mys* in this one sentence.) Immediately God spoke one sentence in reply to the king, "The kingdom is departed from thee." Within an hour, the king was removed from the palace because he had become instantly insane. As Daniel had predicted, he remained in this mental state for seven years until, the Bible says, he turned to God and praised and honored Him. At that moment, his reasoning returned and he was healed. God restored to him his kingdom; and this time, he testified in true repentance. His entire account of his experience can be read in the fourth chapter of Daniel; verses 34 and 37 sum up his testimony well.

> "And at the end of the days I Nebuchadnezzar lifted up mine eyes unto heaven, and mine understanding returned unto me, and I blessed the most High, and I praised and honored him that liveth for ever, whose dominion is an everlasting dominion, and his kingdom is from generation to generation…Now I Nebuchadnezzar praise and extol and honour the King of heaven, all whose works are truth, and his ways judgment: and those that walk in pride he is able to abase."

We are much like Nebuchadnezzar when we live our lives thinking that God does not see or care what we say and do. Like he, we become angry and unreasonable when our personal kingdom is threatened or when we are told that our lives are not our own to do with as we please. When we believe we earn a place of importance or respect by our own strength and power, we will fight whoever threatens to uproot us and will see the source of opposition as fate rather than God. That God makes even our enemies to be at peace with us when our ways please Him is the furthest thing from our minds when we ignore the presence of God. And when we take pride in our accomplishments and possessions as if God had nothing to do with them, we are not likely to yield our possessions or ourselves to the cause of Christ.

Paul addressed this same tendency in the Corinthian believers and asked them, "For who maketh thee to differ from another? and what hast thou that thou didst not receive? now if thou didst receive it, why dost thou glory, as if thou hadst not received it?" (*1 Corinthians 4:7*) If everything we have is a gift of God, then nothing we have is ours to keep. Contentment is being thankful and enjoying what God gives, but freely giving up that which He requires.

Provoked by Problems

One of the most common tendencies in those who struggle to control their anger is to tolerate irritations and problems until tension builds and rises to the "explosion" point. When it seems a situation cannot be tolerated another minute, they suddenly react with intensity by verbally attacking whoever is involved, hitting something, loudly stomping out of the room, refusing to cooperate, crying, sulking, or engaging in some other response that expresses extreme displeasure. Once the tension is expended, remorse often sets in as those who have reacted in this way realize their outrage has hurt others or themselves, or that they have sinned in some way. Some deal with their guilt by immediately rationalizing, blaming, or "forgetting" what just happened, while others beg for forgiveness or "make up" by doing kind things or attempting to please those they have wronged.

No amount of determination, resolution, or self-flagellation lessens the grip explosive anger has on those who get caught in the cycle of tolerating, exploding, and then sorrowing, because tolerating or ignoring problems does not gain self-control. Self-control develops as believers learn how to walk in the Spirit and resolve problems in biblical and righteous ways. It is the by-product, not the goal. **The goal is to recognize, face, and resolve problems biblically.** In this way, we use our energy to attack the *problem*, not people.

When we are faced with any kind of trial or problem, our human tendency is to blow up in anger because we do not like what is happening, run the opposite direction because we do not want to deal with it, clam up out of fear and despair, or attempt to circumvent the trial in an effort to find an easier way to deal with it. God's way is to acknowledge and confront the problem directly, seek God's Word for direction in finding the way of escape God has provided, obey the scriptural admonition for dealing with the particular problem, and then wait and trust God to intervene to do what we are powerless to do.

Paul tells us something that not only helps us understand how we are to react, but why we are to react in a certain way. This is extremely important if we are going to learn godly self-control. "There hath no temptation [trial] taken you but such as is common to man: but God is faithful, who will not suffer [allow] you to be tempted [tried] above that ye are able; but will with the temptation also make a way to escape, that ye may be able to bear it" (*1 Corinthians 10:13*).

Notice that God uses specific words to express the emphatic certainty of the truth—*no, will not, will*. Our God is faithful: He is dependable, and He cannot lie. Therefore we can be certain what He says to us is true. There will be *no trial* too big, too difficult, too mundane, or too unusual allowed in a believer's life. Whatever the difficulty, God *will always* provide a means of escape. It may look like a huge brick wall in front of us, and it may seem like we are in a box with no way out—but look again. There is *always* a little door somewhere in that brick wall that leads to freedom. God will *never* allow an irritation, problem, or difficulty in a believer's life that is beyond our God-given ability to handle. If we do not have the strength, God will provide the strength. If we do not have the resources, God will provide the resources. We are *never* alone or forsaken in *any* trial, no matter how big or small!

David understood this and testified, "The righteous [those who are saved] cry, and the Lord heareth and delivereth them out of all their troubles" (*Psalm 34:17*). Notice again the little word *all*—not some, not most, but *all*. David tells us that the afflictions of the believers are many. This is not too encouraging unless we hear the statement he makes next, "But the Lord delivereth him out of them *all*" (*Psalm 34:19*).

When Provoked by a Problem

You will discover you are able to divert the energy and tension of anger into constructive problem solving if you develop the habit of slowing down and thinking biblically the moment you recognize the slightest tension of anger. Memorize the following steps and then practice talking to yourself in this way when irritations and difficulties arise.

1. Take God at His Word and believe what He has said—we are never hopeless, we are never alone, we are never forsaken, we are never overwhelmed, we are never without adequate resources to deal with any problem that enters into our life. If a problem exists, so does the grace and resources to deal with it.

2. Recognize the first signs of tension building and the first twinge of irritation, and immediately tell yourself to STOP! Knowing that God is our source of help, begin by calling upon Him in prayer. If "Help, Lord!" is all you can pray, then cry, "Help!" God has a divine order—first we call and then He delivers.

3. Ask yourself, "What am I really angry about?" Many times pausing long enough to honestly examine what it is that is bothering you is enough to put it into a manageable perspective and construct a solution. If you are willing to

scrutinize the irritation honestly, you will often discover that the source of immediate provocation is not the real issue that is troubling us. We tend to ignore things that are bothering us (such as failing to mail the bills or failing to get adequate sleep) and then become overly sensitive when the children are being too loud or the car fails to start. Stop and think—is there something I feel guilty about? Is there something I've put off or something I'm dreading? These things are often the real culprits lying beneath the surface of angry expressions.

4. Determine if there is something you can change to make the situation more tolerable or to solve the problem. Ask God for wisdom, remembering *James 1:5*. Look for the way of escape—it's there!

5. Ask yourself what biblical instruction you might have failed to obey regarding the situation that is confronting you. Be careful to remember that God is not condemning you—Jesus was condemned in your place on the cross. God may, however, be correcting you in love. To admit fault is a mark of humility and elicits God's grace. Do not run from it! Embrace it!

6. Finally, ask yourself if Christ would be angry over this. We are taught to look at Christ, not another person, and find in Him our example. Learn how to find passages of Scripture that encourage and inspire you in times of temptation. Remember that our Lord responded to Satan's taunts with the Scripture and was victorious every time. Learn to tell yourself, "It is written…"

Learn To Be a Problem Solver

Working out problems in a godly way requires us to be humble, to be focused on the issue and not ourselves, to be in control of our own spirit, to be ready to love and forgive. These disciplines do not come naturally to any of us. They must be learned and practiced *deliberately.*

Daniel was a problem solver; Nebuchadnezzar was not. Daniel exuded patience, self-control, and wisdom when confronted with problems. The Bible tells us that Daniel had an excellent spirit. He was faithful, humble, and dependent upon God. Compare Daniel's godly attitude and manner to that of the king. The Bible describes Nebuchadnezzar as hasty (impulsive), proud, self-sufficient, and cruel. He did not act when faced with a problem—he *reacted.* The Bible tells us that he became furious, full of fury, in a rage, very angry. The differences between the two men provide a striking contrast of anger under control and anger out of control. Because Daniel was a problem-solving believer that we want to emulate, let us end our study by examining specific ways six different problems were solved in the book of Daniel.

Problem #1

In the first chapter of Daniel, we are told that Daniel and his three friends were chosen to serve the king of Babylon. They were to be taught the Chaldean language and fed well for three years, after which time they would be brought before the king. The problem—the young Jewish boys were brought food that violated their consciences because it was forbidden by the law of Moses. Because Daniel had purposed, or decided, in his heart that he would not eat the food or drink the wine, he asked the overseer if he and his friends could be provided with different food.

The Bible tells us that because God had already brought Daniel into favor with the overseer, he listened to Daniel's request but explained that his life would be in danger if the Jewish boys' health was inferior because of the food they wanted to eat. Daniel did not argue or complain or become angry. He made a respectful appeal and then offered a workable solution. They would eat the Jewish food for ten days and then submit themselves for comparison with the others who ate the king's food. Then the overseer could look at them and decide if the food was better or worse. He agreed and at the end of ten days discovered they looked better than all the others, and so were fed on a Jewish diet thereafter.

Problem #2

The second problem Daniel faced involved the incident with the dream the king could not remember and his decision to kill all the wise men, including Daniel. The Bible tells us God had given Daniel and his friends both knowledge and skill in learning, and to Daniel, He gave understanding in visions and dreams. This is important for us to see because we need to know that God always paves the way ahead of us and provides whatever is needed in order to enable us to do exactly what He wants us to do. Daniel first asked for time to pray and seek God's wisdom. This is a habit many Christians fail to cultivate; and as a result, many of them make many hasty decisions or say foolish things. Notice too that Daniel enlisted the help of his three believing friends to pray with him. There are times when corporate prayer with the body of Christ is wise. Daniel did everything he knew to do and then simply waited on God. God, of course, provided the answer he needed at exactly the right time.

Problem #3

The third problem involved Daniel's three friends, Shadrach, Meshach, and Abednego. When they did not bow and worship the gold idol that the king had set up, the king became furious and had them brought to him. They had no alternative option to offer the king. They could not obey the command because it superseded God's command not to worship idols. These godly young men were not about to capitulate to the demand of the king because, as you will recall, Israel was destroyed because of their idol worship. Their fear of God conquered any fear they might have had of Nebuchadnezzar. Nevertheless, they were not defiant, disrespectful, angry, anxious, or disgusted. They calmly stated that they could not obey. They told the king that although their God was able to deliver them, if He did not choose to do so, they were willing to die in the fiery furnace that awaited them. Making an appeal to both the king and God, and then willingly committing themselves to God and accepting the outcome solved the problem. Again, they simply did what was right with the right attitude and left the outcome to God. God intervened miraculously to do what they could not. As a result, God was glorified, their lives were spared, they were promoted, and their faith in God was strengthened all the more.

Problem #4

The fourth problem involved the second dream of Nebuchadnezzar. Unlike the first dream that Daniel interpreted, this dream was specifically directed against the king. Daniel faced a most awkward and difficult situation, considering that this was a king who was impulsive and known to kill whoever displeased him. Daniel took the time to carefully word the interpretation, being respectful and wise in the way he presented the information. First, he spoke only when the king urged him to do so. Second, he began by telling the king that his dream pertained to his enemies and those that hated him. After this, he explained that it also pertained to him. Finally, he closed with a humble petition and offered a means whereby the king could escape immediate judgment from God.

Daniel said, "Wherefore, O king, let my counsel be acceptable unto thee, and break off thy sins by righteousness, and thine iniquities by shewing mercy to the poor; if it may be a lengthening of thy tranquility" (*Daniel 4:27*). Daniel wisely understood that putting aside sin does not change a person unless he also puts on its righteous counterpart. The king was proud and needed to engage in acts of humility. This problem required Daniel to be direct, to address the king's specific sin, and to speak the truth in love, as we are instructed to do in *Ephesians 4:15* and *25*. Daniel did this without knowing how the king would react yet being willing to accept the outcome, whatever it might be.

Problem #5

The fifth problem occurred about twenty-five years after Nebuchadnezzar had died and his great grandson Belshazzar had become the ruler. By this time, Daniel was an old man that God had protected and preserved through the reigns of several rulers who came after Nebuchadnezzar. We are not told what took place in Daniel's life during this time, but quite likely he had been demoted and placed in obscurity.

When King Belshazzar decided to host a feast in honor of his gods, he made sure there was plenty of wine, women, and song. In the middle of his drinking orgy, he made a fateful decision: he ordered the vessels that had been taken out of the temple in Jerusalem to be brought to him for their wine, no doubt to make sport of the God of Israel. The laughter and partying stopped short when a hand appeared and wrote a message on the wall. Because the king could not read the message, he called his pagan wise men and offered them a reward to read it to him. When none of them could do so, the queen spoke up and asked Belshazzar to call Daniel, a man that was known to be wise, who had served his father well, and who would know how to read and understand the Word of God.

When Daniel was brought before the king, he was offered gifts, which he declined. Daniel could not be bought for any price, for long ago he had turned his heart from the enticements and glitter that the world offered to serve the living God. Like Moses, he chose "rather to suffer affliction with the people of God, than to enjoy the pleasures of sin for a season" (*Hebrews 11:25*). The solutions Daniel chose when faced with a trial did not include sinful solutions. A true servant of God will not sell God's truth for personal gain and will not bring dishonor to God by using sinful means to accomplish His will. A true servant of God will stand for right though none stand with him—and when he does, he will find that God Himself will stand by his side.

Daniel began his courageous explanation with a recollection of Nebuchadnezzar and the incident involving his pride and God's dealings in his life. Daniel then truthfully and directly addressed Belshazzar and said, "And thou his son, O Belshazzar, hast not humbled thine heart, though thou knewest all this; But hast lifted up thyself against the Lord of heaven; and they have brought the vessels of his house before thee, and thou, and thy lords, thy wives, and thy concubines have drunk wine in them; and thou hast praised the gods of silver, and gold, of brass, iron, wood and stone, which see not, nor hear, nor know: and the God in whose hand thy breath is, and whose are all thy ways, hast thou not glorified" (*Daniel 5:22–23*).

When Daniel was finished speaking, Belshazzar promoted Daniel as he had promised but did not indicate the slightest evidence of repentance. At the same moment, Cyrus of Persia was approaching the gates of Babylon with his army, waiting for the right moment to besiege the city. Before the night was over, Belshazzar was murdered and Darius the Mede became king, just as Jeremiah and Daniel had prophesied would happen. But Daniel's problems were far from over.

Problem #6

The sixth problem occurred when powerful men in the newly reorganized kingdom became jealous of Daniel's promotion and plotted to destroy him. The Scriptures tell us that Darius chose Daniel for the second highest office under the king, because an excellent spirit was found in him. What we as believers know to be the Spirit of God empowering and filling the believer, the world can only describe as an excellent spirit. It is significant that Daniel's character was known and valued even by those who did not know God. In fact, the Bible also tells us that Darius preferred Daniel above others because he trusted him. He said, "And over these three presidents; of whom Daniel was first: that the princes might give accounts unto them [the three presidents], and the king should have no damage" (*Daniel 6:2*). The king knew Daniel would solve problems honestly and with the utmost integrity. Daniel was a man who was brilliant and wise but knew how to serve under authority.

Just when Daniel may have felt things were going pretty well, trouble was brewing. Other members of the king's cabinet plotted and searched for a way to destroy him. Finally, when they realized they could not find fault with him, they turned their attention to Daniel's faithfulness to the law of God, just as wicked politicians do today—casting doubt on a man because of his faith in God, when they cannot find fault with his character. This problem was one that brought false accusations against Daniel with the intention of destroying him. Those who hated him came up with a cleverly disguised method to trick Darius into ordering Daniel's death. They came to him with flattery, not respect, and then exaggerated their claims, implying that more were in agreement with the proposal than in truth were. They cloaked their malice in pious-sounding talk of wanting the king's best interest and wanting prayer to be upheld in the country. So they asked the king to make a decree that no one could ask any petition from any god or anyone but the king for thirty days. When the king signed the decree, Daniel's enemies must have been thrilled. They knew Daniel, bowed toward Jerusalem, prayed to God three times every day.

When Daniel heard of the decree, he faced a serious decision. Would he compromise and hide the fact that he was praying? He had to make a decision between loyalty for the king and loyalty to God. His life, not just his position, was at stake. He was an old man, at least ninety years old. He might have reasoned that he was too old to be put in a situation like this. He could have quit or complained to the king about those who hated him. He might have leveled an accusation against the men, or he could have used his authority to retaliate. But Daniel decided not to solve his problems with unrighteousness or fear. He chose to face them and simply continue doing what he knew was right. He did not act in defiance against the king—he simply continued doing what he had been doing before; and because Daniel would not hide his prayer habits, he was quickly discovered and brought to trial.

Perhaps no other story in the Bible is more loved than the story of Daniel in the lion's den. At one moment we see the three conspirators gleefully watching as Daniel is found guilty and Darius is grieving over what he had been tricked into doing. Daniel is put in the den of lions, the stone is rolled over the opening, and the city goes to bed. But in the next scene, we see the sun coming up and the king hurrying to the lion's den to see what has happened to Daniel. The Bible tells us he called to Daniel with a lamentable voice, "O Daniel, servant of the living God, is thy God, whom thou servest continually, able to deliver thee from the lions?" And we thrill to hear Daniel reply, "My God hath sent his angel, and hath shut the lions' mouths, that they have not hurt me: forasmuch as before him innocency was found in me; and also before thee, O king, have I done no hurt" (*Daniel 6:19, 22*).

God solved Daniel's problem! Yet Daniel was not passive—far from it. He overcame evil with good as we are instructed to do in *Romans 12:21*, he prayed as we are instructed to do in *Philippians 4:6*, and he put his trust in God as we are instructed to do in *Psalm 56:4*. Daniel did exactly what Christ did when he was falsely accused and ridiculed. He committed his case to God Who judges righteously, according to *1 Peter 2:21–23*. "For even hereunto were ye called: because Christ also suffered for us, leaving us an example, that ye should follow his steps: Who did no sin, neither was guile found in his mouth: Who, when he was reviled, reviled not again; when he suffered, he threatened not; but committed himself to him that judgeth righteously."

Daniel may very well have sung the words of a song written by David years before him. "Shew thy marvelous lovingkindness, O thou that savest by thy right hand them which put their trust in thee from those that rise up against them" (*Psalm 17:7*).

There is a wealth of practical lessons we can learn from the life of Daniel, but among them is the tremendous example we have concerning his godly, problem-solving skills. Daniel had an intimate knowledge of God's Word and an intimate relationship with God. Like David, his life is a testimony of God's faithfulness to those who put their trust in Him.

A World Filled with Darkness and Light

Can you imagine a place where the light of day is never seen, where nothing lives and the stench of death is present continually? Imagine what it would be like if God were removed from this world. All would become utter darkness, for God is light. No longer would we enjoy the delights of seeing God's beauty all around us. Never again would we see the morning sunshine illuminate the bright colors of nature or the sweet smile of a little baby. If God were not here, there would be no love at all, for God is love. Without love, there would be nothing but hatred, cruelty, and wrath. In a world without God, there would be no life, for God is life. Sorrow and death would reign in a place where God did not dwell. And without God, the world would be thrown into immediate chaos, for it is God who maintains the order of the universe to our benefit.

In this world in which we live, darkness and light dwell together. Good and evil coexist. There is life and there is death...love and hatred. But in eternity, there will be two worlds—one in which there is no darkness, and the other in which there is no light. In one world, God is present. In the other, He is utterly absent. One world has been prepared for those who have obeyed the gospel and love God. The other has been prepared for those who are disobedient and hate His ways. One place is filled with unspeakable joy and pleasure, the other with weeping and unspeakable torment.

The Bible tells us we are either children of light or children of darkness. We are either lost or saved, a child who belongs to God or a child who belongs to the devil. Each of us is destined to go to his or her own place, either with God or with the father of this world, the devil. At this very moment we are either one or the other. We cannot be both. We are either filled with wrath because we are a child of the night, or we are filled with sorrow for our wrath, because we are a child of light. We might think we are a child of God because we go to church, have said a prayer, or because we believe Jesus is Christ Who died for our sins. These, however, are not the birthmarks that reveal a believer's spiritual parentage. Listen to what John said.

> "This then is the message which we have heard of him, and declare unto you, that God is light, and in him is no darkness at all. If we say that we have fellowship with him, and walk in darkness, we lie, and do not the truth: But if we walk in the light, as he is in the light, we have fellowship one with another, and the blood of Jesus Christ his Son cleanseth us from all sin" (1 John 1:5–7).

The child of God loves God, God's commandments, and God's children. It is evident in the way he lives both openly and secretly. The child of the devil hates the God of the Bible, God's commandments, and God's children. No matter how determined he is to do the right things, win favor with God, or control his outward behavior, inwardly he seethes and hates and resents God's commandments. The Bible says, "He that saith, I know him, and keepeth not his commandments, is a liar, and the truth is not in him. But whoso keepeth his word, in him verily is the love of God perfected: hereby know we that we are in him" (1 John 2:4–5). The child of God delights in God's Word and thirsts for God's righteousness. He grows in grace and increases in love toward God and others.

One who has not been born again deceives himself if he believes he can love God and yet continue to hate others. "He that saith he is in the light, and hateth his brother, is in darkness even until now" (1 John 2:9). How we regard others, how we react when they sin like we do, how we think about them, and how we treat them reveal the true condition of our heart. "We know that we have passed from death unto life, because we love the brethren. He that loveth not his brother abideth in death. Whosoever hateth his brother is a murderer; and ye know that no murderer hath eternal life abiding in him" (*1 John 3:14–15*). "He that loveth not knoweth not God; for God is love" (*1 John 4:8*).

May I remind you that the Bible tells us, "Charity [love] suffereth long, and is kind; charity envieth not; charity vaunteth not itself, is not puffed up, doth not behave itself unseemly, seeketh not her own, is not easily provoked, thinketh no evil; rejoiceth not in iniquity, but rejoiceth in the truth; beareth all things, believeth all things, hopeth all things, endureth all things. Charity never faileth" (*1 Corinthians 13:4–7*). In summary, "love worketh no ill to his neighbor" (*Romans 13:10*).

Which are you, dear reader? Can you say for certain that you know you are a child of God, destined to spend eternity with Him? Do you see yourself as a child of light who walks in the light of God's Word, or as a child of the night who walks in darkness? If you have never truly repented of your sinful ways and turned to Christ for forgiveness of your sin, trusting Him alone for your salvation, no amount of grief or regret will change your darkened heart or give you a spirit of love. You will struggle with rage for the rest of your life and in eternity live in a place where anger and rage will fill your ears forever. Neither this book nor any other is able to transform your inner character or wash you from your sins. Only the Lord Jesus Christ can forgive your sin and give you a new heart like His own.

The Bible says "Hereby know we that we dwell in him, and he in us, because he hath given us of his Spirit" (*1 John 4:13*). No one is given the Spirit of Christ until he comes to God in repentance, believing that Jesus is God, that He died on the cross to pay the penalty for our sins, and that He arose victorious over death and lives today. Except you repent, Jesus said, you cannot be saved (*Luke 13:3*). Repentance is a prerequisite to salvation. Salvation is freely given to those who are repentant and willing to trust Christ, not themselves, for righteousness.

The Apostle Paul spoke of people who were zealous for God yet were not saved. The reason they were not saved was that they went about to establish their own righteousness rather than submit themselves to the righteousness of God (*Romans 10:1–3*). Salvation cannot be received in any other way except as the gift of God. It cannot be earned by our own merit, for it costs the precious blood of One Who is without sin. Salvation is an expensive gift that cost the Giver everything. Only love could motivate God to pay the price for our redemption and then so willingly offer it to us as a gift that costs us nothing. "For God so loved the world that gave His only begotten son, that whosoever believeth in Him should not perish, but have everlasting life" (*John 3:16*).

Friend, if you do not know Christ and want to receive this gift of God's love, you may if you receive it on God's terms. First, salvation is received, not earned. "For by grace are ye saved through faith; and that not of yourselves; it is the gift of God; Not of works, lest any man should boast" (*Ephesians 2:8–9*). It is given to those who are willing to turn away from sin and turn instead to Christ. Jesus said He came to call those who are sinners to repentance, not those who imagine they are of themselves righteous (*Luke 5:32*). "Repent ye therefore, and be converted, that your sins may be blotted out" (*Acts 3:19*). Those who call upon Him in repentance and receive the Lord Jesus Christ as their God and King have this promise: "But as many as received him, to them gave he power to become the sons of God, even to them that believe on his name" (*John 1:12*).

God invites you to call upon Him in prayer, asking Him to forgive you and save you. "For whosoever shall call upon the name of the Lord shall be saved" (*Romans 10:13*). The moment you do, you will be born into the family of God and have all the rights and privileges of those who are called God's children. Your name will be written in heaven and the angels will rejoice. You will be given the potential to become like your new heavenly Father as you obey Him, trust Him, and depend on Him. You will be given the Holy Spirit Who will live with you forever and the Spirit of adoption that will cause you to confidently call God your

Father and make you know you are a child of God (*Romans 8:15–16*). Best of all, you will be given eternal life in heaven where there will be no more sin and no more struggles with a sinful human nature. Jesus promised, "Verily, verily, I say unto you, He that heareth my word, and believeth on him that sent me, hath everlasting life, and shall not come into condemnation; but is passed from death unto life" (*John 5:24*).

To Every Child of Light Living in Darkness

Perhaps you have already settled these matters in your heart and know you are a child of God. It could be that you are a child who is living rebelliously and suffering the consequences of your failure to obey your Father's voice. To you the Apostle Paul was speaking when he said, "For ye were sometimes darkness, but now are ye light in the Lord: walk as children of light" (*Ephesians 5:8*). If you are living like those who live in darkness apart from any conscious awareness of God, repent! Choose to live like a child of light, not a child of darkness. Seek your Father's forgiveness so fellowship with Him can be restored and your prayers unhindered. Then get busy learning so you will grow up in Christian maturity and enjoy the blessings of walking in the light of God's love. Do not think you can be a child of God and not be chastised when you rebel and refuse to love and forgive others as you can and should.

Remember what the Lord has said to us, "Now no chastening for the present seemeth to be joyous, but grievous; nevertheless afterward it yieldeth the peaceable fruit of righteousness unto them which are exercised thereby. Wherefore lift up the hands which hang down, and the feeble knees; and make straight paths for your feet, lest that which is lame be turned out of the way; but let it rather be healed. Follow peace with all men, and holiness, without which no man shall see the Lord; Looking diligently lest any man fail of the grace of God; lest any root of bitterness springing up trouble you, and thereby many be defiled" (*Hebrews 12:11–15*).

If we persist in the ways of darkness, we will naturally experience the grief that always comes as a result. If we are in fact God's children, we will also experience discipline that comes from our Father's loving hand and is intended to bring us to repentance and a right relationship with Him. So we have some choices. We can choose whether or not we will continue to insist it is other people's sins or our circumstances that cause us to react in anger, rather than our own sinful heart with its selfish demands. We can ignore God's warnings and remain alienated from God, estranged from others, and a victim of our own rebellion. Or, we can choose to see our sin as God sees it and deal with it His way. If we choose to rationalize our anger, our lives will simply continue unchanged and leave a trail of devastation and sorrow until it ends prematurely in regret and sorrow. But if we choose to humble ourselves and confess and forsake the many sins that underlie anger, we have God's promise that He will extend mercy and forgive us. Furthermore, He gives promises that will lead us to victory over our angry spirit.

The Precious Promises of God

The little book of second Peter opens with a promise of grace and peace to believers if they will progress in their knowledge of God, and of Jesus our Lord. Peter, that apostle who once cursed with anger and denied the Lord, goes on to say, "According as his divine power hath given unto us all things that pertain unto life and godliness, through the knowledge of him that hath called us to glory and virtue; whereby are given unto us exceeding great and precious promises; that by these ye might be partakers of the divine nature, having escaped the corruption that is in the world through lust" (2 Peter 1:3–4). By what means do we obtain the divine nature of Christ and escape the devastation that comes when people follow their own selfish desires? By the precious promises found in God's Word.

It is in learning God's Word that we learn to think and respond as God's children. It is through the power of *obeying* God's Word that our hearts and lives are miraculously transformed. Apart from the Holy Spirit indwelling us and the Word of God teaching us, we can hope for nothing more than the world hopes for. We might learn strategies for managing anger, but we would be powerless to conquer it. God has a different plan for His children. Peter tells us we are a chosen generation, a royal priesthood, a people who are to be walking examples of lives changed by the power of God, not the power of our own efforts and clever manipulation. Our lives are to be walking testimonies of God's grace and love; for He has called us, Peter said, "out of darkness into his marvelous light" (*1 Peter 2:9*). Because we have received God's mercy and forgiveness, he tells us, "Dearly beloved, I beseech you as strangers and pilgrims, abstain from fleshly lusts, which war against the soul" (*1 Peter 2:11*).

Sin wages its relentless war against us every day of our lives in this world. Each day we choose to either ignore the enemy and thereby give him strategic advantage over us, or we take up our weapons and fight. If we fight with the weapons of this world, we will lose the battle. If, however, we wield the weapons God has provided for our battle, we *will* win; for God's weapons are mighty and powerful and He will undertake for us as we use them. Paul tells us, "For though we walk in the flesh, we do not war after the flesh; (For the weapons of our warfare are not carnal, but mighty through God to the pulling down of strong holds;) Casting down imaginations, and every high thing that exalteth itself against the knowledge of God, and bringing into captivity every thought to the obedience of Christ" (*2 Corinthians 10:4–5*).

Winning the Battle

God's weapons and methods for winning the war against lusts that fuel anger bear no resemblance to the world's. Our armor is described in *Ephesians 6:10–18*, but in *2 Corinthians 10* God describes our plan of attack. We are to cast down human reasoning and every desire in our life that is in opposition to God and then subject every thought to the obedience of Christ. Soldiers win wars by capturing the enemy and taking control of them, making them obedient subjects to the will of their leader. In this same way, Christians win their battles by taking control of every thought and keeping thoughts in captivity as obedient subjects to the will of Christ.

The battle with anger will be won or lost on the battlefield of the mind, for it is with our minds that we feed our hearts, and it is out of the heart that every sinful act and word originates. What we think and how we think matters; for it not only determines the condition of our heart, it determines what controls it. Whatever captures our thoughts, then, will have captured the very source of sin's strength. We cannot win the battle with anger if we allow our minds to wander freely; for if we do, we will soon discover that they gravitate to the very things that ultimately destroy and enslave us. If, however, we capture our thoughts as one would capture a dangerous enemy and make them conform to the mind of Christ, our victory is sure. It is our knowing and obeying God's truth, remember, that sets us free from the grip of sin (*John 8:31–32*).

No wonder Paul exhorted us, "Let this mind be in you, which was also in Christ Jesus" (*Philippians 2:5*), and no wonder the wisdom of Solomon warns, "For as he thinketh in his heart, so is he" (*Proverbs 23:7*). The many habits, beliefs, and desires that lie beneath an angry spirit can be conquered by God's strength when every rogue thought is brought into the captivity of Christ—for whatever conquers our thoughts ultimately conquers us. As those in authority over a soldier give him orders, so the Captain of our faith has given us orders to bring our thoughts into captivity. We are to do what our Captain tells us to do, depend on Him to *use* what we do, and then do for us what we cannot do for ourselves. As we move forward and advance obediently, He will do as He has promised and fight our battles even as we follow Him. We must simply fight on God's terms, using God's methods in God's ways.

What hope and encouragement to know that our victory over sin is won by Christ, Who fights on our behalf as we trust and obey Him. We serve the Lord in His army with the same goals and objectives as He. We learn to hate what He hates and love what He loves, remembering there is no such thing as neutral ground. We recognize that in every order we obey or disobey, we either fight for or against Jesus Christ and His kingdom. And as we pledge our allegiance to the right King and willingly surrender ourselves to His leadership, we will triumphantly give praise to God and say, "But thanks be to God, which giveth us the victory through our Lord Jesus Christ" (*1 Corinthians* 15:57).

WHY AM I
SO
angry?

PART TWO

Applying God's Truth

The believer has something the world does not. He is something the world is not! The believer is a new creature in Christ with a new nature, a new destiny, and a new power within him to change (*2 Corinthians 5:17*). The indwelling Holy Spirit, the grace of God that permeates a believer's life, and the available wisdom and energizing power of God's Word is a believer's birthright. By these means, a believer's desires and priorities are reordered. His mind is bathed in the sunlight of truth; and as a result, his life is profoundly and supernaturally affected. He is no longer a self-willed child of wrath but a surrendered child of the King who can confidently entrust all of his life to His care.

The believer is taught by the Holy Spirit and the Word of God to recognize sin and hate it. But this alone does not deliver him from sin's stubborn grip. The Holy Spirit and the Word of God also work together to renew and transform the way a believer thinks and the things a believer desires, and then teaches him to pursue the righteous behavior opposite of his sin. Simply hating what is wrong and loving what is right does not deliver a believer from sin. The believer must turn from what is wrong and choose to do what is right while relying upon God's power and available strength to transform him. It is our union with Christ and conformity to the mind of Christ that enables us to change from the inside out. Therefore, we are to live in fellowship with Him and rely on Him to produce His nature in us. Jesus promises us, "I am the vine, ye are the branches: He that abideth in me, and I in him, the same bringeth forth much fruit: for without me ye can do nothing" (*John 15:5*). Paul recognized this truth and rejoiced in it. He said, "But thanks be to God, which giveth us the victory through our Lord Jesus Christ" (*1 Corinthians 15:57*).

Anyone can outwardly change his behavior—actors and actresses do it every day. Acting "good," however, is not the same as being "good." Only God can change our hearts and transform our inner beings into His own likeness and goodness. Only God can change us in such a way that we delight to do His will because we love and trust Him. He changes us from the inside out as we walk with Him, talk with Him, and obey His Word. Our desires and beliefs, which make up our heart, are transformed by the renewing of our minds as Paul described (*Romans 12:2*). And when the heart is changed, righteous behavior (the fruit of the Spirit of God) becomes the fiber of our natural personalities and character. This is the believer's joy! The Scriptures tell us, "This I say then, Walk in the Spirit, and ye shall not fulfill the lust [desires] of the flesh [our sinful human nature]. For the flesh lusteth [wars] against the Spirit, and the Spirit against the flesh: and these are contrary the one to the other: so that ye cannot do the things that ye would" (*Galatians 5:16–17*).

Conquering Anger in God's Strength

Those who desire to face and confront problems by God's strength, in God's way, will first want to seek God's wisdom on God's terms. Two excellent chapters to read and study before you begin these applications are *Proverbs 2* and *James 1*. When we acknowledge that our ways fail and that our human reasoning is insufficient to recognize and resolve problems righteously, when we seek humility and wisdom first, when we are certain that we are willing to submit our will to God and allow Him to use the problem for our good and future joy, and when we ask God to help us properly discern the problem or provocation (taking the necessary time to identify the source of anger) then, and only then, are we facing the problems biblically and taking the proper steps toward a godly solution.

Instructions

Prepare a three-ring notebook with lined paper on which to keep notes and record your progress. If you are working with a pastor or counselor, he or she may want to provide extra handouts that you can insert into your notebook. You will need 3x5 cards and a ring or envelope in which to store them, two different-colored highlighting pens, your Bible, and this book. It is important that you work through applications one through seven in consecutive order. The applications following those may be completed in any order, but remember that all of them play an important role in re-orienting your thoughts and actions toward godliness and victory over sinful anger. As you are working through the applications, go back through the first part of this book and using one of your highlighters, mark any specific underlying problem you believe contributes to your difficulty with anger. With the other marker, underline statements you want to remember and any that are especially pertinent to you.

May the Lord bless you as you study and grow in grace!

Debi Pryde
Ephesians 3:14–20

Application #1—Recognizing Hidden Anger

Following is a list of questions that will assist you and your counselor as you begin the work of examining and confronting underlying problems that tend to feed anger. This exercise can reveal some of the subtle ways we tend to misinterpret and overlook emotions that may actually be fueling anger. As you progress in this study, you should be increasingly more able to see the connection between your answers and the specific areas in your life that are in need of God's transforming change.

What frustrates me?

What lingering disappointments do I have?

What/who discourages me?

What irritates/bugs me?

What injustices bother me?

What fears trouble me?

Application #2—Recognizing Anger's Pattern

You may not be aware of it, but the tension and expression of anger is always preceded by specific events and thoughts that recur in your life. Sometimes these are called "triggers" because they tend to produce a seemingly "automatic" and strong emotional response. There is great value in knowing what is happening and what you are thinking *just before* you become aware you are, or are becoming, angry. Not only does pattern recognition reveal the kinds of situations and circumstances in which you are likely to react with anger, it assists you and your counselor in developing specific biblical resolutions that will *prevent* anger. Your counselor or pastor will more clearly understand how to help you if you will take the time to note and document the time and place, as well as what you were thinking and doing before you reacted in anger or experienced the rising tension of anger. You will need to faithfully do this for at least a week, and preferably two or more, in order to gain an adequate understanding of your particular patterns and their significance in your journey to overcome anger.

As you work on this assignment, pay close attention to similarities in themes that trigger anger, patterns relating to days and times that are most problematic for you, and the specific thought patterns that incite rather than resolve anger. You will want to become aware of anger's cycle and how it is being manifested in your life. The repeating cycle of tension "build up" and then "blow up" is especially apparent when anger has become a habit of life or method of expending emotional energy that builds as a result of unresolved problems or physiological hormone changes (in women). Note the way inner tension can gradually build up over a period of days or weeks until it explodes into a destructive rage, after which you become calm, controlled, and sorrowful for your loss of control. Then as you are once again faced with life's daily problems, the inner tension begins to build again until once again it finds its release in a destructive rampage of angry words and actions, typically followed by some measure of sorrow and grief.

Many people repeat this cycle over and over without ever noticing that it is a predictable pattern. By learning what troubles you most and what precedes sinful reactions, you will gain the understanding necessary to begin learning how to solve problems righteously and prevent the cycle from occurring. One skill that you will want to develop in the early stages of gaining mastery over your spirit is the skill of recognizing anger at its *earliest* starting point and responding to it in appropriate pre-planned ways. In this way you will learn to use the energy and tension of anger to *solve* problems, rather than expending it by reacting sinfully to the difficulties in your life.

Watch for cycles, but also watch for endure-and-ignore-until-explosion patterns. If you are more the "endure and ignore" kind of person rather than the "build up and blow up" person, you need to learn to ask yourself what you are enduring and how you might be able to resolve the irritation. People may respond to problems by reacting to them, ignoring them, running from them, or sometimes merely tolerating them. Yet no matter what our pattern might be, anger is the inevitable outcome until we learn how to resolve problems in righteous ways.

Instructions: Record the time and day that angry tension or expressions of anger occurred, what was happening *preceding*, what you were thinking *beforehand*. What, where, why, and who are helpful tidbits of information that will paint a very accurate portrait if you will simply keep a daily "anger" record. Your notations do not need to be long or detailed. Using a calendar that is large enough to write on is usually sufficient, although some prefer keeping notations in a little notebook that you can keep in your purse or pocket. Remember, the more diligent you are at recording your tense moments throughout the week, the more helpful this strategy will be to you. If you are working with a counselor or pastor, this information will form the "battle plan" for succeeding weekly discipleship meetings that should continue until you have sufficiently developed skills and habits that will enable you to continue growing without a high level of assistance.

Application #3—Evaluating Anger's Impact

Read each question and then underline the word that best describes your response. This self-discovery exercise will help you and your counselor explore many common problems that are often related to anger. Your answers will help you and your counselor more accurately assess core beliefs and desires that trigger angry reactions and to what degree they are a problem for you. Becoming more aware of these will help you deal with problems that contribute to anger. Remember that your efforts to conquer anger will succeed only if you deal with the many *underlying* problems that feed and trigger it.

Am I experiencing physical problems related to anger such as chronic fatigue, recurring headaches, unexplained gastrointestinal disorders, chronic respiratory disorders, circulatory disorders, unexplained heart palpitations or chest pain?

- ☐ Often
- ☐ Sometimes
- ☐ Seldom
- ☐ Not at all

Do my thoughts gravitate toward people and situations that I am angry about?

- ☐ Often
- ☐ Sometimes
- ☐ Seldom
- ☐ Not at all

Do I often feel sad, unhappy, fed up, annoyed, hurt, or harassed?

- ☐ Often
- ☐ Sometimes
- ☐ Seldom
- ☐ Not at all

Do I often talk about being frustrated, disappointed, or ready to explode?

- ☐ Often
- ☐ Sometimes
- ☐ Seldom
- ☐ Not at all

When I am confronted, do I tend to quickly become defensive, shift blame to someone else, or point out others who are doing the same thing or worse?

- ☐ Often
- ☐ Sometimes
- ☐ Seldom
- ☐ Not at all

Is confessing fault, asking forgiveness, or admitting error difficult for me?

- ☐ Often
- ☐ Sometimes
- ☐ Seldom
- ☐ Not at all

Are the faults and weaknesses of others difficult for me to overlook?

- ☐ Often
- ☐ Sometimes
- ☐ Seldom
- ☐ Not at all

Is the thought of failure or not living up to a standard I've set for myself something that produces anxiety in my life?

- ☐ Often
- ☐ Sometimes
- ☐ Seldom
- ☐ Not at all

Do I become angry when people fail to live up to standards and convictions that I believe are important?

- ☐ Often
- ☐ Sometimes
- ☐ Seldom
- ☐ Not at all

Am I sometimes depressed or overwhelmed with problems that I am having difficulty resolving?

- ☐ Often
- ☐ Sometimes
- ☐ Seldom
- ☐ Not at all

APPLICATION #4—CONFRONTING ANGER

Once you have spent some time noting and recording the circumstances that prompt and surround your experiences with anger, you are ready to move ahead and begin confronting yourself with questions that will gradually bring your thinking into harmony with a godly (and consequently happy) outlook. **Do not begin this exercise until you have completed applications one through three.**

During the first week, answer the following five questions in a notebook each time you become aware you are angry (or beginning to sense the rising tension that precedes anger). The second week, write these five questions on several 3 x 5 cards and keep them where you can refer to them to prompt your memory when you need to. The more you read the card when you sense you are becoming angry, the more quickly you will begin to memorize the questions and be able to recall them when needed. You will want to get to the place where you think through the questions without having to refer to your cards at all. After you have done this enough to begin automatically talking to yourself in a constructive way, you are ready to go on to the next step in becoming adept at thinking biblically about the provocation quickly. For now, these are the five questions you will need to concentrate on.

1. What am I angry about?

2. Is there something I can change that will resolve the problem or make the situation I am facing more tolerable?

3. Is there something I can change about me?

4. What biblical instructions do I know I have failed to obey regarding this situation?

5. Would Jesus be angry over this?

Application #5—Taking Thoughts Captive

On a 3x5 card or in your notebook, write the following passage of Scripture, noting the meanings of several key words.

There hath no temptation [trial or problem] taken you [come into your life] but such as is common to man [others have faced the same problem and dealt with it successfully]: but God is faithful [God cannot not lie; therefore His promises are absolutely reliable], who will not suffer [allow] you to be tempted [tried] above that ye are able; but will with the temptation [trial or problem] also make a way to escape, that ye may be able to bear it.—*1 Corinthians 10:13*

On the back of this verse card, write the following questions that you will ask yourself *after* you have answered the five questions listed above and *after* you have reread the verse card. If you have difficulty answering the questions, enlist the help of your counselor or pastor.

1. Do I believe this promise?

2. What, specifically, is the trial or problem I am facing at this moment?

3. Have I prayed for or looked for the way of escape that God has provided?

4. What resources and practical solutions has God given me that might help me face and resolve this problem righteously? [List as many solutions as you think of.]

5. Am I willing to trust God to give me all I need to confront this problem in a godly way?

6. Am I willing to acknowledge that God can and will turn this trial into something that will serve a good purpose and glorify Christ if I trust Him to do so?

7. Am I willing to thank God right now for the good outcome of this problem even though I do not see or understand how it will be resolved?

APPLICATION #6—UNDERSTANDING ANGER BIBLICALLY

Following are eight biblical concepts that form the basis for a truly biblical perspective of anger. Look up and read the passages of Scripture under each heading so you will thoroughly understand the concept. Remember that nothing equals the power of God's Word to change your heart and re-orient your thinking. Once you have read through the eight concepts, write the concept and the passages of Scripture under each one on a 3x5 card. Read them once in the morning and once before you go to sleep. After four weeks, write a paragraph in your notebook describing how the Lord is working in your heart and life and how He is helping you conquer anger in His strength. Note any instances where these concepts and passages of Scripture came to mind and changed the way you responded to some form of difficulty or provocation.

1. **Anger Begins in the Mind**. (*Leviticus 19:17–18; Ephesians 2:3*)

   Biblical Application: Notice how God draws our attention to the significance of our private thought lives in relation to anger. In *Leviticus 19,* God gives specific instructions that will prevent sinful expressions of anger. First and foremost, we are reminded that God forbids us to harbor hatred toward another in our hearts (minds). He instructs us to confront problems directly and honestly, going to one who sins against us for the purpose of helping him see his offense. Next, God forbids us to take matters into our own hands by avenging ourselves or retaliating, and forbids us to harbor any kind of grudge against others. Finally, God commands us to love our neighbor in the same way we naturally love ourselves. To merely stop holding a grudge or to ignore a sin is not enough. God's way is to put off sinful behavior and actively and deliberately choose to put on its righteous counterpart, which in this case is love.

2. Anger Is to Be Controlled / Mastered.
(*Proverbs 16:32; 25:28*)

Biblical Application: Paul tells us that he has to work at disciplining himself. In 1 Corinthians 9:27 we read, "But I keep under my body, and bring it into subjection." Later he tells us how to win our battles with the flesh: "Casting down imaginations [reasonings], and every high thing that exalteth itself against the knowledge of God, and bringing into captivity every thought to the obedience of Christ" (2 Corinthians 10:5). Bringing ourselves under subjection to Christ requires a deliberate choice to discipline ourselves for that purpose. Successful people work hard to accomplish their goals. Athletes, soldiers, and professionals of all kinds spend painstaking efforts to develop their particular proficiency. The Christian life is a disciplined life, intended to reap the joys and privileges of victory. While the world admires the accomplishments of its heroes, heaven recognizes the true greatness of a Christian who has learned to govern his own inner spirit and emotions through God's strength and power.

God compares the Christian who fails to build up the protective walls of discipline around his life with an ancient city that neglected to build and repair protective walls around it. Such carelessness left the city open to the easy access and destruction of the enemy. In the same way, the Christian who does not work hard to rule his spirit leaves himself open to destructive enemies that will take advantage of such an easy entrance into his life.

Venting anger by beating a pillow, screaming, or swearing does not resolve a problem or bring the peace that believers seek. Victory is found in learning to harness anger's energy and redirect it to solve problems in tangible and biblically consistent ways.

3. **Anger Never Accomplishes God's Will or Brings about God's Blessing**. (*James 1:19–22*)

Biblical Application: Anger NEVER accomplishes God's will and is NEVER blessed by God. Anger does not produce the righteousness of God. It does not change people. It does not build up homes or churches or organizations or governments. It only tears down and destroys. Anger may intimidate and stop behavior, but it can never change another person's heart or behavior.

God gives a solemn warning to women when He says in *Proverbs 14:1*, "Every wise woman buildeth her house: but the foolish plucketh it down with her hands." The *tearing down* referred to in this passage is not referring to a physical house being pulled apart brick by brick. God is talking about the foolish woman who tears down people and relationships within her home in an effort to control, rather than build up. To lash out at others with cruel words and cutting accusations is a wicked and dangerous thing, for words can never, never be taken back. Very often, though they are later regretted and cried over with bitter tears, the damage those words brought remains; and relationships are never restored to what they could have been.

4. **Anger Is a Work of the Sinful Flesh and the Mark of an Immature Believer.** (*Proverbs 14:17; James 3:13–17; Galatians 5:19–21*)

Biblical Application: The unbeliever is characterized by anger, according to Ephesians 2:3. Before salvation, we are, by nature, the children of wrath. When a sinner repents and turns to God for forgiveness, God gives him a new inner nature, one like His own. The old nature dies and the new nature brings everything in life into a new perspective. This new perspective and awareness of one's freedom from the penalty and guilt of sin dispels anger. Nevertheless, the new Christian nature still lives in the same mortal body that is contaminated by the effects of sin.

While sin no longer has dominion over a believer or keeps him locked in an escape-proof box, sin is still an enemy out to destroy him. There is wonderful hope for the child of God because God gives His children everything they need to overcome sin's control. As they grow in their knowledge of Christ and learn how to appropriate truth into their lives, anger is chipped away. A supernatural spirit of gentleness, patience, and love characterizes the maturing believer. This is called the "fruit of the Spirit" and is the natural byproduct of one who lives his life in harmony with God's Word. The fruit of God's Spirit is the Christ-likeness that God desires for every believer. Unlike anger, which comes naturally to human beings, the fruit of God's Spirit does not.

The more immature we are spiritually, the more our reactions will look like the world's reactions. The more mature we are spiritually, the more our instantaneous reactions will pattern those of our Lord Jesus Christ. Peter asks, "For what glory is it, if, when ye be buffeted for your faults, ye shall take it patiently? but If, when ye do well, and suffer for it, ye take it patiently, this is acceptable with God. For even hereunto were ye called: because Christ also suffered for us, leaving us an example, that ye should follow His steps." If you were mistreated, as Jesus was the day He was crucified, would you have been able to accept it quietly without cursing under your breath or hating your persecutors? One of the most incredible things about Jesus' crucifixion is the fact that in spite of all the gross injustice, humiliation, and cruelty leveled against Him, He "did no sin, neither was guile found in His mouth: Who, when He was reviled, reviled not again; when he suffered, he threatened not; but committed himself to him that judgeth righteously" (*1 Peter 2:20–24*). This is the mark of miraculous love and forgiveness which is a natural part of God's nature, not our own.

5. **Sinful Anger Is a Result of Our Proud Self-Will.**
   (*Proverbs 13:10; James 4:1–3, 5–8*)

Biblical Application: Anger and pride are mentioned in the same context in Scripture almost invariably. The Bible teaches us that contention *always* stems from pride (self-interest). Love and forgiveness (which is the righteous counterpart to anger) stems from self-denial and a correct estimation of self (such as the understanding that one is undeserving of God's love and forgiveness and that he possesses a deceitful and wicked heart that he must never trust but instead must always keep under subjection to God's authority). Contempt for others stems not from *their* failures or sins, but from *our* esteem of self.

A disagreement, or conflict, is not necessarily contention or contempt. Contention develops when one or both disagreeing parties are not able to regard the other with love and respect even though there is a disagreement. When one is unable to resolve problems calmly and rationally with another in a spirit of kindness and respect, he is being governed by pride and self-will, not by a godly spirit of love. Whenever disagreements become personal attacks rather than efforts to resolve an issue, pride and ungodliness are involved.

When we believe that our views make us more lovable, righteous, or superior than others, we will exhibit a spirit of anger or intolerance when we are corrected or when offenses and differences in opinions arise. When we are prideful, we cannot disagree with others in matters of emotional significance without feelings of tension, hostility, or disrespect. Disagreements are a normal part of life. Anger and intolerance toward those who disagree are not "normal" in the godly sense and are a manifestation of pride. This is why people who try to control their anger without dealing thoroughly and biblically with the greater root issues involving sins such as their pride, fear, and jealousy, cannot ever conquer their anger. To learn to restrain their angry outbursts if sufficiently motivated (fear of being fired, rejected, or arrested for assault and battery) is sometimes possible, but they never conquer the inward feelings of tension or restlessness. Instead, they end up redirecting the anger in yet another destructive way, often with great physical manifestations stemming from the chemical changes that the body automatically triggers whenever anger arises internally.

6. **Anger Destroys the Atmosphere of a Home.**
   (*Proverbs 5:17;21:19*)

   Biblical Application: Anger destroys the atmosphere that God intended the home to provide. It is rooted in hostility toward others, in a lack of love, and in an unwillingness to overlook or forgive sin. Until a man or woman faces and deals biblically with his or her own sin of anger, none of the problems in a marriage or home will be resolved. Peace, love, and family intimacy cannot coexist with anger. A loving family so poor that all they can afford to eat for dinner is Campbell's soup is far better off than an angry family so rich they can afford to eat filet mignon steak every night.

7. **Angry People Influence Others to Be Angry.**
   (*Proverbs 22:24; Ephesians 6:4*)

   Biblical Application: Anger is contagious. It is as much a learned habit as it is a natural human response. The more we expose ourselves or our children to people characterized by anger, the more we will be influenced to react in similar ways. Men who abuse their wives and women who abuse their husbands typically learned their demanding and cruel ways in childhood—from parents, friends, or family. Because anger comes so naturally to sinful and self-centered humans, it is easily learned and incited by exposure to it. Thankfully, because anger is a learned habit, it can be unlearned.

8. **Love and Forgiveness Overcome Anger.**
   (*Proverbs 15:1; Psalm 37:8; Colossians 3:8–10, 12–15*)

Biblical Application: Anger is a powerful energy that can be extremely destructive both internally (physically) and externally if it is not directed toward solving problems in righteous ways. God promises believers that He will never allow them to go through a trial without also providing a way of escape and His own supernatural power to meet problems head on through His own grace and strength (*1 Corinthians 10:13*). He assures us that problems of every sort are common to all people, Christians included. Yet only the Christian has God's promise that He is ever present to provide strength, faith, and specific ways to respond. Only a believer can have the assurance that God will always ultimately turn every problem around for good.

When problems arise, as problems will, God wants us to face them and seek His direction and power to resolve the problem His way rather than our own. When we ignore the problem God has allowed, run from it, circumvent it, blow up at it, or hide from it, we become prone to sinful expressions of anger, bitterness, and despair. Instead, God instructs us to find the godly means of escape that He has provided to us, so that we might deal with or resolve any problem that comes into our lives. Conquering problems God's way requires us to put off our own ways of dealing with life's difficulties and put on God's ways. Anger is man's way of dealing with problems. Love and forgiveness is God's way.

APPLICATION #7—THINGS I NEED TO REMEMBER

Underline the sentences below that you most need to remember when you become angry. Write these on 3x5 cards and read them every morning for a month. Together with someone who can help you, find passages of Scripture that instruct and encourage you to apply each instruction. A *Nave's Topical Bible* would be helpful to use with this exercise.

- Cease justifying anger.

- Quickly recognize and admit anger and practice principles of repentance.

- Follow repentance with restitution to those whom you have offended and with thanksgiving for God's love, mercy, and forgiveness.

- Learn to obey God's rules concerning anger and look for righteous solutions to problems and trials.

- Attack the problem, not the person, and not yourself.

- Cease demanding perfection in others.

- Recognize God's sovereignty. God will deal with both the wicked who oppress His children and other Christians who oppress His children. He will do this in His own way, in His own time.

- Do all you can to work out problems with others in a biblical way with a biblical attitude, and then entrust your case to God. Rest in the knowledge that He is faithful to deal with others. God alone can accurately judge hearts and administer correction.

- Replace acts of anger.

- Put off bitterness, abusive words, wrath, and self-centeredness. Replace them by putting on acts of love such as patience, kindness, humility, and forgiveness. This replacing is one of the most important keys to overcoming anger. We only conquer habitual anger, unkindness, and malicious words by developing new habits of deliberate acts of kindness, love, and forgiveness. New godly reactions and habits must replace the old, sinful ones. Therefore, the primary focus must be on developing godly actions rather than pouring effort into merely trying to control ungodly reactions.

- Remember that a failure to discuss problems or work them out biblically eventually produces tension and discouragement, which leads to various expressions of anger. Ignoring problems that God has commanded us to deal with in a particular way leads to unhappiness and irritability because we are not living obediently toward God, and thus cannot receive the peace of the Holy Spirit.

APPLICATION #8—LEARNING TO RECOGNIZE SELF-WILL

- Self-will (stubbornness) is the enemy of God's will.—*2 Kings 22:1–23:30; 2 Chronicles 34:1–35:27*

- Self-will is forbidden.—*2 Chronicles 30:8*

- Self-will proceeds from unbelief.—*2 Kings 17:14*

- Self-will proceeds from pride.—*Nehemiah 9:1-33 (16, 29)*

- Self-will is manifested in refusing to listen to the messengers of God.—*1 Samuel 8:1–22 (19); Jeremiah 44:15–16; Zechariah 7:11*

- Self-will is manifested in refusing to walk in the ways of God.—*Nehemiah 9:17; Isaiah 42:24; Psalm 78:10*

- Self-will is manifested in refusing to listen to parents.—*Deuteronomy 21:18–21*

- Self-will is manifested in refusing to receive correction.—*Jeremiah 5:1–4; 7:25–28*

- Self-will is a characteristic of the lost.—*2 Peter 2:10*

- The end result of self-will is destruction.—*Proverbs 1:24–31; 29:1; 2 Chronicles 36:15–16*

Bible Study:

Read the passages of Scripture below and then write a paragraph in your notebook describing the outward manifestations of the people's self-will and the consequences they suffered as a result.

1. Simeon and Levi—*Genesis 34; 49:5–7*

2. The nation of Israel—*Psalm 78; 95:8–11; Hebrews 3:8, 15; 4:7*

3. Israel under judges—*Judges 2:1–23*

Application #9—Learning to Deal with Failure Successfully

After filling in the appropriate blanks and studying the following outline and passages of Scripture, write a paragraph or two describing how this information applies to your life in particular and what changes you want to make as a result of your study.

Paul, the failure?

- Paul, the mature believer, delights in the _____ _____. *Romans 7:22*

- Yet Paul, who still lives in a mortal body, discovers a conflict between his new nature that was given birth when he was saved and the remnant of his old nature that still begs to govern his life. *Romans 7:19*

- Because Paul is a mature believer who deeply desires a walk of faith and obedience to the Lord, he laments over his failure and inability to control his sinful nature by his own will power alone. *Romans 7:24*

- Paul asks who, not what, will rescue him and then answers his own question by giving the only solution to this dilemma. _____ _____ _____ _____ is He Who enables us to live as He lived. *Romans 7:25*

Why do we "feel" like a failure?

- Because we fail so often, being human

- Because we sin

- Because _____
  (Give your own ideas.)

What is it that believers want?

- We want to please God.

- We want to "succeed" in the eyes of others.

- We want to avoid pain and suffering that comes as a result of failure.

- We want to "feel" good about our efforts and ourselves.

- We want to _____
  _____. (Give your own ideas.)

- Which of these is a godly or ungodly motive to succeed? Why or why not? What passage of Scripture does this violate or adhere to? (See remaining outline.)

Learn to recognize and divide sins from weaknesses.

- Things that trigger sorrow over failure in my life that are not sins:

- Things that trigger sorrow over failure in my life that ARE sins:

Human weakness:

- Exalts God, not self—*1 Corinthians 1:26–31*

- Puts our confidence in the right place—*Philippians 3:3; Hebrews 4:16; Ecclesiastes 7:14*

- Promotes humility; establishes our position as the student, not the teacher, the clay, not the potter. *2 Corinthians 4:7*

- Turns faith to Christ, not self—*Acts 3:12,16*

Sin...

- Reveals our human heart—*Romans 7:13; 1 John 1:8–10*

- Reveals our need—*James 4:6; Hosea 13:9*

- Forgiveness of sin reveals the heart of God—*Psalm 130:4; Isaiah 1:18; Acts 13:38; Hebrews 8:12*

What pleases God?—*John 6:28–29; Hebrews 11:6; Hebrews 13:16*

What is success in the eyes of others?—*Galatians 1:10*

What good comes of suffering?—*Psalm 119:71, 75; Hebrews 5:8*

Why do I not need to "feel" good about my righteousness?—*Philippians 3:8–9; Galatians 6:14–15*

> The perfectionist is driven by a desire to excel to such a degree that he does not experience the pain of human failure, weakness, or sin. Perfectionism is characterized by a desire to sense or feel one's self to be righteous on the basis of one's own self-denial, discipline, and moral excellence.

Failure teaches, disciplines, and forces us to grow. Failure produces growing pains. Growth is *good*.—*2 Corinthians 3:18; Galatians 3:1–3; Ephesians 3:19–21; Philippians 2:13; 2 Thessalonians 2:16–17; Hebrews 12:2*

The grace of God *teaches* us to live godly.—*Titus 2:11–14*

Guilty feelings...

The repentant conscience—*2 Samuel 24:10*

The hypersensitive conscience—*1 John 3:20*

The immature conscience—*Hebrews 9:14*

True Guilt	False Guilt
Comes as a result of becoming aware we have violated God's law, sinned against God and others.— *Genesis 3:6–13*	Comes as a result of fearing the judgments and suggestions of men or becoming aware we have violated their judgments.
Comes from divine judgment.—*2 Samuel 24:10*	Comes from judgments of men (and self).
Comes when we fear God's judgment and have a desire to please God.	Comes when we fear man's judgment and have a desire to please man.
Holy Spirit produces real guilt and conviction of sin in order to build us up.—*John 16:8*	Satan accuses us of sin (true and false) to confuse us and tear us down.
True guilt causes us to take responsibility for our own sin.	False guilt causes us to accept responsibility for someone else's sin or judgment.
Purpose of true guilt is to bring us to a right relationship with God and others.	False guilt drives us further from God and drives a wedge between ourselves and others.

Application #10—Learning to Deal with Injustice

How we deal with injustice beyond our control often reveals what and where we are spiritually, whether or not we trust God's ways.

- Those who oppress others do not go unnoticed by God—or unpunished.—*Psalm 1:4–6; 10:13–14; 1 Thessalonians 4:6–8*

- God uses the unjust and even injustice for His own purposes.—*Genesis 50:20; Proverbs 16:4; Isaiah 45:1; 55:8*

- The just should expect mistreatment from the unjust.—*Psalm 37:1,12; 73:2–17; Luke 17:1; 2 Timothy 3:2–3,12–13; 1 Peter 4:12–13*

- The oppressed are rewarded and comforted.—*Psalm 9:9–10; Proverbs 20:22; Matthew 5:10–12; Luke 6:22–23; Romans 12:19–21; Hebrews 12:2–3; 1 Peter 3:9; 4:19*

- Judgment may be delayed, but payday always comes unless the offender repents.—*Ecclesiastes 8:11–12; 1 Timothy 5:24; 2 Peter 2:9*

- Judgment and recompense for works is inevitable, and God's books are always ultimately balanced.—*Proverbs 12:2–3, 7; 24:19–20; 1 Corinthians 4:5; Colossians 3:25; Hebrews 2:2; Revelation 2:23*

Deal with injustice by—

- Expecting it

- Understanding the nature of the world, sinners

- Living as peaceably and justly as possible with all men

- Committing your case to God, believing He is in control

- Enduring it with patience

- Expecting a reward for suffering

- Knowing injustice does not slip by God
- Recognizing it is God's responsibility to correct or take vengeance, in His time, *not yours*

Application #11—Learning to Deal with Criticism

When You Are Your Own Worst Critic

To judge ourselves with the intent of correcting known sin is productive; to criticize ourselves because we fail to meet our own personal expectations is self-destructive.

- What you dwell on, think about, and act like, you will become.—*Proverbs 23:7*

- Focus on the assets and gifts God has given you, not those He's given to someone else.—*Romans 12:4–6; 2 Corinthians 10:12*

- Learn to recognize your strengths and work at polishing them.—*Psalm 138:8*

- Minimize your weaknesses and accept your humanity.—*2 Corinthians 12:9–10*

- Dwell on Christ's adequacy, not your inadequacy.—*Hosea 12:6; John 15:4–5; Philippians 4:13*

- Praise God continually for the growth and work He's doing in your life.—*Colossians 1:9–11*

- Ask for and accept God's forgiveness on a daily basis and always forget the past.—*Philippians 3:13–14*

If the Criticism Was Justified

As a general rule, do NOT respond quickly to criticism, especially if you are inclined to defend yourself. Pray about it. Be humble and willing enough to take the time to consider it. Only then decide if it is valid. Do not judge its validity by the attitude of the critic. Sometimes our worst enemies are our best critics, and we can learn something from them.—*Proverbs 14:29; 18:13; 19:11*

- Defuse anger by answering quietly and gently.—*Proverbs 15:1; 25:15; Ecclesiastes 7:8–9*

- Be very quick to admit fault.—*Ecclesiastes 10:4; Lamentations 3:39; Proverbs 12:1; 15:5,10,12,31,32; 27:5*

- Remember that anger and defensiveness lead to bitterness and spiritual blindness.—*Ephesians 4:31–32; 1 Thessalonians 5:12–15*

- Thank your critic for bringing the matter to your attention. Do not engage in any lengthy explanations on the matter, however.—*James. 5:16*

- Dwell on the good that can come out of the criticism, not on your hurt feelings.—*2 Corinthians 7:9*

- Do not consider one who is trying to help you and who is willing to be truthful with you as your enemy.—*Galatians 4:16*

- Thank God for using the criticism to correct you.—*1 Thessalonians 5:18*

- Ask for and expect God's grace to cope with hurt.—*1 Peter 5:6–7; James 4:6–7*

- Ask for forgiveness, wisdom, and help; then make deliberate steps to correct yourself.—*Isaiah 43:25; Psalm 119:59–60*

If the Criticism Stems from a Misunderstanding

- Consider first how you could have contributed to the misunderstanding.—*2 Corinthians 8:21*

- Accept responsibility for giving a wrong impression and admit this to your critic.—*Acts 24:16*

- Take whatever steps are necessary to correct the misunderstanding and right any wrong you have done.—*Luke 6:31; Mark 9:50*

If the Criticism Is Unjustified

- Tell your critic you appreciate his concern for you and his willingness to be honest. Tell him you will certainly consider the matter and talk to the Lord about it. Then DROP it. Do not attempt to defend yourself.—*1 Peter 2:19–23; 1 Peter 3:8–9*

- Display a quiet, humble attitude. If you defend yourself, you will cause him to stubbornly defend HIS position and feel justified in his criticism.—*1 Peter 3:16–17*

- Do not accept or dwell on unjustified criticism. Remember, you do not owe anyone an apology or explanation for each of your actions. Allow God to work on your behalf and convince your critic of his error.—*Romans 14:22; Proverbs 19:1*

If the Criticism Is Slanderous

Whenever appropriate, confront your critic by asking if you have done something to offend him. Listen patiently to his response and determine if the slander might not stem from a misunderstanding. Always hear the matter before you assume anything or respond to anything slanderous. If the slander is definitely not due to a misunderstanding and your critic is not willing to respond to your efforts to correct the situation scripturally.

- Refrain from bitterness by forgiving your enemy.—*Acts 7:59–60*

- Wish the best for your enemy, invest good in your enemy (do not avoid him), and pray for your enemy.—*Matthew 5:44,46; Romans 12:17–21*

- Call on God for His intervention on your behalf; and if you have followed His directions for dealing with enemies, you can definitely expect Him to take up for you and vindicate

you one way or another. Entrust your reputation to God.—
Psalm 37:7–9; Proverbs 24:17–18

- Keep slander in perspective; in other words, do not allow yourself to take it personally. Do not dwell on it.—*Luke 6:35–38*

- Remember that criticism may be a compliment in disguise if it is provoked by your desire to live right.—*Matthew 5:10–12; 1 Peter 4:13–15,19; 2 Timothy 3:12*

APPLICATION #12—LEARNING TO DEAL WITH BITTERNESS

Definition

In the Old Testament, the word *choler* is used to describe bitterness stemming from anger and intense hatred (*Daniel 11:11*). A self-willed and bitter person who turns away from the Lord is described as a poison, "a root that beareth gall and wormwood," that infects other people. In the New Testament, Simon the sorcerer is referred to as being in the "gall of bitterness," describing a heart poisoned with sinful self-pleasing (*Acts 8:23*). The human heart, apart from God, is naturally bent toward anger expressed by "cursing and bitterness" [hateful words and anger] (*Romans 3:14*). Bitterness is linked together with "wrath [fierce indignation], and anger [vengeance], and clamour [an outcry], and evil speaking" (*Ephesians 4:31*). It is described in *Ephesians 4:22* and *29* as behavior originating in the naturally sinful and rebellious heart ("the old man" who indulges in "corrupt communication"). Bitterness is to be replaced with its righteous counterpart— tenderhearted kindness and forgiveness (*Ephesians 4:32*). Husbands are instructed not to be "bitter" toward their wives (*Colossians 3:19*), meaning they are not to harbor a grudge or irritation. A "root of bitterness" (*Hebrews 12:15*) is a person or a sinful disposition that leads to unbelief and rebellion toward God and ultimately influences others to rebel as well.

Biblical Perspective

Bitterness results when anger is justified with unbiblical assumptions, thus allowing anger to be nurtured and prolonged. Bitterness quickly develops into hatred and a deep-rooted wish to see the offender punished for wrongs committed. This often becomes an obsessive desire that manifests itself in the thought life and speech of a bitter person. He has a difficult time committing the responsibility for punishment to God, but rather assumes the right to punish that which God alone has the authority to correct. It is not unusual for the alleged offender or object of a bitter person's rage to be innocent and quite possibly unaware of the resentment toward him. Bitter people typically dwell on perceived wrongs or insignificant flaws or oversights until an assumption is built in his mind which results in horribly twisted or exaggerated conclusions. Bitter people typically manifest an intense desire to blame others for their unhappiness or failure. They tend to go to great lengths to avoid accepting personal responsibility for their hateful thought lives and attitudes and cling to their perceived "right" to be bitter, the way an alcoholic clings to his alcohol.

It is quite possible for bitterness to begin to take root when an offense is confusing to the offended one, or when responsibility for the offense is not clearly understood. This may lead to assuming guilt for someone else's sin or a pattern of self-blame and despair over perceived failures or past sins. If this is not resolved, the embittered person often attempts to manage the resulting emotional pain of self-blame by directing his anger toward someone else.

Bitterness typically results when we do not fully comprehend or believe God's promises to His children but instead, adopt a negative attitude toward the offender rather than a positive attitude toward the promised good outcome of the trial or offense. There is no antidote to bitterness and despair more powerful than simply knowing God. God-given peace is always based in our confidence in God's promises and God's character, not in our circumstances or other people. Those who have a difficult time trusting God in adversity do not know God well, for if they did, they would not struggle to trust Him. Notice the divine order in *Psalm 28:7*. First the psalmist states His confidence in God's promises of strength and protection, then he trusts, then he is helped, and finally he is filled with peace and joy. "The LORD is my strength and my shield; my heart trusted in him, and I am helped: therefore my heart greatly rejoiceth; and with my song will I praise him." Study *1 Corinthians 4:8–9* and *Psalm 27:13* and note the basis for both Paul and David's hope and encouragement in times of great trouble.

The heart that is focused on pleasing self rather than pleasing God is always vulnerable to anger and bitterness when life does not turn out as expected. Those who are bitter must choose between refusing to give up what is wanted or submitting to what God wants to accomplish in their lives. The bitter person must make a deliberate choice to believe God is good and will use the disappointment for his ultimate good, or he will persist in believing God is cruel and is using the offense for his destruction. Sadly, to wrongly believe God is cruel and designs trials to destroy His children, or to refuse to deal biblically with sin in our lives or someone else's life, is to engage in morbid self-destruction and needless despair.

Four occasions when bitterness commonly creeps into our lives:

1. When our reputation is damaged

2. When pain is inflicted on us or on a loved one

3. When our expectations are frustrated

4. When others do not live up to our standard of perfection

- Kill the root of a plant, and the plant will die. Kill the roots of bitterness; and the plants of anger, resentment, and depression will die.—*James 3:14; Hebrews 12:15; Ephesians 4:31*

- Bitterness becomes hatred; hatred must be replaced with love.—*Leviticus 19:17–18; Matthew 5:43–44; John 15:18; Proverbs 10:12; 13:10; 22:10; 26:24; Matthew 18:15; James 3:14; 1 Thessalonians 5:14*

- Bitterness is overcome with forgiveness. True forgiveness is manifest when we return good to those who wronged us. Forgiveness is an act of love, an act of the will. We learn to forgive by forgiving!—*Exodus 23:4; Proverbs 25:21; Matthew 5:7, 39–46; 6:12; Mark 11:25; Luke 17:3*

- Bitterness is produced when we assume the right to punish, a right we do not have. Forgiveness means we stop trying to make other people pay for their sins and offenses against us. Forgiving a person requires us to transfer to God the responsibility for any punishment due that person.— *Romans 12:14; 1 Corinthians 4:12; Colossians 3:13; 1 Peter 3:9; Jude 9; Proverbs 20:22; 24:29*

-

- Bitterness is produced when we have a negative attitude toward the offender, rather than a positive attitude toward the offense.— *Job 2:10; James 5:11; 1 Peter 4:12–19; 5:6*

- Bitterness is produced when we focus on what we want, rather than what God wants for us.— *Psalm 75:6–7; 115:3; 1 Chronicles 29:11–12; Jeremiah 18:6*

APPLICATION #13—LEARNING TO DEAL WITH MY PRIDE

Definition of Pride

A frame of mind and attitude in which an individual believes his opinions, worth, or status is superior. A proud person regards himself as possessing greater reasoning powers, worth, standing, focus, character, position, beauty, or abilities than is permitted by God's Word. Pride causes us to depend on our own reasoning, our own strength, and our own efforts to obtain joys and blessings that can only come as we obey and depend on God's reasoning, strength, and will. Pride blinds us to the dangers of our self-will and generates an attitude of false confidence and determination to live our lives however we please, often in defiance of God's instructions or with a hypocritical surface compliance to God's instructions. Pride produces anger and rebellion when people or circumstances interfere with our desires or plans.

Manifestations of Pride

Pride often manifests itself in lofty airs, distance, reserve, rude treatment or contempt of others, or in a refusal to cooperate with others. In the Bible, it is associated most often with sinful anger, sometimes well hidden from others. There are many other evidences of a prideful heart: impatient intolerance of failings or imperfections of others; a refusal to recognize pride in oneself; flattery; lying; strife; cursing; slander; unwillingness to admit fault or sin or to defer to others or serve others; lust for the approval and admiration of others; jealousy of others' status, possessions, or accomplishments (thinking you deserve what others have more than they do); prayerlessness; lack of dependence on God; self-efforts apart from God; not recognizing God's sovereignty and right to govern one's life; taking credit for one's abilities, accomplishments, and possessions which belong to God alone; boastful speech; and an unwillingness to submit to legitimate God-given authority.

Our Ways Are Not God's Ways!

In the Christian life, the way **up** is really **down**.

- The way to be **exalted** is to be **abased**.—*Matthew 23:12*
- The way to **get** is to **give**.—*Luke 6:38*
- The way to **lead** is to **follow**.—*1 Corinthians 11:1*
- The way to **fight** is to **love**.—*Matthew 5:44*
- The way to **gain** is to **lose**.—*Matthew 10:39*
- The way to be **honored** is to **serve**.—*Matthew 20:27*
- The way to **conquer** the devil is to **submit** to God.—*James 4:7*
- The way to be **great** is to be **small**.—*Matthew 18:4*
- The way to be **strong** is to be **weak**.—*2 Corinthians 12:10*
- The way to be **rich** is to be **poor**.—*2 Corinthians 6:10*
- The way to be **openly praised** is to **secretly pray**.—*Matthew 6:6*
- The way to be **first** is to be **last**.—*Mark 10:31*
- The way to **conquer** the fear of man is to **love** and **fear** God.—*Luke 12:4–5*

To submit to God and govern our lives by principles such as these requires humility.

- Paul—"I know that in me (that is, in my flesh) dwelleth no good thing" (*Romans 7:18*).
- David—"I am poor and needy" (*Psalm 86:1*).
- Jacob—"I am not worthy of the least of all the mercies, and of all the truth, which thou hast shewed unto thy servant" (*Genesis 32:10*).

The connection between pride, anger, and unhappiness is certain.

> Why can't I live the Christian life? Why aren't my prayers answered? Why am I so unhappy?

> James reminds us that God resists (is opposed to) the proud, but gives grace (unmerited favor; ability and desire to do God's will) only to the humble—only to those who are dependent on Christ rather than self.—*James 4:6*

The humble are dependent on Christ, not self.

- Without God's grace, we cannot be saved, for we are saved by grace through faith and that not of ourselves.—*Ephesians 2:8–9*

- Without God's grace we cannot understand the Scriptures, let alone obey them or please God in any way. We are dependent upon God for every breath we take and for every move we make. "In him [Jesus] we live, and move, and have our being" (*Acts 17:28*).

- Jesus, our Lord and Savior and example to follow declared, "I can of mine own self do nothing...I seek not mine own will, but the will of the Father which hath sent me" (*John 5:30*).

- Paul reminds those who have privileges, abilities, or desirable qualities that it is God Who gives all of these things; and because God gives them through no merit of our own, there is absolutely nothing for anyone to boast about.—*1 Corinthians 4:7*

- Moses reminded Israel not to say, "My power and the might of mine hand hath gotten me this wealth." Instead he beseeches them to remember the "Lord thy God; for it is he that giveth thee power to get wealth, that he may establish his covenant which he sware unto thy fathers, as it is this day" (*Deuteronomy 8:17–18*).

God has a divine order to receiving His grace and blessings.—*1 Peter 5:5–6*

Humility means:

- One has a right estimation of himself and a right understanding of one's dependence on God and unworthiness in God's sight.

- Humility always produces submission to God's divine will and always gives up its own perceived rights.

- Humility is connected to fearing God and giving Him the respect and honor and submission that is due Him.

The treasures of humility are beyond our comprehension.—*Proverbs 22:4; 1 Peter 3:4; Numbers 12:3; Hebrews 11:24–26*

Spurgeon: "If you and I empty ourselves, depend on it, God will fill us. Divine grace seeks out and fills a vacuum. Make a vacuum by humility, and God will fill that vacuum by His love. I believe every Christian has a choice between being humble and being humbled."

Directed Bible Study—Pride

A prideful person can be described as follows:

1. One who believes he can rebel against _____ and His Word without incurring God's correction.—*1 Samuel 15:1–23*

2. One who _____ on his own _____ and is _____ in his own eyes.—*Proverbs 3:5–7*

3. One who refuses _____.—*Proverbs 10:17*

4. One who goes his own way and becomes an _____ to the Lord.—*Proverbs 16:1–5.* (See *Proverbs 3:32*; "froward" —having an unwillingness to yield or comply with what is required; more than going aside from what is right, but going the opposite way.)

5. One who expresses or exhibits a _____ demeanor toward others.—*Proverbs 16:18*

6. One who stirs up _____. — *Proverbs 28:25*

7. One who uses _____ speech. —*Psalm 75:4–5*

8. One who believes he can avoid suffering _____ even though he has persecuted others.—*Psalm 10:2*

9. One who hates _____.—*Psalm 12:3*

10. One who thinks he is _____. —*Isaiah 47:7–10*

11. One who loves to have _____. —*Matthew 23:6–7,11–12*

12. One who thinks of himself more _____
    than he ought to—*Romans 12:3*

13. One who refuses to humbly admit specific _____
    and ask _____ or make
    restitution.—*2 Corinthians 7:9–10; 12:21*

14. One who loves to _____
    himself with others in order to build himself up in the eyes of
    others.—*2 Corinthians 10:12,18*

15. One who takes _____ for possessions,
    abilities, or accomplishments that are gifts and blessings of
    God.
    —*2 Corinthians 10:17–18; James 1:17; Galatians 5:25–26;
    Proverbs 27:2*

16. One who does not believe he deserves the same
    _____as others.—*Galatians 6:3*

17. One who resists the exercise of _____
    _____.—*James 4:6*

Application #14—Learning to Suffer Graciously

Bible Study from 1 Peter

Before you read through this study, read the book of *1 Peter*. This book of the Bible was written to people who were suffering great hardship and injustice. It was intended to encourage them and give them a much broader perspective of the trials they were facing. Some were suffering personal loss of property, violence committed against them or family members, or oppression of various sorts due to their faith in Christ. Peter wanted to assure those hurting people that there was a reason behind the suffering, there was grace and strength in the midst of it, and there was a great reward ahead of it. The same principles are true for us today. Keep in mind that God loves to heal people who have been hurt and loves to forgive people who have sinned and repented. As you read this book, make a note of each verse you come to that encourages the people to focus on the future or on heaven, rather than on the present suffering or offense.

To suffer means "to bear or undergo pain, inconvenience or loss; endure distress or injury; permitting; allowing."

> *1 Peter 3:1–6*—Chapter three begins with the word *likewise*, or in other words, *therefore*. *Likewise* means God is about to compare one concept to another. The key to the submissive behavior in chapter three is found in the comparison of submissive behavior in chapter two.

> *1 Peter 2:18–23*—There are to be no strings attached as conditions for giving patience, love, respect, or reverence. Difficult circumstances are not grounds for anger, resentment, disrespect, or abusive behavior. Rather they are an opportunity to display the character of Christ, grow in grace, and obtain a sure reward.

When you are misunderstood, mistreated, falsely accused, ignored, or used, how do you usually react?

1.

2.

3.

4.

5.

Study Christ as your example.—*1 Peter 1:15–16; 2:21; 4:1*

Refuse to harbor anger or use deceit.—*1 Peter 2:1–2*

Begin to overcome bitterness toward your oppressor with reverence to God first.

- Submit yourself to God.—*1 Peter 4:19*

- Submit yourself to others.—*1 Peter 5:5*

- Submit yourself to your authority.—*1 Peter 3:5*

- Submit yourself to every ordinance of man for the Lord's sake.—*1 Peter 2:13*

- Submit yourself to your master, with all fear.—*1 Peter 2:18*

Endure grief and overlook faults.—*1 Peter 2:19–20; 4:8*

Do not retaliate! Look to God for understanding and justice, not to your abuser.—*1 Peter 2:23*

Refuse to fight, tear down, or engage in a destructive war of words.—*1 Peter 3:9–10*

Have compassion and pity on your abuser; God *will* hold him responsible for his sin!—*1 Peter 3:8; 4:18*

Be active, while submitting to God. Being submissive does not mean we are to be passive.

- Pray.—*1 Peter 3:12*
- Appeal by reason.—*1 Peter 3:15*

Make sure you are suffering for well doing, not evil doing. Keep a clear conscience; quickly right your wrongs.—*1 Peter 3:16–17; 4:15*

Rejoice and be thankful, no matter how ridiculous it seems or how you feel!—*1 Peter 3:14; 4:14, 16*

Expect to give an account of how you handled your suffering.—*1 Peter 1:17*

Expect a future reward for suffering graciously.—*1 Peter 1:7; 3:9; 4:13*

Recognize that God allows your suffering.—*1 Peter 2:15; 3:17; 4:19*

Recognize that suffering is temporary.—*1 Peter 1:6; 5:10*

Recognize that there is always purpose in suffering and always a promise that God will change to good that which Satan meant for evil when we look to Him to do so.

- To promote your spiritual growth, faith, maturity, strength, and peace.—*1 Peter 5:10*

- To win the conversion or repentance of your oppressors.—*1 Peter 2:12; 2:15; 3:1; 3:16*

- To glorify God by your faith and trust.— *1 Peter 4:11*

Learning to Suffer Graciously—Verse Study

- Suffering steers us away from error.—*Psalm 119:67*

- Suffering motivates us to draw near to God.—*Psalm 57:1–2; James 4:8–10; Matthew 11:28*

- Suffering teaches us to pray.—*Psalm 50:15; 61:1; 116:1, 3–4*

- Suffering gives us the opportunity to see God's power.—*Jeremiah 32:17; 33:3; Psalm 27:13; 28:7*

- Suffering is God's way of correcting us.—*Revelation 3:19; Proverbs 28:13; Isaiah 59:1*

- Suffering provokes us to recognize and judge sin in our lives.—*1 Corinthians 11:31–32*

- Suffering teaches us obedience that we may be blessed.—*Hebrews 5:8*

- Suffering deepens bonds of friendship and love within the church body.—*Hebrews 10:34*

- Suffering develops inward character—faith, patience, wisdom.—*Romans 5:3–5; James 1:3; 1 Peter 1:6–7; Psalm 119:72–73, 75*

- Suffering redirects our attention from temporal to eternal.—*2 Corinthians 4:16–18*

- Suffering conquers our pride and generates humility.—*Proverbs 13:10; 29:23; Luke 14:11; 1 Peter 5:6–7; 2 Corinthians 12:7*

- Suffering openly demonstrates and warns of sin's consequences.—*Proverbs 16:6; Galatians 6:7; 1 Corinthians 11:28–30*

- Suffering reveals our ability or inability to trust God.—*Matthew 8:25–26*

- Suffering teaches us how to appropriate God's promises and comfort so that we in turn may comfort and guide others.—*2 Corinthians 1:3–4*

- God often uses suffering to change the direction of our lives. See the lives of Esther, Joseph, Daniel, Joseph and Mary, and Ruth. Suffering was used in these people's lives to put them in the right place at the right time so that they might be used of God and receive great reward.

- Suffering reveals satanic oppression and alerts us to the reality of our enemy.—*Ephesians 6:11–18; 1 Peter 5:8–9; 1 John 4:4; James 4:6–7*

- Suffering makes us understand our human frailty and God's strength and ability. —*2 Corinthians 12:7–10; Psalm 108:6*

- Suffering is evidence that God loves us.—*Hebrews 12:6–7, 10–13*

- Suffering enables God to ultimately bless us and reward us.—*1 Peter 4:12–13, 19; 5:6–7*

- God uses suffering to conform us to Christ-likeness.—*Romans 8:28–29; Ephesians 2:10; Philippians 2:13; Isaiah 64:8*

- All suffering is allowed by God and in God's control.—*Job 2:10; 1 Corinthians 10:13*

- All suffering can be used for our ultimate good.—*Romans 8:28*

- Not all suffering is necessary.—*Jeremiah 2:19; Galatians 6:7–8; 1 Corinthians 11:31–32*

Read *Romans 12:9–21*. List twenty-three things God wants us to do when people mistreat us, and list six things He does not want us to do when we are mistreated.

APPLICATION #15—LEARNING TO DEAL WITH ENVY

Six Easy Steps that Lead to Anger and Misery

Step One

Always demand your own rights, putting yourself and your own interests first in your life. This will lead to envy, jealousy, and covetousness. You will covet:

- Other people's things
- Other people's position, status, prosperity
- Other people's circumstances in life, family, trials, etc.
- Other people's personality, physical endowments, talents, spiritual gifts

Step Two

Concentrate on what you do not have, what others have, your disappointments, and how unfair life is. As you perfect envy and covetousness, you will soon become *discontent* with your own:

- Things
- Position, status
- Circumstances, family, personal problems, etc.
- Personality, physical endowments, talents, spiritual gifts

Step Three

As you become more and more discontent, indulge in larger daily doses of destructive "thinking" (which is really brooding). This in turn will make you increasingly more self-centered, which will cause you to spend still greater amounts of time in *self-pity*. Everything and everybody will soon start to get on your nerves. You will have no tolerance for people's imperfections, let alone their mistakes and offenses. Complaining, whining, and attention seeking (please feel sorry for me!) will most likely become a way of life; and you will seek out friends to feed your self-pity further (just sharing the misery). Or, you may be the type who likes to party alone and isolate yourself with your "thoughts."

Step Four

Next, perfect little acts of unkindness or the cold shoulder so you can direct your displeasure toward those who do not see things your way. This will help you move toward *anger* with others, with yourself, and with God. Usually, by this time you will not recognize your anger as anger; you will feel perfectly justified in your "thinking," but you will notice yourself becoming increasingly more irritable and discontent with people, especially those who "bug" you.

Step Five

The result of irrational pent-up anger will sow seeds of *bitterness*, which will spring up like weeds. By all means, refuse to forgive people who bug you or hurt your feelings, and keep your focus on your hurt feelings rather than on God's grace. This will give bitterness a chance to really flourish and choke out the last bit of joy in your life and any intimacy you may have had with God.

Step Six

Neglect responsibilities and refuse to direct your attention toward wholesome activities so that you can spend more time thinking about yourself and your emotional pain. This entire process will ultimately send you into a tailspin of *depression* which will make you feel worthless, lethargic, and sad. If you can keep this up, it will affect you physically and sap all your strength. Congratulations! You've succeeded in making yourself thoroughly miserable!

How to Conquer Envy

1. Cultivate thankfulness. Using a good concordance, locate passages of Scripture that contain the words thank, thankful, thanks, and thanksgiving. Find ten that command the believer to be thankful and five that describe the attitude of thankfulness. Copy these onto 3x5 cards and add to your notebook or memory collection. Read in the morning or before going to

bed, or before praying for the purpose of giving praise to God. Practice giving thanks for everything even if it is only to give thanks for what God is going to do through a difficult situation. Recognize that we deserve nothing and are dependent on God for everything.

2. Pray for the welfare of others (be specific). Make a list of specific things you will begin praying about with regard to others.

3. Look for whatever good you can find in others; give thanks to God for that person's gifts.

4. Verbally express your appreciation to others for their good qualities. In your notebook, write a description of the response you received when you did this.

5. Recognize God's control and sovereignty in all the circumstances of your life. Develop your understanding of the love and mercy of God, as well as His faithful work in your life for your own good and His own glory. Accept it!

6. Talk about your difficulties only when you are talking with someone who will be objective and can help you resolve them with concrete solutions. Do not talk in an effort to pacify your anger—it will not.

7. Allow yourself only two minutes (time it) to think about a sad situation in your life. Conclude your thoughts with prayer, casting all your care on Him. Then immediately force yourself to get up and busy yourself in some enjoyable activity or work.

8. Study and memorize appropriate Scriptures relating to specific spiritual weaknesses that feed jealousy. Write the verse on one side of a 3x5 card and what it means and how you can apply it specifically on the other side.

Verses on Jealousy and Envy: *Exodus 20:17; Psalm 73:2–3; 119:36; Proverbs 14:30; 19:3; 23:4–5, 17; Ecclesiastes 5:10; Song of Solomon 8:6; Ezekiel 33:31; Luke 12:15; 1 Corinthians 3:3; Galatians 5:26; 1 Timothy 6:4–8; Hebrews 13:5; James 3:14; 5:9*

Application #16—Learning about God's Love

The Treasures of God's Love

- "Mercy unto you, and peace, and love, be multiplied" (*Jude 1:2*).

- "No fear in love; but perfect [mature] love casteth out fear" (*1 John 4:18*).

- In the fear of the Lord is strong confidence.—*Psalm 36:7*

- "And to know the love of Christ, which passeth knowledge, that ye might be filled with all the fullness of God" (*Ephesians 3:19*).

- "In whom are hid all the treasures of wisdom and knowledge" (*Colossians 2:3*).

- *1 Corinthians 13*

- Five reasons to keep ourselves in the love of God...

  * To stand strong in an evil world

  * To be filled with all the fullness of God

  * To be confident; without fear; assured

  * To be comforted

  * To show us how to love God and others (*Titus 2:4*— husbands and children)

The Character of God

God's character and heart are revealed by

- What He says—*Psalm 119:103, 130*

- What He does—*Psalm 145:17*

- What He thinks—*Jeremiah 29:11*

- What He loves—*Psalm 33:5*

- What He hates—*Zechariah 8:17; Proverbs 8:1; 11:1, 20; 12:22*

God's character is in contrast with man's.—*Isaiah 55:8–9*

Man's character and heart are revealed by

- What He says—*Matthew 12:37*
- What He does—*Titus 1:16*
- What He thinks—*Psalm 94:11*
- What He loves—*Proverbs 1:22; 2:14*
- What He hates—*John 3:20; 7:7*

Salvation changes the heart and character of man. What he says, does, thinks, loves, and hates is transformed by the grace of God.—*2 Corinthians 5:17; Psalm 40:3*

Christians are happiest when they know and imitate God's ways.—*Psalm 40:8; 95:10; 103:7; Jeremiah 9:24*

All that God is can be summed up in this statement: God is love. *1 John 4:7–12; Jeremiah 31:3; Song of Solomon 5:16*

He loves us, not because we are lovable, but because He is loving.

A God Who Gives

The nature of love

- Love longs for expression.
- Love is not satisfied with words.
- Love manifests itself in actions.
- Love gives of itself.
- Love delights in sacrifices.

We first perceive God's love by understanding the cross. —*1 John 3:16; John 3:16; 10:11*

Christ voluntarily died in our place, even though there was nothing lovable in us, even though we would not love him for doing so and would utterly reject His great love and sacrifice if left to ourselves.—*1 John 4:10; Ephesians 2:4–7*

Christ willingly left heaven to espouse our cause and become one with His chosen people.—*Philippians 2:5–8; Hebrews 2:16–18*

Christ had compassion on the hopeless plight of sinful man, on man's humanity, and on his weakness.—*Hebrews 4:15; Psalm 103:14; Mark 6:34*

God gives of Himself to save us from our sin, but gives further by…

- Taking upon Himself all our debts and exchanging them for all His riches—*2 Corinthians 8:9*

- Providing the means for us to be with Him where He is and share His joy forever—*John 14:3*

- Undertaking responsibility for our continual care and protection—*Psalm 37:25; Isaiah 41:10; 1 Peter 5:7; Philippians 2:20*

- Providing all that we need to live a blessed and joyful life—*2 Peter 1:2–3*

- Giving beautiful gifts for our enjoyment—*1 Timothy 6:17; James 1:17*

- Providing the ability to exercise the fruit of the Spirit and be like Christ in character and deeds—*Philippians 2:13; John 6:63*

My love for others—*Ephesians 5:2*

A God Who Hears

Believers are united to a God Who hears and understands.

- Love makes itself readily available.—*Psalm 145:18; Jeremiah 23:23; Deuteronomy 31:8; Isaiah 58:9; Acts 17:27; Hebrews 4:16*

- Love takes a special interest in the unique qualities of the one loved.—*Psalm 138:6; 139:1–10; Luke 12:7*

- Love endeavors to thoroughly know and understand the one loved.—*Psalm 44:21; 142:4–5; Nahum 1:7; Matthew 6:8; Romans 8:26; 2 Timothy 2:19*

- Love listens carefully.—*Psalm 10:17; 22:24; 34:4, 17; 50:15; 86:5; 116:2; 138:3; Jeremiah 33:3*

- Love delights in hearing the one loved.—*Jeremiah 33:3; Proverbs 15:8; Song of Solomon 2:14; John 9:31*

My love for others—*1 Peter 1:22*

A God Who Speaks

- Speech is a unique attribute of God, given to man.

- Words are extremely important.—*Psalm 33:6; Matthew 12:36–37; Luke 6:45; John 12:48*

- Words are the medium God uses to reveal Himself and His will.—*Deuteronomy 13:3; Psalm 40:7; 119:24, 130; Proverbs 6:22; Isaiah 8:20; Acts 17:11*

- Words are the means God uses to communicate love, to bring joy and intimacy to our relationship, and to engage in exclusive fellowship with His beloved.—*Psalm 19:8; 119:14, 92, 97, 103, 165; 138:2; Jeremiah 15:16; John 8:47; 14:23; Luke 24:32*

- Words are the means God uses to instruct, reprove, comfort, and strengthen.—*Psalm 107:19–20; 119:50; Hebrews 4:12; Matthew 4:4; 22:29*

- Loving words are always gracious and truthful. Love always finds expression.—*Psalm 33:4; Luke 4:22; Proverbs 16:24; Jeremiah 20:9; Song of Solomon 8:7*

My love for others—*Ephesians 4:29*

Application #17—Learning to Forgive

All of the following people are professing believers who have received God's salvation by grace through faith in Jesus Christ. At a particular point in their lives, they recognized they were helpless sinners who needed a Savior. They repented of their sin and turned to Christ for forgiveness, believing He alone could save them from their sins and change their hearts. All of them attend church regularly and are involved in church activities. How many of them are having trouble with the issue of forgiveness?

- Says a young couple on the verge of divorce after numerous attempts at counseling have failed, "I know I am critical of my wife…" and "I know I resent my husband's lack of understanding…"

- Says a middle-age woman who has been tormented with depression most of her life, "I could never forgive my abusive father for what he did to me…"

- Says a young mother who has just had her children taken by CPS, "I love my children, but they just make me so mad at times that I can't control myself…"

- Say two women at odds with one another for years, "I don't have a problem with Mrs. So-and-So; it's she who has a problem with me."

- Says a single woman, who is dying with a sexually transmitted disease, "I know God has forgiven me, but I can't forgive myself for what I did and how I messed up my life."

- Says a contentious church member about to leave his church, "I love my church and pastor, but I just can't tolerate his lack of sensitivity toward some people."

All of the people above have a problem with forgiveness. They do not understand what it is or how their failure to forgive biblically is bringing torment and destruction into their lives. Let's see if we cannot find some answers for them in the Scriptures.

We are to forgive as God forgives us.—*Colossians 3:13*

How does God forgive and on what basis?

- Repentance is always a condition to the granting of forgiveness and restoration of fellowship.—*Psalm 86:5; Proverbs 28:13; Luke 13:3*

- When we willfully choose to disobey God and insist on our own way, God holds us responsible for our behavior until we confess and forsake the sin. In *1 John 1:9* the word *if* means "conditional; provided that."

How does God treat the unrepentant?

- God forgives in the sense that He does not treat offenders the way they deserve to be treated, nor does He withhold kindness and mercy toward them.—*Luke 6:35–37*

- Jesus' prayer was that the Father would not at that time exact vengeance upon those who were killing Him. Not all those who took part in the crucifixion ever repented of their sin and received the forgiveness that accompanies salvation. They were, however, spared the immediate judgment of God and were given a space of time to repent.—*Luke 23:34*

- Jesus did not hate those who were wronging Him unjustly. He did not retaliate in any way, threaten them with vengeance, hold a grudge against them, or in any way treat them with anger or resentment. Rather, He grieved for them and pitied them; for He knew that unless they repented of their evil ways, they would one day suffer the just recompense of their sin that is the Father's prerogative alone.—*1 Peter 2:22–23*

How does God treat the repentant?

Psalm 32:1–2, 5; 103:11–13; Exodus 34:6; Isaiah 1:18; Isaiah 55:7; Hosea 14:4; Romans 8:1; Galatians 4:4–7

How are we to treat those who sin against us?

1. First, we are to strive to overlook petty human frailties in a spirit of mercy and patience.—*Proverbs 13:10; 19:11; 25:15; Psalm 130:3; 1 Thessalonians 5:14; Romans 12:18*

2. Second, we are to humbly confront those who cause divisions by specific sins or who are bringing destruction upon themselves by sinning, with the motive of restoring them in a spirit of love and kindness. Those who are spiritual are those who are able to confront sin without regard for himself or herself, without anger, and without a spirit of contempt or condemnation.—*Galatians 6:1; Luke 17:3–4; Matthew 18:15–16; Ephesians 4:25*

3. Third, we are commanded to forgive from our hearts any who repent and to consider the matter closed and forgotten, never to be brought against the offender again.—*Matthew 18:21, 33–35; Ephesians 4:32*

How are we to treat those who do not repent?

Leviticus 19:18; 1 Corinthians 4:12; Exodus 23:4–5; Proverbs 20:22; 24:17, 29; 25:21; Romans 12:20; Luke 6:27–34; Matthew 6:12; Mark 11:25; Romans 12:14, 17–19; 1 Peter 2:20–22, 3:9; James 3:14; Hebrews 12:15; Ephesians 4:29–32

Study Questions

1. Read *Matthew 18:21–35*. On what basis did the Lord tell the servant he should have forgiven his fellow servant?

2. Read *1 Samuel 24:10–12; 26:9, 23;* and *2 Samuel 16:9–13*.

   a. David told Saul, "I have not sinned against thee; yet thou _____ ____ _____ _____ ____ ____."

b. Whom did David say would avenge him of the wrong done to him? _____

c. When Saul's life was taken by God, did David rejoice?

d. How did David show love by "covering a transgression"?

3. Read *Genesis 45:5–15* and *50:19–21*. What did Joseph mean when he said to his brothers, "Am I in the place of God?"

Answers to Application Questions

#9—Learning to Deal with Failure Successfully

law of God

Jesus Christ our Lord

#13—Recognizing Pride
Directed Bible Study

God

leans; understanding; wise

instruction or correction

abomination

haughty

strife

boastful or arrogant

persecution

truth

invincible; in control

preeminence

highly

sin; forgiveness

compare

praise; glory

burden; weakness; treatment; frailty

grace

14—Learning to Suffer for Righteousness Sake

Verse 51—ridiculed; did not forsake God's law or quit doing as God's law said

Verse 61—robbed; did not forsake God's law

Verse 69—lied against; kept God's precepts with his whole heart

Verse 78—dealt perversely with; meditated on God's precepts

Verse 86—persecuted wrongly; trusted in God's faithfulness and went to Him for help

Verse 87—almost consumed him; did not forsake God's precepts

Verse 95—waited to destroy him; would think on and consider God's testimonies

Verse 110—laid a snare or trap for him; did not err from God's precepts

Verse 157—had many persecutors and enemies; believed and acted on God's testimonies

#17— Learning to Forgive

Study Questions

1. On the basis of how his heavenly Father had forgiven him

2. a. huntest my soul to take it

   b. the Lord

   c. No

   d. David stayed the hand and mouth of his men who sought to harm Shimei (of the house of Saul) who cursed David.

   e. He would not step into the place of God to avenge himself.

ALSO AVAILABLE
BY DEBI PRYDE

Why do Christians suffer from depression? Is there hope? Does the Bible really have the answers? Debi Pryde answers these questions plus addresses key issues surrounding depression such as loss, failures, self-indulgence, despair, doubt, suicide, drug therapy, and much more. Designed to be an all-in-one resource for counselors and counselees, *Why Am I So Depressed* is filled with biblical principles and practical applications that will help readers grasp the trustworthy truths that will set them free from the torments of depression.

Abuse is scary and unsettling, whether you are the pastor or counselor offering hope and instruction, the woman facing the abuse in her home, the friend wanting to help, or the abuser struggling to change. *What to Do When You Are Abused by Your Husband* offers a biblical perspective of hope and lasting peace, concepts often foreign to abuse situations.

The Titus 2 Series, consisting of *The Secrets of a Happy Heart*, *Happily Married*, and *Parenting with Wisdom*, is designed to be effective as a personal study book, a group Bible study, a one-on-one counseling tool, or as a Sunday School curriculum. The memory verses, workbook questions, and textual content will provoke thought and encourage Christians to be more Christ-like in all aspects of their life.

ORDERING INFORMATION

Ironwood
49191 Cherokee Road
Newberry Springs, CA 92365
760.257.3503
www.ShopIronwood.org

Made in the USA
Columbia, SC
18 February 2018